THE LIES
OF THE
LAND

Also by Adam Macqueen

The Prime Minister's Ironing Board and Other State Secrets

Private Eye: The First 50 Years, an A–Z

The King of Sunlight: How William Lever Cleaned Up the World

THE LIES OF THE LAND

A BRIEF HISTORY OF POLITICAL DISHONESTY

Adam Macqueen

Atlantic Books
London

Published in hardback in Great Britain in 2017 by Atlantic Books, an imprint of Atlantic Books Ltd.

10 9 8 7 6 5 4 3 2 1

A CIP catalogue record for this book is available from the British Library.

Hardback ISBN: 978 1 78649 249 4
E-book ISBN: 978 1 78649 250 0

Printed in Great Britain by TJ International Ltd, Padstow, Cornwall

Atlantic Books
An Imprint of Atlantic Books Ltd
Ormond House
26–27 Boswell Street
London
WC1N 3JZ

www.atlantic-books.co.uk

CONTENTS

For my brother Andrew
who likes 'books which are true'
and isn't keen on politicians who lie.

'An old gentleman had been serving on a battleship as a young rating in early 1940 when Churchill had come aboard. Put in a group to question the great man, he had nervously asked, "Is everything you tell us true?" The answer, he alleged, was: "Young man, I have told many lies for my country, and I will tell many more."'

Anecdote recounted by former
Cabinet Minister William Waldegrave
in his memoirs, 2015

'Truth is a difficult concept.'

Ian McDonald,
official at the Ministry of Defence,
in evidence to the Scott Inquiry, 1993

'I only know what I believe.'

Prime Minister Tony Blair
on his approach to events after 9/11
and the Iraq War, speech, 2004

'You are fake news!'

President-elect Donald Trump
refuses to answer a question from CNN,
press conference, 2017

INTRODUCTION

How do you know when a politician is lying? runs the age-old joke. Answer: Their lips are moving. Always gets a big laugh in the saloon bar, that one. Bet Nigel Farage has trotted it out more than once.

Like most jokes, it's 90 per cent nonsense wrapped around a hard kernel of truth.

There are plenty of elected representatives out there living perfectly upright lives. They do their best for their constituents, balance their beliefs with the demands of office and professionalism, speak truth to power and attempt to wield what power comes their way in a manner that brings the greatest benefit – or at least does the least damage – all round.

So why are we convinced otherwise? Why, as the Brexit referendum and an embarrassment of elections in recent years have repeatedly demonstrated, have we become so determined to think the very worst of those who aspire to serve us?

Some of it is down to the extraordinary polarization of contemporary politics. Many voters have evacuated the centre ground for entrenched positions held independently of the traditional redoubts of the party system. If you bolster your own righteousness by dismissing the other side as inherently evil and beyond salvation, what can their every utterance be but a lie? Trump's army of 'deplorables' call it 'fake news'. Hard-core Brexiteers rail against 'project fear'. The cult of Corbyn dismiss the 'smears of the mainstream media'. And the laser-focused EU negotiation team offered to the nation by Theresa May in the summer of 2016 appeared to deem any and all alternative points of view as something not far short of treason.

As sure as night follows day, the louder you shout about your opponents' lies, the less obliged you feel to tell the truth yourself. The book is far from closed on the presidential team's links to Russia. There is not, and there was never going to be, £350 million a week to solve the problems of the NHS. Leaders are capable of looking incompetent all by themselves. And the prime minister could boast of as big a parliamentary majority as she likes, but it's not even a minority interest of Guy Verhofstadt, Michel Barnier, Donald Tusk or anyone else beyond our borders.

But while downright dishonesty may have increased in volume and visibility in recent years, it is not a new development in politics. For decades now we have felt that our elected representatives speak with forked tongues. There is a very good reason for that. It is the other 10 per cent of the joke. It is the fact that they do.

Of course they don't lie *all* the time. That's only true in a few cases, those of pathological liars programmed to believe whatever happens to be coming out of their mouth at any given moment. We'll see some examples in the stories of Jeffrey Archer and Donald Trump, both of whom have built a well-deserved reputation for their lying. We'll also see it in the tales of Mohamed Fayed, who though he is not a politician himself has nevertheless been the facilitator and funder of more than one incident of spectacular lying which appears in these pages.

But then, very few people out there are listening *all* the time either. Beyond the wonks of Westminster, the loyal partisans and the dedicated readers and viewers of political journalism (who for the most part – let's be honest – tend to be other political journalists), most of politics coalesces into a shapeless ball of noise. The bulk of the population perceive only something we might call 'Politicians with a capital P' (followed by a sigh). Politicians with a capital P are a not trustworthy but nevertheless authoritative mass, always there on the nightly news and in the papers and the Facebook feed, getting in the way of the sport and showbiz gossip and your friends' family pictures. Very occasionally a clear statement, pledge or personality breaks out of the background noise. In spin-doctoring circles, these are known as the moments with 'cut-through'.[1] All too often, these moments are not exactly the ones the spin doctors want us to be focusing on.

As one prime example, how often these days do you hear people bring up the topic of how tirelessly Tony Blair worked first to corral George W. Bush and then to get the UN Security Council to pass Resolution 1441 condemning Saddam Hussein's 'non-compliance' to ensure the US didn't go into Iraq without some international backing?[2] Probably not much. But it is an unbreakable rule of these first decades of the twenty-first century that any conversation about British politics, on almost any topic, on- or offline, will at some point default to the claim that the former prime minister lied about WMDs in order to take us into an illegal war. I happen not to believe that is true – don't worry, I'll explain why in chapter 7 and you'll have every opportunity to denounce me as a Blairite lickspittle neocon. But as we have already seen, one of the curious things about the loudest accusations of lying is that those making them don't feel obliged to tell the whole truth.

It's always the bad behaviour that sticks. Can you name one achievement of the Nixon administration other than Watergate? Do you have any idea what government positions John Profumo held before he had to resign from them in disgrace? Which action taken in the Oval Office by Bill Clinton is the first to spring to mind? And those are just the classics. Within these pages you will find many less well-known incidents of chicanery, double-dealing, alternative facts and outright falsehoods. En masse, they form the folk memory that has ushered us into the much-vaunted 'post-truth' era. They are the reason so many of us feel unable to believe anything a politician says.

The bigger question is why politicians lie, dissemble, mislead or simply go to great efforts to avoid telling us the truth in the first place.

Discipline obliges dishonesty. I write this introduction from the midst of an election campaign which the incumbent party are fighting in the form of a stuck record, repeating nothing but the phrase 'strong and stable' for fear that anything else might offer hostages to fortune and doing their best not to answer the very few questions that make it through their fortified defences. If their own foot soldiers make it into government they will face immense pressure to keep up a similar parroting of the party line. The system is rigidly enforced with the carrot of career advancement and the stick of a media mauling.

It is that same fear – imposed both by party whips and by a lobby press with a shameless, symbiotic relationship with the hierarchies it ought to be holding to account – that ensures politicians who are under-informed, unprepared or unable to think on their feet (a bit like most of us, most of the time) are reduced to bullshitting their way through everything. Their unstudied interviews, once broadcast or printed, acquire an authoritative status that might as well be carved in tablets of stone. Entire policies and political crises have been constructed around the inability of a powerful person to admit, in the moment, 'I don't know.'

There is also the sheer overweening arrogance that overtakes the elected once they reach a certain point in their careers. Being driven everywhere, having an army of civil servants to attend to your every need, flying in and out of receptions and banquets where everyone wants to talk to you and toast your eminence is not a good diet for the ego. It is especially bad for those whose egos were big to start with. A calling can all too easily turn into a mission; a mission in time can mutate into a conviction that you, and only you, have the answers that will save the world. It is a quality that singles out our best prime ministers – Winston Churchill, Margaret Thatcher, Tony Blair – and also simultaneously makes them our worst. Self-belief can convince you that everyone else should believe you too. Then things like empirical truth are for the little people.

And marching behind the righteous are the reckless, those whose own personality flaws manifest in an extraordinary desire to play with fire – be it sexual affairs, financial fiddles, or the sheer thrill of risk itself. From Jeremy Thorpe to Jonathan Aitken, they did not so much sow as scatter the seeds of their own destruction.

Some of them were simply greedy, unhappy to settle for the spiritual rewards of public service when the potential pecuniary ones remain much more generous. Yet, however those of us who pay their wages might feel about it, the rules say that being an MP is not a full-time job. It is perfectly possible for a politician to be straightforward and honest about exploiting opportunities for enrichment. The ones who have lied about it did so for a different reason. MPs like Aitken and Neil Hamilton are often described as shameless. The opposite was the case. It was shame that made them deny their sins so loudly for so long, just as it was a collective, institutional shame that prompted Parliament to resist perfectly reasonable enquiries about its expenses system, until finally, in 2009, the curtain was whipped back to expose our ruling class in all its naked, squirming venality.

From Nixon onwards, it has always been the cover-up that does for them. A fear of how transactions might be perceived has led both Tory and Labour leaders to try to keep the whole 'murky business' of political donations and honours (the description is Tony Blair's) out of sight and out of public mind.[3] A vicious cycle – public mistrust leading to private dissembling leading to greater public mistrust – has been established. They tell us lies because they know they can't expect us to believe them.

The result is that the one profession in whom we are regularly required to register our trust at the polls, is the one the polls show we least trust. At the end of 2016 just 15 per cent of the British public said they trust any politicians to tell the truth; the next least trusted profession, with 20 per cent, was 'government ministers'. You can take my word for this, even though, as a journalist, I'm right there in third place with 24 per cent credibility.[4]

With trust all round at such a dismal low, we enter the realms of farce. In April 2016, Secretary of State for Culture, Media and Sport John Whittingdale faced some embarrassment. It was revealed – perhaps belatedly, since he was in charge of implementing press regulation after the Leveson inquiry, and this may have made the papers less keen on exposing his peccadillos – that the minister had been going out with one Olivia King, a dominatrix who worked under the professional name 'Mistress Kate'. 'Between August 2013 and February 2014, I had a relationship with someone who I first met through Match.com,' Whittingdale admitted. 'She was a similar age and lived close to me. At no time did she give me any indication of her real occupation and I only discovered this when I was made aware that someone was trying to sell a story about me to tabloid newspapers. As soon as I discovered, I ended the relationship.'[5]

It turned out that Mistress Kate was not the only one who had fibbed about their occupation, however. Another woman, called

Stephanie Hudson, came forward to say she too had gone out with the veteran politician after meeting him on the same website. But she said Whittingdale – who had worked as political secretary to Margaret Thatcher, been an MP since 1992 and headed the influential select committee on culture before ascending to the cabinet – had not revealed what he actually did for a living.

He told her he was an arms dealer instead.[6]

How the hell did we get here?

1

OUT OF DEFERENCE

There is a famous political interview from the General Election of 1951 in which the BBC's Leslie Mitchell promises to 'cross-question' senior Conservative Sir Anthony Eden. 'I would like to feel that I am asking, so far as possible, those questions which you yourselves would like to ask in my place,' he told viewers. Then he goes in with a real zinger: 'Well now, Mr Eden, with your very considerable experience of foreign affairs, it's quite obvious that I should start by asking you something about the international situation today, or perhaps you would prefer to talk about home. Which is it to be?'[1]

Paxman he was not. It would be a further four years before Robin Day on the new ITV jump-started the sort of adversarial political interview to which we have become accustomed. Day-to-day political reporting consisted mostly of producing page after page of transcripts of parliamentary speeches, taken down at shorthand speed and reproduced verbatim, thus allowing MPs – and their unelected counterparts in the hereditary House of Lords – to effectively write their own accounts of their activities.

None of this seemed remarkable at the time. Hierarchies, and the deference that was due to them, were embedded and enforced in every institution: the arcane pecking order of the public schools was echoed in the state sector by the eleven-plus division, which defined the course of a pupil's life. And whether they then found themselves on a factory floor or in a professional body, they were locked into a rigid system of willing conformity. National service, which lingered as a hangover of the war right up until 1960, trained every man to unquestioningly accept the authority of his elders and betters, while women were expected to know their place, which, once married, was in the home.

Through everything ran the vast system of self-regulation that is class in Britain. As if stamping down on the brief socialist aberration of Attlee's government, when Winston Churchill was re-elected in 1951, he appointed two marquesses, four earls, four viscounts and three barons as ministers. The commoners in the cabinet seemed to work on the hereditary principle too. Anthony Eden married Churchill's niece Clarissa in 1952 before following her uncle into Number 10, and Duncan Sandys, another of his cabinet colleagues, married Churchill's daughter Diana.

In such an atmosphere, is it any wonder that honesty and openness to one's social inferiors was not a priority for politicians? But voters did demand that their rulers be accountable for their actions. And that was a lesson Britain's political elite were about to learn the hard way.

* * * * *

'For a long time the Prime Minister has had no respite from his arduous duties and is in need of a complete rest. We have therefore advised him to abandon his journey to Bermuda and to take at least a month's rest.'

Lord Moran and Sir Russell Brain, doctors to Sir Winston Churchill, press bulletin, 27 June 1953

The prime minister was on fine form that night. He had been knocking back the booze in his customary manner, and when he rose to say a few words in honour of his Italian counterpart, Alcide De Gasperi, the guests in Downing Street agreed it was a classic of its kind. 'He made a speech in his best and most sparkling manner, mainly about the Roman Conquest of Britain,' noted his principal private secretary Jock Colville, who not so long before had been worrying that the increasing amount of speechwriting he had been asked to do was 'a sign of advancing senility' in his seventy-eight-year-old boss.[2] The mood in the room was boisterous and joyful as the meal concluded and Churchill stood up again to urge his guests through from Number 10's dining room to the drawing room. But he only made it a few steps before he staggered and sat down heavily on a recently vacated chair. Elizabeth Clark happened to be beside him at that moment, and he clutched her hand. 'I want a friend,' he muttered, not quite focusing on her face. 'They put too much on me. Foreign affairs…' Then he tailed off into silence.[3]

She kept it together. Although she couldn't spot Churchill's wife, Clementine, in the melee, his daughter Mary was still in her seat at the opposite end of the long table, and Elizabeth dispatched her husband – the eminent art historian Sir Kenneth – to quietly attract her attention. Mary sent her own husband, Christopher Soames, to retrieve his mother-in-law from the crowd next door. Not wanting to cause a diplomatic incident in front of the Italian prime minister, he told her, slightly pointedly, that Winston was 'very tired'. Perhaps thinking her husband had had too much to drink, Clementine nodded and said, 'we must get him to bed then.' She soon realized it was something more serious when Soames whispered: 'we must get the waiters away first. He can't walk.'[4]

He couldn't walk properly the next morning either, when his personal physician, Lord Moran, came to his bedroom for a check-up. Wanting a second opinion – his own – Churchill insisted that the doctor open the door of his wardrobe so he could see his own unsteady efforts in its mirror. 'What has happened, Charles?' he asked sadly. 'Is it a stroke?'[5]

It was. And Moran told him that walking might be the least of his problems: 'I could not guarantee that he would not get up in the House and use the wrong word; he might rise in his place and no words might come.' The doctor might also have been tempted to say 'I told you so': just one day previously he had warned Churchill that he was 'unhappy about the strain' upon him, that 'it was an impossible existence.'[6] As well as his own duties, the prime minister had insisted on shouldering those of the foreign secretary too: Anthony Eden was off sick after an operation to remove gallstones went disastrously wrong. Churchill, whose main medical complaint was a deafness that became particularly acute when colleagues mentioned the word 'retirement', was rather chuffed about this fact: Eden was twenty-three years his junior and his chosen successor, although his boss was determined to make him wait for his promotion as long as possible.

Thankfully the cabinet were an unobservant lot, because none of them noticed the state the prime minister was in when he insisted on chairing a meeting that morning. Despite the fact he was slurring his speech and unable to move his left arm, the chancellor only noticed that he was 'very white' and didn't speak much.[7]

By lunchtime Churchill had difficulty getting out of his chair. The following morning Moran found him, 'if anything, more unsteady in his gait' and 'becoming more blurred and difficult to follow' when he talked. But Moran's main concern does not seem to have been medical: 'I did not want him to go among people until he was better. They would notice things, and there would be talk.'[8]

So a plan was hatched – or rather a plot hardened around Soames's first instinct for discretion over resuscitation. The prime minister's illness must be covered up at all costs. That afternoon he was driven down to his private residence, Chartwell, in Kent, accompanied by Clementine and Colville, who noticed sadly that his boss was now having difficulty finding his mouth with his trademark cigar. By that evening the paralysis had spread over most of Churchill's left side; by the next day, he could barely move. Moran gave his professional opinion that he didn't expect the PM to live through the weekend. But they had their orders, slurred to them by Churchill himself: they were under no circumstances to let it be known that he was incapable of running the country. Government was to continue as if he were in full control.

Certain people did have to be told. Colville telephoned the Queen's private secretary to pass on a message that the monarch – herself in the job for just eighteen months at this point – might find herself having to appoint a new prime minister at very short notice. The US president had to be told too. Churchill was due to hold a summit in Bermuda with Eisenhower on 9 July, the first face-to-face manifestation of the 'special relationship' since the death of its wartime third wheel, Joseph Stalin, in March. In January Churchill had travelled by boat to meet the newly elected president after Moran warned him that air travel posed a danger to his circulation; now that the risk had become a reality, there could be no question of him going at all. 'You will see from the attached medical report the reasons why I cannot come to Bermuda,' the prime minister – or rather Colville on his behalf – telegrammed the White House.[9] The US administration could at least be trusted to keep the secret. After all, they had helped disguise the extent of Franklin D. Roosevelt's paralysis, brought on by polio, from voters for years.

But it certainly wasn't the sort of thing the whole government needed to be told about. Instead, only two men were told. Chancellor Rab Butler and Lord President of the Council Lord Salisbury were summoned to Chartwell that Saturday, where Colville solemnly handed them a formal letter:

> I write, very sorrowfully, to let you know quite privately
> that the PM is seriously ill and that unless some miracle
> occurs in the next 24 hours there can be… little
> [question] of him remaining in office. It was a sudden
> arterial spasm, or perhaps a clot in the artery, and he has
> been left with great difficulty of articulation although
> his brain is still absolutely clear. His left side is partly
> paralysed and he has lost the use of his left arm. He
> himself has little hope of recovery.[10]

With Buckingham Palace at the other end of the telephone line, the trio neatly sorted things out. If Churchill died, or had to resign, then Salisbury – who owed his place in Parliament to the favours his ancestors had performed for James I and George III – would take over running the country; not as prime minister – everyone agreed Eden was the best fellow for that job – but as 'chairman' of a caretaker government that might hold the fort until the foreign secretary had made a full recovery and himself moved into Number 10. There was no question of involving the electorate – or even the Conservative Party – in the matter. That was not how things were done.

The two cabinet ministers cast an eye over the bulletin that Moran and a specialist neurological surgeon, the aptly named Sir Russell Brain, proposed to issue to the press. 'For a long time the Prime Minister has had no respite from his arduous duties,' it read. 'A disturbance of the cerebral circulation has developed, resulting in attacks of giddiness. We have therefore advised him to abandon his journey to Bermuda and to take at least a month's rest.'[11] The statesmen agreed that this would not do at all: great war heroes didn't get giddy, and the medical terminology might make people think Churchill was at death's door. He was, of course, but there was no need to say so. The middle sentence was excised completely and replaced with the bland phrase 'and is in need of a complete rest'. Moran himself was dubious – he wrote in his diary, 'if he dies in the next few days will Lord Salisbury think his change in the bulletin was wise?' – but he was just a doctor, and was easily overruled.[12]

Now all they needed to do was ensure that no journalists asked any awkward questions. Thankfully, that was a simple task: Colville had already gone over their heads. Twenty-four hours before Butler and Salisbury arrived at Chartwell, Colville had hosted the men with the real power in the country: Lord Camrose, owner of the *Daily Telegraph*, Lord Beaverbrook, who owned the *Daily Express* and *Evening Standard*, and Lord Bracken, who chaired the company which owned the *Financial Times*. All three were 'particular friends' of Churchill. Camrose had bought the very house they were meeting in and presented it to the prime minister when he found himself suffering from financial embarrassment, and Bracken and Beaverbrook had been co-opted into the cabinet during the war. As well as pledging to keep all news of the seriousness of the prime minister's illness out of their papers, they also promised to persuade their fellow proprietors to do the same. And they were as good as their word. 'His trouble is simply tiredness from over-work', the *Sunday People* assured its readers on 28 June.[13] 'They achieved the all but incredible, and in peace-time possibly unique, success of gagging Fleet Street, something they would have done for nobody but Churchill,' wrote Colville many years later, after the truth had come out.[14]

When Tony Blair suffered a considerably less serious health scare exactly fifty years later, his official spokesman was briefing journalists on how to spell 'supra ventricular tachycardia' the next day. But in 1953 the country was just eight short years on from the days of loose lips sinking ships and keeping calm and carrying on. When it came to the wartime leader, journalists were content to slip back into discreet and deferential mode.

At that point everyone imagined they were involved in a very short-lived deception. No one expected the prime minister to make it through the weekend. But much to everyone's surprise, he did. 'By Monday morning, the Prime Minister, instead of being dead, was feeling very much better,' wrote Colville years later. 'He told me that he thought probably that this must mean his retirement, but that he would see how he went on.'[15] He certainly had no intention of going anywhere before the Conservative Party Conference that October. And so there was no choice but to continue the prevarication.

The cabinet were informed in the afternoon that the prime minister's condition was more serious than originally thought, but the revelation was carefully not minuted. 'It was a terrible shock to us all,' wrote future prime minister Harold Macmillan. 'Many of us were in tears or found it difficult to restrain them.'[16] But they were also informed that despite his debility, Churchill remained very much in charge. Red boxes full of official papers continued to be sent down to Chartwell over the next month, and then to the PM's official country residence, Chequers, for three weeks after that, as Churchill recuperated. He never saw much of their contents. Instead Colville – a civil servant – and Soames, a mere backbench MP, dealt with the prime ministerial paperwork. 'The 33-year-old Soames… quite unobtrusively, took a hundred decisions in Churchill's name without once breaching the trust which such a heavy responsibility involved,' writes the PM's admiring biographer Martin Gilbert.[17] 'There is some ambiguity about whether Colville and Soames faked his initials on papers,' notes Gilbert's more sceptical counterpart Roy Jenkins.[18]

Churchill did not return to Downing Street until 18 August, the day after the *Daily Mirror* – implacably opposed to the Tory prime minister – finally broke ranks and demanded to know: 'WHAT IS THE TRUTH ABOUT CHURCHILL'S ILLNESS?' The impudent query had been prompted after an American newspaper dared to use the word 'stroke' in a report on rumours about the PM's health. Why, the *Mirror* demanded, should the British 'always be the last to learn what is going on in their country? Must they always be driven to pick up their information at second hand from tittle-tattle abroad?'[19]

Apparently so. For while Churchill raged that the *Mirror*'s report was 'rubbish, of course', he had already ensured that the White House was fully acquainted with facts that would not emerge on his own side of the Atlantic for years to come. 'I had a sudden stroke which as it developed completely paralysed my left side and affected my speech,' he had written to Eisenhower way back on 1 July. 'Four years ago, in 1949, I had another similar attack and was for a good many days unable to sign my name. As I was out of office I kept this secret'.[20]

'His case has been the subject of close investigation. No evidence has been found to show that he was responsible for warning Burgess or Maclean. While in Government service he carried out his duties ably and conscientiously. I have no reason to conclude that Mr. Philby has at any time betrayed the interests of his country, or to identify him with the so-called "third man", if, indeed, there was one.'

Harold Macmillan,
House of Commons, 7 November 1955

Russian spy Donald Maclean had more than one lucky escape. Both the British and American secret services knew from a series of intercepted and decoded messages that the Soviets had an agent going by the code name 'Homer' working in the British embassy in Washington in the late forties. Maclean, who had been recruited to the Foreign Office straight out of Cambridge, was first secretary there. But it was taken as read that no high-ranking diplomat would betray his country. Only the lower classes did that sort of thing. Far better to look into the typists and clerks, the janitors and chauffeurs. One of them had to be Homer.

Even when Maclean underwent a spectacular breakdown after being relocated to Cairo in 1948, no one thought any the worse of him. All right, so he went on day-long drinking benders where he ranted about the awfulness of Americans, attacked his wife in public and broke into a stranger's flat and trashed it.... Nothing that a recall to London and a spell under the care of a top Harley Street psychiatrist couldn't sort out.

In early 1951, however, the evidence became undeniable when a US cryptographer managed to decode a Russian message dating back to 1944. It revealed that Homer's wife was pregnant at the time and had gone to stay with her mother in New York. Only one man fitted the bill: Maclean, now working on the American desk at the Foreign Office in London. The CIA relayed the information to their British counterparts, with whom they enjoyed a good relationship – a relationship overseen at the Washington end by top MI6 man Harold Philby, known to his many friends as Kim.

The news came as a particular blow to Philby, because Maclean was an old friend; although they hadn't seen each other in years, they had been students together in the early thirties. Philby was so shaken by the revelation of his pal's treachery that he had to share the news with another mutual friend from Cambridge who, as it happened, was living in the basement of his home having recently completed a stint at the British embassy. The friend's name was Guy Burgess. Neither man could bear to think of Maclean back in Britain, his home and office bugged, and officers from MI5, who dealt with enemy agents, following him everywhere to gather evidence for when he inevitably went on trial for treachery.

It wasn't the only bad news Burgess had received in recent days. He had just lost his job, after a litany of bad behaviour and drunkenness culminated in him being caught speeding three times in a single day and rowing with the traffic cops when he tried to claim diplomatic immunity. The night before he went back to London in disgrace, he and Philby dined together at a Chinese restaurant, rather a tacky place where the piped music was so loud it was impossible to hear what other people were saying. Afterwards Philby drove him to the station and dropped him off with a somewhat unusual farewell: 'Don't you go too!'[21]

But Burgess did. On the night of Friday 25 May 1951, the very day the foreign secretary gave formal approval for MI5 to bring Maclean in for interrogation, Burgess turned up at Maclean's home in Kent with a rented car. Astonishingly, the surveillance on Maclean was a nine-to-five job: his MI5 tail saw him from his office and onto his train at Victoria station, and then knocked off for the night. Thus no one saw the two men driving off into the darkness, headed for Southampton and a cruise ship sailing for France at midnight. The luggage that Burgess had carefully packed made the return trip to Britain, but he and Maclean did not. Instead, they took various trains to Switzerland where, with the help of false passports they picked up at the Russian embassy, they boarded a plane for Prague, where the Iron Curtain closed behind them. The first clue anyone at MI5 had about it was when Maclean failed to get off his commuter train on Monday morning. They had been planning to seize him that morning: his first interrogation was scheduled for 11 a.m.

Both Burgess and Maclean had been spying for the Russians since 1935. Recently, however, their controller, Yuri Modin, had concluded that they were both 'burnt-out'.[22] Even before Maclean's cover was blown, both men had been making a spectacle of themselves with their drunken antics. Burgess was particularly unsuited to being a spy: permanently sozzled, he drew attention to himself everywhere he went; when he wasn't picking fights, he was seducing anything in trousers. Since neither man could be trusted to keep shtum under questioning – quite the opposite, in fact – Modin felt he had no choice but to pull them out. But if their disappearance was bad news for Britain, it was terrible news for Kim Philby, who knew suspicion would inevitably fall on their old friend. He expressed his horror in a phone call to an MI5 contact, Guy Lidell, who dutifully reported back to his superiors: 'There is no doubt that Kim Philby is thoroughly disgusted with Burgess's behaviour.'[23] Privately, Philby reassured himself that 'there must be many people in high positions… who would wish very much to see my innocence established. They would be inclined to give me the benefit of any doubt'.[24]

And they were. Philby was recalled to London to discuss his friends' exploits, but he was given the news in a friendly note from his boss ahead of the official telegram. The same boss accompanied him to his MI5 interview, where he was offered tea and allowed to smoke his pipe. A couple of days later they had him back for a slightly more frosty chat: the CIA were kicking up a fuss and saying they didn't want him back in Washington. He had been helped by his long-running friendship with one of the top men in the CIA, James Jesus Angleton, who had assured his superiors that there was no way Philby could possibly have known about Burgess's treachery. Yet the Americans were still insisting that the British 'clean house regardless of whom may be hurt'.[25] As for his MI6 colleagues, they were standing 100 per cent behind him. 'Philby had not run away, he was happy to help, and he was, importantly, a gentleman, a clubman and a high-flier, which meant he must be innocent,' writes Ben Macintyre in *A Spy Among Friends*, his superb account of Philby's career. 'Many of Philby's colleagues in MI6 would cling to that presumption of innocence as an article of faith. To accept otherwise would be to admit that they had all been fooled; it would make the intelligence and diplomatic services look entirely idiotic.'[26]

So instead they chose to blind themselves to the truth. Philby had volunteered to spy for the Russians long before he 'dropped a few hints here and there' and bagged himself a berth at MI6 in 1940. The background checks done at the time of his recruitment turned up the result 'nothing recorded against': a chat with his father, an adviser to the king of Saudi Arabia, had been enough to convince recruiters that his flirtations with communism at Cambridge in the thirties were 'all schoolboy nonsense. He's a reformed character now.' Besides, no less a figure than MI6's deputy head, Valentine Vivian, had provided a reference of the most unquestionable kind: 'I was asked about him, and I said I knew his people.'[27]

Philby in turn had passed Burgess and Maclean's details on to the NKVD, precursor to the KGB. And it was he who had tipped off his Soviet contact in the US that Maclean's cover had been blown, and he who arranged for Burgess to get Maclean to the extraction point. When Philby realized Burgess, to whom he was directly and obviously connected, had gone too, he had considered fleeing himself. In the end, he had decided to stay put and bluff.

He had come close to discovery before and got away with it. In 1937, when he was still filing reports on the Spanish Civil War for *The Times* as well as more secret ones for Moscow, a defector had described a 'young Englishman, a journalist of a good family' who was out in Spain, but no one made the connection. In 1945 Konstantin Volkov, the deputy chief of Soviet intelligence in Turkey, announced to staff at the British embassy that he wanted to come across too, and offered a list of Russian agents in Britain which he said included 'one fulfilling the functions of head of a section of the British counter-espionage service in London', a description which Philby swiftly recognized as himself. That time, he had been in a position to do something about it: the report about Volkov landed on his own desk at Section IX, which was dedicated to the 'professional handling of any cases coming to our notice involving communists or people concerned in Soviet espionage'. He arranged to go to Istanbul himself to extract Volkov and his wife. Naturally, he made sure that the Russians got there first, and the couple were spirited away to

Moscow where they were tortured and killed. A '"nasty piece of work" who "deserved what he got"' was Philby's considered, and psychopathic, opinion.[28]

His dual lives continued along weirdly parallel lines: in 1946 he was awarded both the OBE *and* the Soviet Order of the Red Banner in recognition of his work for the country's respective secret services. By then he was even being talked about as a future head of MI6, not least by his biggest fan, Sir Stewart Menzies, who currently held the role of 'C'. As a stepping stone on the way he was sent to Washington to serve as MI6's 'linkman' with the newly created CIA. This gave him complete access to the secret communications between Britain and America. Immediately, a great many bilateral operations started to go wrong: agents working in Ukraine, Lithuania, Estonia and Armenia disappeared in mysterious circumstances, while CIA-funded insurgents in Albania were picked up by secret police who seemed to already know the details of their plans. It is estimated that Philby's actions directly resulted in the deaths of up to two hundred guerrillas in Albania, plus thousands of their relatives and associates. He just shrugged. 'They knew the risks they were running. I was serving the interests of the Soviet Union and those interests required that these men were defeated. To the extent that I helped defeat them, even if it caused their deaths, I have no regrets.'[29]

This was the man MI6 closed ranks to protect. But they couldn't keep him on, they sadly concluded. His association with Burgess was just too close, and, now that MI5 had actually bothered to look properly, they had discovered all sorts of other dubious things about him – such as the fact he had not only moved to Vienna in 1933 to hang out with revolutionaries, but actually married one of them, Litzi Kohlmann. Nonetheless, Menzies had personally assured his MI5 counterpart, Sir Dick White, that his protégé could 'not possibly be a traitor'.[30] He made it clear to

Philby that he was leaving with honour, awarding him a generous £4,000 payoff. Newly unemployed, he retreated to a cottage in the countryside. MI5, still suspicious, bugged his phones. All they heard were a series of calls from former MI6 colleagues wanting to commiserate.

The whereabouts of Burgess and Maclean became the subject of frenzied speculation in the summer of 1954, after a KGB colonel defected in Australia and claimed to have evidence not just that the pair were living in the Soviet Union, but that they had been tipped off about Maclean's imminent arrest by a 'third man' who was a British official. MI5 and MI6 both started lobbying the foreign secretary: MI5 urging him to go public in the hope of flushing out Philby; MI6 assuring him the whole thing was just a vendetta got up by their domestic rivals. Menzies' successor as 'C', Sir John Sinclair, blustered: 'It is entirely contrary to the English tradition for a man to have to prove his innocence… in a case where the prosecution has nothing but suspicion to go upon.'[31]

Across the Atlantic, the bombastic and deeply peculiar head of the FBI, J. Edgar Hoover, had got a bug up his ass about the whole affair, and decided to leak Kim Philby's name to the New York *Sunday News*. Equally uninhibited, thanks to the custom of parliamentary privilege (which means no one can sue for libel over any remarks made in the Commons), was Labour MP Marcus Lipton. He stood up on 25 October 1955 and asked: 'Has the Prime Minister made up his mind to cover up at all costs the dubious third man activities of Mr. Harold Philby…?'[32] As foreign secretary, Harold Macmillan was instructed to make a statement in response. In a briefing paper circulated to the cabinet he maintained that it would be very unwise to start too scrupulous an inquiry into the whole affair. 'Nothing would be worse than a lot of muckraking and innuendo,' he fretted. 'It would be like one of the immense divorce cases which there used to be when

I was young, going on for days and days, every detail reported in the press.'[33]

This was certainly the view of the man chosen to brief Macmillan ahead of the debate, MP Richard Brooman-White, whose career might be summarized as Eton, Cambridge, MI6, Conservative Party. He was an old friend of Philby, and, in the double agent's own words, was one of those who was 'absolutely convinced I had been accused unfairly. They simply could not imagine their friend could be a communist. They sincerely believed me and supported me.'[34] The fact that everyone had thought exactly the same about Donald Maclean does not seem to have occurred to them.

'No evidence has been found to show that Mr Philby was responsible for warning Burgess and Maclean,' Macmillan assured the House. 'While in Government service he carried out his duties ably and conscientiously. I have no reason to conclude that Mr Philby has at any time betrayed the interests of this country, or to identify him with the so-called "third man," if, indeed, there was one.'[35]

Lipton and a few Labour colleagues protested. 'Whoever is covering up whom and on what pretext, whether because of the membership of a circle or a club, or because of good fellowship or whatever it may be, they must think again and think quickly,' said Frank Tomney, a trade unionist who had walked the whole way from Bolton to London in search of work in the thirties.[36] He was howled down by the Tory benches, where a taunting chant of 'Say it outside!' was soon got up. Philby himself repeated the invitation to Lipton at a press conference the following day, and the MP had little choice but to withdraw the accusation, saying he 'deeply regretted' it.[37] 'The last time I spoke to a communist, knowing him to be a communist, was some time in 1934,' Philby lied to the assembled journalists, all of whom were utterly charmed.[38]

Burgess and Maclean finally surfaced in Moscow the following February, when they were triumphantly presented to the world's press to read a script about how they 'came to the Soviet Union to work for the aim of better understanding with the West'.[39] Philby's luck did not run out for a further seven years. Following up a tip-off from yet another defector, an old friend of Philby's from his MI6 days, Nicholas Elliott, was dispatched to Beirut, where Philby was working as a journalist and hitting the bottle in a big way – like Burgess and Maclean before him. Philby finally shared all in January 1963 with the words: 'Okay, here's the scoop.'[40] After providing Elliott with a signed confession running to several pages, he contacted his KGB handler and was quietly smuggled on board a Soviet freighter. Two months later, the British government was forced to admit that he, too, had gone missing. And in June, beneath the provocative headline, 'HELLO, MR PHILBY', the state-owned Russian paper *Izvestia* revealed that he was not only a resident of Moscow, but a newly sworn citizen of the Soviet Union. He died in 1988 and was buried with a full KGB honour guard, just ahead of the collapse of the country and system he had devoted his life to.

In 1968 a trio of *Sunday Times* journalists published *The Philby Conspiracy*, which for many years stood as the definitive work on the scandal. By way of demonstrating how most people grew out of their youthful dalliances with communism and went on to lead the most respectable of lives, the book mentioned the names of a few other Cambridge friends: 'men who are now diplomats, millionaires, bulwarks of the Church, the Establishment and the established'. One such was 'Anthony Blunt, now Keeper of the Queen's Pictures'.[41] A decade after the book's publication, Margaret Thatcher was forced to confirm in the Commons that Blunt had also spied for the Russians. He had even helped to organize Maclean's defection to Moscow. Although the British security services had allowed him to keep his job at Buckingham Palace, they had known he was a Soviet agent since 1964 – a year after Philby had been unmasked, and a full thirteen years after Maclean had eluded his half-hearted pursuers.

If a mistake is worth making, it is worth making again and again.

> 'I want to say this on the question of foreknowledge, and to say it quite bluntly to the House, that there was not foreknowledge that Israel would attack Egypt – there was not.'

Sir Anthony Eden,
House of Commons, 20 December 1956

Anthony Eden needed an excuse. He knew full well that Colonel Gamal Abdel Nasser, who had seized power in Egypt in a coup in 1954, was bad news. When, two years later, he nationalized the Suez Canal – a vital trade route controlled by the UK since the Victorian era – it only went to prove exactly what sort of a man Nasser was. 'We all know this is how fascist governments behave, and we all remember, only too well, what the cost can be in giving in to fascism,' thundered the prime minister in a BBC broadcast on 8 August.[42] Eden had made his name as a vocal opponent of Neville Chamberlain's policy of appeasing Hitler back in the thirties; now, he was determined to refight the defining battle of his youth.

No matter that Nasser did not intend to stop shipping using the canal – he needed the income from it to fund his plan for a hydroelectric dam on the Nile – or that he offered to keep on all its staff on the salaries and terms they had previously enjoyed and pay all shareholders the full price of their shares as recorded on the Paris stock exchange the day before his nationalization. The canal, which linked the Red Sea and the Mediterranean, knocking more than four thousand miles off a journey that would otherwise take ships the full length of Africa and back again, was too important to trust to a man who, for all Eden's talk of fascism, was leaning dangerously leftwards and making friendly overtures to both the

Soviet Union and China. More than half of Europe's oil came through the canal, giving Nasser an effective stranglehold on Britain's energy supplies. More to the point, like so many former colonial subjects, he was challenging British power, and as such he needed to be swiftly and definitively crushed.

What Eden lacked was an actual justification for an aggressive response. 'We should be on weak ground on basing our resistance on the narrow argument that Colonel Nasser had acted illegally,' reads a cabinet briefing note drawn up by government lawyers. 'From the legal point of view, his action amounted to no more than a decision to buy out the shareholders.'[43] What they needed, concluded the special Egypt Committee that Eden convened of his most hawkish colleagues, was 'some aggressive or provocative act by the Egyptians'.[44] But as the months went past, and the British Army drilled its troops and painted its vehicles in desert colours, Nasser obstinately refused to provide one.

So they had to create one themselves. On 14 October two French diplomats visited Chequers. Eden told his private secretary that there would be 'no need' for any notes to be taken of their meeting and the visitors' book was quietly doctored to excise their names. Six days later the foreign secretary, Selwyn Lloyd, cancelled his official engagements, claiming to be ill. Instead of resting up at home he caught a flight from RAF Hendon to a military airfield in France. From there he was driven to a villa in the Paris suburb of Sèvres where the French prime minister, Guy Mollet, and the Israeli prime minister, David Ben-Gurion, were waiting. France, which had overseen the canal's construction in the nineteenth century, and which remained a major shareholder right up until Nasser's action, was committed to military action alongside Britain; the top secret agreement, signed in the villa's kitchen two days later with a champagne toast, brought Egypt's neighbour fully on board. The existing peace between Israel and Egypt was already uneasy: Nasser had demanded 'Israel's death' a year before.[45] But, thanks to the terms of the Protocol of Sèvres, it would be Israel which struck first.

The agreement did not beat about the bush. And it came with a full timetable and detailed instructions:

1. The Israeli forces launch in the evening of 29 October 1956 a large scale attack on the Egyptian forces with the aim of reaching the Canal Zone the following day.

2. On being apprised of these events, the British and French Governments during the day of 30 October 1956 respectively and simultaneously make two appeals to the Egyptian Government and the Israeli Government on the following lines:

A. To the Egyptian Government
   a) halt all acts of war.
   b) withdraw all its troops ten miles from the Canal.
   c) accept temporary occupation of key positions on the Canal by the Anglo-French forces to guarantee freedom of passage through the Canal by vessels of all nations until a final settlement.

B. To the Israeli Government
   a) halt all acts of war.
   b) withdraw all its troops ten miles to the east of the Canal.

...It is agreed that if one of the Governments refused, or did not give its consent, within twelve hours the Anglo-French forces would intervene with the means necessary to ensure that their demands are accepted.[46]

On 29 October, just as agreed, Israeli forces invaded Sinai, the peninsula between the Egyptian border and the Suez Canal. The next day, putting on their most surprised faces, the British and French governments demanded a ceasefire from both sides. When Nasser refused, British planes unleashed hell, practically destroying the Egyptian air force. On 5 November ground troops went in.

The invasion had one immediate effect – the exact effect Eden had been trying to avoid: Nasser did finally close the canal, scuttling all forty ships that were currently in it for good measure. The canal would not reopen to shipping until well into the following year. But the invasion had a second unwanted consequence: it whipped up an unprecedented frenzy of condemnation back home. The prime minister was booed in the Commons as he arrived to debate a Labour motion: 'That this House deplores the action of Her Majesty's Government in resorting to armed force against Egypt in clear violation of the United Nations Charter'.[47] Eden was forced to fall back on his own record to defend himself. 'I have been personally accused of living in the past and being too much obsessed with the events of the 'thirties,' he told baying MPs. 'However that may be, is there not one lesson of that period which cannot be ignored? It is that we best avoid great wars by taking even physical action to stop small ones.'[48] This overlooked a fairly enormous point: that Eden had actually started the small war to justify an action he had been itching to take for months.

But as yet, no one knew this. All they knew was that almost everyone seemed to think it had been a bad idea. Eden's protests that he had taken nothing more than a 'police action' in intervening to 'separate the belligerents' cut little ice. There were protests against the war across the Middle East, and as far afield as China and Indonesia. The UN General Assembly convened its first emergency session, with sixty-four nations voting to demand an immediate ceasefire. Thirty thousand people crowded into Trafalgar Square to hear Labour's shadow foreign secretary, Aneurin 'Nye' Bevan, spit fire at the prime minister: 'If Sir Anthony is sincere in what he says – and he may be – then he is too *stupid* to be Prime Minister.' The chant 'Law not war!' rang out around the square. A breakaway group marched down Whitehall singing, 'One, two, three, four, we won't fight in Eden's war.' They had to be held back by police at the entrance to Downing Street.[49]

It wasn't the domestic protesters that did for Sir Anthony; it was the Americans. The US had been quite happy to intervene when Iran's first democratically elected leader, Mohammad Mosaddeq, had tried a similar trick in 1951 and seized control of British-owned oil companies within his borders. The CIA had fomented a revolt which ended with Mosaddeq in prison and a much more 'friendly' regime in Tehran that didn't bother with silly notions like voting. But this time, Dwight D. Eisenhower was president of the US, and he had been clear from the outset that he (and by extension, America) wanted nothing to do with military action in the region. 'I hope that you will consent to reviewing the matter once more in its broadest aspects' was Ike's magnificently diplomatic message to Eden when he learned the Brits were determined 'to drive Nasser out of Egypt'.[50] In the White House, he was said to use somewhat more 'barrack-room language' to describe Eden's decision. But the prime minister and his colleagues seemed to have their fingers in their ears. 'We must keep the Americans really frightened…. Then they will help us to get what we want,' wrote Chancellor Harold Macmillan in his diary after a particularly discouraging conversation with the US secretary of state early in the crisis.[51]

The problem was a massive and disastrous overestimation of Britain's influence in global affairs a decade after World War II. Eden, Macmillan and the other cabinet hawks had failed to notice that the world had rearranged itself: there was a new war on, a Cold one, in which the UK would be no more than a minor and subservient player. Treaty obligations threatened to draw America into the conflict on Egypt's side: the USSR was already threatening to pile in and 'crush the aggressors by the use of force'.[52] Eisenhower finally put the kibosh on it all when he threatened to invoke oil sanctions against Britain unless they withdrew. Having already managed to stop supplies via the canal itself, the country simply would not be able to get by if it lost the rest. (As it was, petrol rationing had to be reintroduced later in the month.)

'That finishes it!' remarked Macmillan, finally getting the message.[53] A ceasefire was announced on 6 November, by which point nearly one hundred British and French soldiers had lost their lives. When the full and humiliating British withdrawal from the canal zone was announced on 22 November, it was not Eden who broke the news to the Commons: pleading ill health, he had handed over the reins to his colleague Rab Butler and gone off to recuperate in the Jamaica home of his friend Ian Fleming, creator of James Bond, whose undiplomatic adventures overseas never seemed to end like this. Eden finally resigned as prime minister the following January. Suez finished him.

He continued to lie through his teeth about his foreknowledge of the invasion,[54] but the evidence was out there. Ben-Gurion and his team had insisted on each party taking away a written copy of the Sèvres protocol: the last thing the Israelis wanted was for their European allies to have second thoughts and abandon them after they had fulfilled their half of the bargain. It would not be until twenty years later that one French and one Israeli official who had helped negotiate the protocol spoke out about its existence, and not until 1996 that the Ben-Gurion archives in Israel released the only surviving copy, which had been kept under lock and key ever since.

And the British copy, that solid evidence of both Eden's perfidy and his inherited conviction that he could do what he wanted and the world would just fall into line? It had been burned in a Downing Street fireplace forty years earlier. The ashes were left for the servants to clear away.

2

SEX LIES

Do politicians have more adventurous sex lives than the rest of us? Probably not. But there is a lot more pressure on them to pretend that they don't. If you and I get caught in a cruising spot or bondage dungeon (I don't mean together; you haven't even bought me a drink yet) the only ones likely to care are our partners and gossipy friends. For our elected representatives it will always be more of an issue.

Not that it is necessarily those who elected them who are most bothered: the public typically prove themselves quite capable of separating the professional and personal lives of their MPs. The problem is the tabloid press, who seemed to have taken over the job of policing the nation's morals from the established church at some point midway through the twentieth century. Maybe more politicians should have mimicked the brass-necked Lord Lambton, who, after being caught in bed with two prostitutes in 1973, shrugged and told the press corps that 'people sometimes like variety'. Yet, twenty years later, romps, shame and love children did as much to bring down John Major's government as the more serious corruption which enveloped his ministers. Tim Yeo, Robert Hughes, Rod Richards and Richard Spring all resigned from government positions after extramarital exposés, while ironically the only minister to ride out the scandal was the one with the most mistresses: Steven Norris. (He had five.)

Only in the very recent past have prime ministers become confident enough to act like grown-ups – and accept the fact that their colleagues sometimes do the same. In 2006 then opposition leader David Cameron decided that his environment spokesman Greg Barker leaving his wife for a man was not worthy of public comment, while Barker's mother-in-law dismissed any fuss with the immortal words, 'It's modern life isn't it? Men seem to think they can get away with it now.'[1] Barker was re-elected at the next election with a majority of nearly thirteen thousand, and that was in Bexhill-on-Sea.

These days you need to do something really extreme – one thinks, and then rapidly wishes one hadn't, of the 'bizarre sex act too revolting to describe' committed by, or rather on, Lib Dem Mark Oaten that same year – in order to shock anyone.[2] But being less than honest about it can still, *sometimes*, do the trick.

* * * * *

> 'There was no impropriety whatsoever in my acquaintanceship with Miss Keeler.'

John Profumo,
House of Commons, 22 March 1963

There was one small problem with the 'personal statement' that Secretary of State for War John Profumo read out to Parliament the morning after two Labour MPs brought up the rumours which were circulating about Christine Keeler, who had recently failed to turn up as a witness in a criminal trial: it was complete nonsense.

Let's compare his account, as solemnly delivered to the Commons,[3] with her version of events:

PROFUMO: My wife and I first met Miss Keeler at a house party in July, 1961, at Cliveden [the country house owned by Conservative peer Lord Astor]. Among a number of people there was Dr. Stephen Ward, whom we already knew slightly...

Keeler told the ghostwriter of her autobiography *Nothing But...* that she had been taken to Cliveden by Stephen Ward, who was not only her friend and landlord but the man who had educated her about 'the orgies that were the rage in upper-crust London'.[4] Ward rented a cottage on the estate, and had free use of Lord Astor's swimming pool – where, on the fateful night, he had dared her to swim in the nude. During this interlude two figures in evening dress – Astor and Profumo – turned up and proceeded to chase Keeler, still stark naked, around the pool. Having caught her, Profumo 'offered to give me a conducted tour.... He started cornering me. It was only for a kiss and a little surreptitious grope and really a million middle-aged men have done it before when they've had a few.'[5]

PROFUMO: … and a Mr. Ivanov, who was an attaché at the Russian Embassy.

The only other occasion that my wife or I met Mr. Ivanov was for a moment at the official reception for Major Gagarin at the Soviet Embassy.

Keeler claimed these two men from opposite sides of the Iron Curtain spent much of the following day's pool party 'vying for my attention'. The Russian won out first. 'That night Ivanov and I made marvellous, passionate love.'[6]

PROFUMO: My wife and I had a standing invitation to visit Dr. Ward.

Between July and December, 1961, I met Miss Keeler on about half a dozen occasions at Dr. Ward's flat, when I called to see him and his friends.

According to Keeler, Profumo himself lost no time: he phoned her the next day and took her out in his chauffeur-driven car and showed her all the sights: '10 Downing Street, which I had never seen before, and the barracks he was in charge of where the War Ministry was housed.' In the process, he 'made his attraction to me very clear'.[7] His wife, unsurprisingly, did not come along for the ride.

PROFUMO: Miss Keeler and I were on friendly terms.

They had sex for the first time a couple of days later at Profumo's house in Regent's Park. 'He was a strong, forceful lover,' she said, 'the kind of man who knows what he wants.'[8]

PROFUMO: There was no impropriety whatsoever in my acquaintanceship with Miss Keeler.

There was impropriety on regular occasions thereafter. 'Jack Profumo came round for a straightforward screw, no more, no less,' claimed Keeler. 'As he came through the door he had only one thing in mind, and that was to get me into bed.'[9]

PROFUMO: I last saw Miss Keeler in December, 1961, and I have not seen her since.

According to Keeler, she broke off the affair after a month or so, when Profumo proposed 'setting me up in a flat of my own' – not because of any growing commitment or affection towards her, but because he had been warned by the cabinet secretary, Sir Norman Brook, that he should steer clear of Ward, who 'apparently had close connections with the Assistant Russian Naval Attaché and MI5 were not entirely sure he was the diplomat he made out to be.' By this point Ward had started priming her with questions for her lover about 'atomic secrets'. Out of loyalty she refused Profumo's offer and did not see him again.[10]

PROFUMO: I have no idea where she is now. Any suggestion that I was in any way connected with or responsible for her absence from the trial at the Old Bailey is wholly and completely untrue.

That last bit at least was the truth. Although everyone suspected Profumo of being involved in her failure to appear in the witness box – even the attorney general had asked him about it – the person actually responsible for driving her to Spain was Paul Mann, who was attempting to broker the sale of Keeler's story to Fleet Street.

The trial concerned Johnny Edgecombe, another of the many dodgy men that Keeler – always described by the Holly Golightly-ish euphemism 'callgirl' – had unwisely got involved with. A jailbird who had earlier taken a knife to a fellow West Indian man who had become violently obsessed with Keeler, Edgecombe had started stalking her himself. He had been charged with attempted murder after firing a gun at Stephen Ward's home when Keeler refused to let him in. Having fallen out with Ward, who dexterously combined his adventurous private life with a career as osteopath to a number of high-profile clients, Keeler was now willing to spill the beans to anyone who would listen – but not necessarily for free. Mann hoped to increase the value of her story (and his cut of the proceeds) by preventing details from coming out in court, where any Tom, Dick or Harry would be able to report them. He wanted an exclusive. Now Profumo was living in fear of his own part in Keeler's story coming out. He wrapped up his oration to the Commons with an ominous warning: 'I shall not hesitate to issue writs for libel and slander if scandalous allegations are made or repeated outside the House.'

His statement could, of course, be reported, and Keeler read it in one of the British papers at her hideout in Spain. She claimed that her first question was 'What's impropriety?' She got the answer 'Screwing.' The trio of senior Conservatives who had interrogated Profumo ahead of his speech had been even blunter: as Iain Macleod, leader of the House of Commons, put it, 'Look, Jack, the basic question is: did you fuck her?'[11] He said no, and they made the mistake of believing him. After saying his piece in the Commons, Profumo and his wife, Valerie Hobson, headed off to the racing at Sandown Park in the company of their good friend the Queen Mother.

But he was not the only one lying about his affair at this point. Stephen Ward was denying everything too. Keeler, when she finally did sign a contract for an exclusive with the *Daily Express*, initially claimed she and the minister had merely had 'a friendship no one can criticise'.[12] In the end it was the conviction with which Profumo argued his own innocence to his colleagues that undid him. Home Secretary Henry Brooke wanted something done about Ward, who had used the publicity to show off about his friendship with Yevgeny Ivanov, claiming to have passed on information to MI5 about the Russian. The subject was a sensitive one: just a few months earlier a British civil servant, John Vassall, had been convicted of spying on the naval attaché at the British embassy in Moscow after the Russians blackmailed him over compromising pictures of him naked with no fewer than three other men. His boss, Thomas 'Tam' Galbraith MP, had been forced to resign as a minister on the grounds that he had addressed a letter 'My Dear Vassall' – which was enough to convince colleagues he was also gay.[13]

Thinking his cabinet colleague was in the clear, Brooke ordered a police investigation into Ward in the hope of pinning something on him. The most anyone could dig up in the way of spying was a passing comment to Keeler that she should ask Profumo about atomic secrets being passed from America to West Germany. This was a bit of a non-starter, so instead officers plumped for a charge of living on the earnings of prostitution. When interviewed by police, both Keeler and Ward had admitted that she had had sex with Profumo; Ward knew all the details, because one of his particular kinks had been that she should tell him all about her sexual encounters. There was no evidence he ever took a cut of her earnings from them, however. In fact she testified that the opposite had been the case: Ward had given her so much spending money that she was still in his debt.

Realizing he was being set up as a fall guy, Ward wrote to Brooke and the leader of the opposition, Harold Wilson, informing them that Profumo had lied to Parliament, which was a far more serious crime than a bit of extramarital nooky. On 3 June the war minister was called back from a holiday in Venice with his wife. He resigned from the government the next day. 'Daddy's decided to stop being a politician' was how Valerie, who had only learned of her husband's adultery during the holiday, broke the news to their seven-year-old son, David. 'He told a lie in the House of Commons, so now we're going to have a little holiday in the country'.[14]

Profumo, who had been talked about as a potential prime minister not so long before, withdrew entirely from public life. He spent the next forty years working discreetly as a volunteer for Toynbee Hall, a charity in the East End of London. In his absence, the country went potty. *The Times* thundered, 'It is a moral issue', and declared that Britain had been reduced 'spiritually and psychologically to a low ebb'.[15] The *Sunday Mirror* railed against 'the Upper Classes [which] have always been given to lying, fornication, corrupt practices and, doubtless as a result of the public school system, sodomy'.[16] The dam of deference that had for so long protected the ruling classes had finally, and permanently, been breached. In the Commons, Harold Wilson opportunistically frothed about 'disclosures which have shocked the moral conscience of the nation' and 'a sordid underworld network' getting its claws into the government.[17] The prime minister himself wrote a near-hysterical letter of apology to the Queen, assuring her: 'I had of course no idea of the strange underworld in which other people, alas, apart from Mr Profumo had allowed themselves to become entrapped. I begin to suspect in all these wild accusations against many people, Ministers and others, something in the nature of a plot to destroy the established system.'[18]

What definitely existed was a plot to destroy Stephen Ward, who was made the official scapegoat for the whole affair. He was arrested a few days after Profumo's resignation, refused bail and thrown into prison. His many friends in high places turned on him and refused to serve as character witnesses. His trial was held at the end of July. There was a scrum of photographers present on the morning after the judge's summing-up, as he was carried into an ambulance having taken an overdose of barbiturates. He died three days later, but not before the jury found him guilty on several charges.

For her own part, Keeler got a criminal conviction – but in another case altogether. She was sentenced to nine months for perjury during the trial of a man who had raped her and held her prisoner. All she had done was go along with a story suggested to her by the officer leading the investigation, Samuel Herbert, who was keen to gather evidence against Stephen Ward. By that point, having been denounced by the press as a 'shameless slut' and an 'empty-headed trollop' who would 'turn your house into a brothel, with coloured layabouts all over the place, drug orgies and all that jazz', the twenty-three-year-old welcomed it as a relief. 'I would be safe in prison, it would give me time to sort out the terribly confused state I was in.'[19]

'He repeated his question, "Will you marry me?" I asked if he really meant it. "I give you my solemn word of honour," he said. He even said he would put it in writing if I did not believe him. "Don't be ridiculous", I said. "Your word of honour is good enough for me."'

Sara Keays,
account of conversation with Cecil Parkinson, 9 June 1983

Mrs Thatcher's favourite cabinet minister, Cecil Parkinson, was often described as a 'love rat', just as the child he fathered with his secretary was always called his 'love child'. Since he never showed that child, Flora Keays, any love, and refused to even meet her until the day he died, the second bit of tabloidese seems inappropriate. The Queen's English also provides a better description than the first. Cecil Parkinson behaved like a shit.

That certainly is the descriptor that would be recognized among the classes in which the whole scandal played out. Sara Keays, the young woman who fell so heavily and unwisely for her boss when she arrived to work in his Commons office in 1971, was a solid product of the twinset-and-pearls, sherry-after-church Tory shires. She grew up in a large house in rural Somerset with parents who she introduces as 'Colonel and Mrs Hastings Keays' in her book about the affair; her brother-in-law was shortlisted as a Conservative candidate in the 1983 general election, and Sara hoped to be selected too, though she was happy to step aside when told it would be 'better to have a man as their candidate'.[20] Parkinson had the looks of a matinée idol and was praised by the *Daily Telegraph* for his monogrammed shirts; he had been a successful businessman both before and during his career as an MP and was plucked out as a protégé by Thatcher, who raved that he was 'dynamic, full of common sense, a good accountant, an excellent presenter'.[21] (More than one observer thought Thatcher had the hots for him.) When he became Conservative Party chairman in 1981, he had been married for twenty-four years and had three young daughters – as well as a long-standing bit on the side in the form of Keays, sixteen years his junior.

Not that that was how she saw herself. 'It was a genuine love affair,' she wrote in her memoir. 'I wanted so much to marry him and have his children.'[22] And Parkinson repeatedly assured her that was exactly what he wanted too, although after eight years she had stopped believing him, and left both him and London in 1979 for a year-long placement in Brussels. He didn't keep his promise not to contact her – instead, he called, begged her not to hang up and made a new promise. As she relates in her book:

> He could not leave it any longer, he wanted to ask me if I would marry him.... I was overjoyed, tremendously happy and elated. Of course, I said yes.... He said I must be patient as it would be some time before we would be able to marry. His Ministerial job [as a junior trade minister] would require him to travel a great deal over the coming year, but he would see me whenever he was in Brussels for Council meetings and we could meet in England for weekends. He said that we would start our new life together when I came back.[23]

Do you see what he did there? Parkinson had managed to install his mistress safely overseas, complete with a cover story for when he wanted to see her, just by telling her what she wanted to hear. All he had to do was extract himself from his obligation when her time in Belgium was up, which he duly did a week before her return: 'half way through lunch he suddenly said that he could not marry me after all, and that he could not leave his wife.'[24]

He did not intend to stop seeing her, however. Their affair went on for a further two and a half years, with Keays forced to jump through ever more elaborate hoops on Parkinson's behalf. Once, he took her on holiday to the Bahamas, but made her fly out a full ten days ahead of him, only joining her for 'a few blissful days' after a ministerial trip to South America.[25] On another occasion, when his car was stolen with two of his ministerial red boxes inside during an overnight stay at her London home, he refused to let her enlighten the police about where it had been taken from, 'saying that if the boxes were not found it would be the end of his political career and that was quite bad enough without revealing his affair with me as well'.[26] Leaving the boxes unattended was a serious breach of the rules and Parkinson got a deserved ticking-off from the home secretary for it. He then told Keays the whole incident was her fault. She decided that she didn't want to see him any more. Undeterred, he took to turning up and banging on her front door in the early hours; the second time he did so, she let him in. Despite the obvious trajectory of his career after Thatcher promoted him to chairman of the party in September 1981, Keays believed him when he offered her yet another promise: he would give up politics and marry her after the next general election.

By the time the campaign for that election was under way, Keays was pregnant. 'It was dreadful,' she recalled of breaking the news to him. 'He begged me to have an abortion, saying that if I had the baby I would destroy his career.... He said that I had better understand that he would never marry me and that if I had the baby he would never have anything to do with me again and never wanted to see the child.'[27] That was the only promise Cecil Parkinson made to Sarah Keays that he would keep.

For the next few weeks Parkinson pestered Keays to abort their baby from every possible angle, 'ringing me up late at night and early in the morning, and coming to see me'.[28] He brought his wife, Ann, and three grown-up children into it, demanding 'whether it was right to set the life of one person against the life of four others'.[29] He told her the baby 'would hate me for destroying his or her father's career'.[30] And then, on polling day itself, 9 June 1983, he changed tack, and pledged that he would leave his wife, marry Keays and help her bring up their baby together. What's more, he was about to go in and tell Mrs Thatcher so. 'He begged me to believe him, saying he knew he had behaved abominably, but that he had come to his senses and hoped that I would be able to forgive him,' wrote Keays two years later, admitting that 'even now I think he did mean what he said then.'[31]

Parkinson did tell the prime minister about his affair that afternoon – but it may have been because he didn't have much choice. Already sure her victory was in the bag, she had him in to Number 10 to offer him one of the top jobs – 'Foreign Secretary for two or three years, then Chancellor' – and Parkinson, in the account he later gave to Mrs Thatcher's authorized biographer, said he told her that having 'two Special Branch men next to me all the time' would not be helpful while he was dealing with the 'very big personal problem' he had to tell her about.[32] Instead, he left Downing Street with the promise of a new job in charge of the Department of Trade and Industry; what he was going to do about the baby was left unresolved. According to Parkinson, 'Mrs Thatcher was immensely sympathetic, not at all censorious.'[33]

The following day, Parkinson's fortunes changed. A few hours after inviting Parkinson to join her in victoriously waving to the crowds from the window of Conservative Central Office, Mrs Thatcher opened the first set of red boxes of her second term as prime minister and found inside one a ferocious letter from Sara

Keays' father telling her all about her new secretary of state's behaviour. 'Some five years ago he came to see my late wife and myself to tell us he was in love with Sara and intended to divorce his wife and marry her,' Colonel Keays informed her. 'For some undisclosed reason he changed his mind. However, he continued to pursue my daughter in spite of our very determined efforts to get the whole situation terminated.'[34] Parkinson was called to a 'most ghastly meeting' with Thatcher. 'He said some terrible things about me,' Parkinson protested to Sara in a phone call afterwards.[35] Parkinson phoned the prospective grandfather the following day to assure him he 'intended to do the right thing by Sara'. According to Sara's retelling, Parkinson said, 'I am not a rat, Colonel Keays – you are speaking to your future son-in-law.'[36]

Anyone remotely familiar with the situation could have been forgiven for not rushing out to buy a hat for the wedding. In August Parkinson summoned Keays, three months pregnant, to his solicitors' office and informed her that he was staying with his wife after all. 'Then he reverted to the line he had taken before polling day, reproaching me for not agreeing to have an abortion, saying that I had tried to destroy his career and his marriage, but that I was not going to succeed,' recalled Keays.[37]

With this turn of events, Keays finally – and rather admirably – decided to test the proposition. With 'frightful men' from the tabloids circling, she insisted on a joint statement being put out about her pregnancy, making it clear that their relationship had not only lasted 'a number of years', but that during it Parkinson had 'told Miss Keays of my wish to marry her' and then gone back on his word.[38] The statement was issued on 5 October, along with a terse one from Downing Street saying that Mrs Thatcher considered it 'a private matter. Mr Parkinson is a member of the Cabinet, doing a good job, and the question of resignation does not and will not arise.'[39] The Iron Lady could not have been more wrong. Versions of the story sympathetic to Parkinson began to appear in the press, and Keays was enough of a political insider to be able to read between the lines and spot the activity of government aides. More than one paper directly, but falsely, accused her of getting pregnant deliberately in order to entrap her man, while 'he was praised for his courage and his handling of his "ordeal",' she fumed. 'The entire Save Parkinson campaign was dependent on the destruction of my reputation.'[40] And she wasn't having it. The full, unedifying details of their twelve-year relationship were unveiled to readers of *The Times* the following week, right in the middle of the Conservative Party Conference. 'I've had it, haven't I?' said Parkinson to a colleague when he saw the first edition.[41] He resigned that night.

Cecil Parkinson's daughter Flora was born on New Year's Eve 1983. As promised, he supported her financially, but he never had any contact with her. As a single mother, Sara Keays coped with diagnoses of Asperger's and epilepsy as well as a major operation when Flora was four to remove a brain tumour. Around Flora's tenth birthday, renewed press interest led to Parkinson and Keays – communicating through their lawyers – to take out a joint injunction to protect their daughter's privacy. Sara subsequently fought against the injunction when she realized how restrictive it was. The result was a second court order specifically aimed at Sara. The effects, she later claimed, were so draconian that Flora could not appear in her school photo, or have her name printed in the programme of an ice-skating show she took part in. When the order finally lapsed on Flora's eighteenth birthday, Flora took part in a documentary in which she said, 'I would like to meet my Daddy. I would like to see him…. I would like to go to the cinema with him and have some fun.'[42]

She never got to. In January 2016, Parkinson's death was announced in the *Daily Telegraph*. The obituary said he was the

'Beloved husband of Ann' and listed his children, grandchildren and even step-grandchildren.[43] There was no mention of Flora whatsoever.

> 'My wife Judith and I have been experiencing difficulties in our marriage and we want to sort the situation out for the sake of each other and especially for our two young children. This I hope we can do in private. We both further hope these sensationalised disclosures in today's newspapers will be put aside and that we can be left to resolve these matters in private. We will be making no further comment.'

David Mellor,
statement to the press, 19 July 1992

David Mellor sometimes seems to go out of his way to behave appallingly. For instance, in 2014 a recording made public by *The Sun* in which he hurled abuse at a taxi driver: 'You've been driving a cab for ten years; I've been in the Cabinet, I'm an award-winning broadcaster, I'm a Queen's Counsel – you think that your experiences are anything compared to mine?'[44] But in the episode that made him most famous, he was just one of a huge cast of people behaving pretty disgracefully.

For one, there was Nick Philp, the landlord who bugged the flat where Mellor cheated on his wife and who sold the recordings to a Sunday tabloid. Then there was Antonia de Sancha, the thirty-one-year-old Mellor was cheating with. She didn't exactly cover herself with glory by announcing, 'I would never stoop so low as to do anything to get money in this situation,' then signing on with publicist Max Clifford. There's nothing to be said in favour of

Clifford, who has since been jailed for a series of sex offences. And finally there were the tabloid editors who competed to buy both the landlord's and de Sancha's stories in the gleeful knowledge that Mellor, as the minister responsible for the media, was considering new privacy curbs on the press. In fact, the only entirely innocent people were probably Mellor's wife, Judith, and their kids, as the politician pointed out the day after his affair was revealed while making not one, but two requests in the course of four short sentences that their privacy be respected.

Exactly five days later, Mellor marched Judith and his sons, aged twelve and eight, out in front of a mob of journalists to pose for photos with him. He even threw in his in-laws, Edward and Joan Hall, for good measure. The elderly couple's gritted-tooth smiles were rather at odds with their own comments to the press a few days earlier, which had appeared beneath the *Sun* headline 'IF HE'LL CHEAT ON MY DAUGHTER, HE'LL CHEAT ON THE COUNTRY'.[45] In the intervening period, Mellor had taken the precaution of making a phone call in which he ranted: 'if you talk about me again you will not see your grandchildren.'[46]

Before the flashbulbs had faded there were signs Mellor realized the appearance was a bad idea. 'I don't want it to look too much like a cynical photocall,' he told the press who had been summoned to his home by 'sources close to the minister', a traditional Fleet Street euphemism in which the first three words are completely redundant.[47] When Mellor was asked – not unreasonably – about how he was getting on with his family, he had the gall to reply, 'we are all resolved that all these matters are going to be discussed in private.'[48]

Other members of the motley cast made decidedly different resolutions. De Sancha, whose career as an actress had never quite got off the ground, suddenly became one of the most famous people in the country. She now found herself dumped by Mellor after what she claimed to have thought was 'a genuine relationship based on deep affection'[49] and reading concocted tales in the tabloids of past jobs in 'seedy vice dens' and roles in 'soft porn movies' – and barely recognizing herself in them.[50] 'She said so much had been written about her that was wrong, and she asked me to put the record straight,' Clifford recalled.[51] He quickly set about doing exactly the opposite.

The exclusive deal he brokered for de Sancha with *The Sun* kicked off on 7 September with the headline 'MELLOR MADE LOVE IN CHELSEA STRIP!' It came complete with a mocked-up photo of the minister in the kit of his favourite football team. Further revelations were staggered throughout the week, including the lie that the couple liked to suck each others' toes. 'Complete and utter garbage', de Sancha admitted later. 'I hate feet.'[52] As for the football kit claim, 'It was all rubbish made up by Max. I was in his office when he first came up with the soccer strip story to a *Sun* journalist. I was amazed.'[53] Having been outbid for her story, other papers naturally lined up to denounce her as 'shameless' and 'tawdry' for selling it. Clifford also took de Sancha around the TV studios, touting imaginary biopic offers from 'top Hollywood film executives'.

De Sancha did, however, manage to quash some of her publicist's suggestions, chiefly that she pretend to be pregnant with Mellor's child in order 'to keep the story hot'. 'It was just awful, awful, awful,' she said later.[54] On this her ex-boyfriend Mellor agreed. 'It should be quite clear to everybody who knows about Max Clifford and his antics that all this so-called new information are fantasies worked up to justify the large fee obviously being paid,' he announced in the week of the *Sun* series. 'It's disgusting that such a man can be accepted by newspapers as a witness of truth.'[55]

His statement hit on the point that elevated this particular sex scandal from the tabloids to the broadsheets. When the story first broke, it had been difficult to perceive anything in the minister's behaviour that had any bearing on his job, and Prime Minister John Major – a close friend of Mellor's – had been quick to turn down his offer to resign. But among Mellor's responsibilities at the newly created National Heritage department was oversight of the media. This was in an era when surreptitiously taped phone calls by both Charles and Diana were turning up in the papers, along with long-lens photos of their sister-in-law Fergie, and Mellor had only a few months earlier commissioned a review of press regulation – including consideration of the vexing suggestion that regulation be taken out of the industry's own hands. Mellor had earlier made it pretty clear which side of the argument he was on by warning that 'the press – the popular press – is drinking in the Last Chance Saloon'.[56]

Patsy Chapman, the former *News of the World* editor who now worked at the existing watchdog, the Press Complaints Commission, claimed his announcement of the review had come just twenty-four hours after the *News of the World* put allegations of Mellor's affair with de Sancha to Mellor, and received the answer – via Tory PR man Sir Tim Bell – that it was 'rubbish'.[57] The PCC ostentatiously downed another glass, announcing: 'In the case of politicians, it is right for the public to be informed about private behaviour.'[58] 'The Mellor affair demonstrates why MPs of all parties join the clamour for a privacy bill – They don't want the press's torch of freedom shone into the dark crannies of their own lives,' declared a leader column in *The Sun*, whose own editor, Kelvin Mackenzie, was shortly afterwards discovered to be cheating on his own wife with a much younger girlfriend.[59] The *Mail*'s Sir David English – found guilty of 'gross misconduct' by the press watchdog a few years earlier for waving his chequebook at relatives of a serial killer and then lying about it – announced that Mellor's position was untenable and he must resign from the government.[60]

He didn't – that is, not until a more substantial scandal, regarding a holiday the Mellor family had taken at the Marbella villa of the daughter of a financial backer of the Palestine Liberation Organization, burst into the headlines towards the end of September. After loudly demanding on *Newsnight*, 'Who decides who is to be a member of the British cabinet – the prime minister or the editor of the *Daily Mail*?', Mellor answered his own question by quitting the following morning.[61] 'TOE JOB TO NO JOB' was *The Sun*'s rather magnificent take.

Early on, the *Financial Times*, while rising above the murkier details, had declared that 'most observers at Westminster believe that whatever happens to Mr Mellor, the row has postponed indefinitely any prospect of the government introducing new privacy legislation.'[62] They were right. When Mellor's reviewer, Sir David Calcutt QC, reported back the following year that the PCC was ineffective, could not command public confidence and ought to be replaced with statutory controls on the press, the issue was kicked very far into the long grass.

The tabloids had won.

> 'I want you to listen to me. I did not have sexual relations with that woman, Miss Lewinsky. I never told anybody to lie, not a single time, never. These allegations are false.'

Bill Clinton,
White House news conference, 26 January 1998

You can understand quite how excruciatingly embarrassing it must have been for Bill Clinton. They were, as he pointed out, 'questions no American citizen would ever want to answer'.[63] And it was hard to see how his fooling around with a twenty-two-year-old intern in the Oval Office three years previously could have anything to do with the topic – some real estate investments Clinton and his wife Hillary had made in the seventies – that Independent Counsel Kenneth Starr had been appointed to look into four years earlier. Over the course of his inquiry, however, the thing had just kept mutating and expanding, taking in lurid conspiracy theories about the death of one of their former colleagues, the finances of the White House travel office, the use or misuse of FBI files, a number of businesses in Clinton's home state of Arkansas and, it started to seem, any other area of the president's past in which Starr thought he might be able to dig up dirt. Finally, with lifelong Republican Starr having long since crossed the line from diligent lawyer to obsessed stalker at the cost of some $25 million to public funds, the investigation had metastasized, enveloping another long-running embarrassment for Clinton: a case for sexual harassment brought by an Arkansas state employee called Paula Jones. Already Jones' harassment suit had entailed having the supposedly 'distinguishing characteristics' of the presidential penis aired in legal documents, and Lewinsky had been called to give evidence in the case. Now, Starr was asking whether or not the president had asked Lewinsky to lie in her deposition. The questions had got very personal. And he didn't want to answer them.

So the president lied, although he would do almost anything to avoid admitting that he had done so. From the moment allegations about an affair with Lewinsky broke in January 1998 and he informed his top advisers that 'There's nothing going on between us,' he was parsing his own sentences like the world's most pedantic English teacher. 'It depends on what the meaning of the word "is" is,' he insisted to Starr's grand jury when he was finally dragged in front of them seven months later. 'If "is" means "is and never has been," that is one thing. If it means "there is none," that was a completely true statement…. If someone had asked me on that day, "Are you having any kind of sexual relations with Ms. Lewinsky?", that is, asked me a question in the present tense, I would have said "no." And it would have been completely true.'[64]

Clinton even tried to quibble over exactly what did and didn't count as sex, a topic most of us haven't had to argue about since teenage sleepovers. As the official record summarized it:

> the President acknowledged 'inappropriate intimate contact' with Ms. Lewinsky but maintained that his January deposition testimony was accurate….

> As to his denial in the *Jones* deposition that he and Ms. Lewinsky had had a 'sexual relationship,' the President maintained that there can be no sexual relationship without sexual intercourse, regardless of what other sexual activities may transpire. He stated that 'most ordinary Americans' would embrace this distinction.

… In the President's view, 'any person, reasonable person' would recognize that oral sex performed on the deponent falls outside the definition.[65]

And, because as the president put it, 'I had a very careful thing I said, and I tried not to say anything else,' that meant he wasn't technically lying.[66]

He had backed himself into a dead end with no room to manoeuvre, and dragged along all of his closest aides and supporters, including his wife, Hillary, who was literally standing by his side when he made his fateful January statement to the public. The next night, she had gone on TV by herself to deny 'unequivocally' everything her husband had been accused of and tell people to 'be patient and take a deep breath… the truth will come out.'[67]

And the truth always does find its way out, even from dead ends. On the evening of 17 August, President Clinton made another broadcast, this time on his own. Lewinsky had admitted everything – that she had had an affair with the president and that she had lied about it – after striking a deal with Starr that she would not be prosecuted over her false affidavit in the Jones case. Having been issued with a subpoena requiring him to answer Starr's questions about Lewinsky under oath, Clinton had appeared in front of his nemesis. No sitting president had been legally compelled to do such a thing in US history. (Nixon had resigned rather than meet such a fate.)

'While my answers were legally accurate I did not volunteer information,' he told the American people. 'I did have a relationship with Miss Lewinsky that was not appropriate. In fact it was wrong.' He had the grace to add: 'I misled people, including even my wife. I deeply regret that.' But he couldn't resist defending himself: 'It is nobody's business but ours – even presidents have private lives.'[68]

Starr begged to differ. His 445-page report, published the next month, gave full lip-smacking details of ten separate sexual encounters between Clinton and Lewinsky, including the number of times he ejaculated, how often she orgasmed, what exactly the stains on her dress consisted of and, possibly most humiliatingly for him, the position he preferred so as not to aggravate his bad back.

But there was one thing that all the legalese and sanctimony of the Starr report couldn't disguise: sneaking snogs with your boss under the pretence of delivering important paperwork, exchanging gifts he could display in public as a secret signal and having rudies in the Oval Office when someone might walk in at any moment – it all sounds quite fun. Compared with other activities that have been conducted there over the years, it's also pretty harmless.

> '**I merely made a telephone call to find someone who could make themselves available for the entrusting of a person who had aroused the sympathy of us all.**'

Silvio Berlusconi, account of his contact with Milan police after arrest of teenager, 29 October 2010

It was a fairly routine night's work for the Milan police: a seventeen-year-old girl had been arrested after an accusation of theft. Her name was Karima El Mahroug. She had run away from home in her early teens and had since spent time in a succession of children's homes. Now she told police she was living independently, earning money working as a belly dancer in nightclubs. Yet she could not provide either identity papers or a permanent address, and the police computer turned up details of an earlier arrest on suspicion of theft. Because of her age, the child protection authorities were contacted.

Annamaria Fiorillo, an official with the juvenile court, ordered that El Mahroug be kept in custody until a place at a children's home could be found for her. It was already nearly eight o'clock at night, so that was unlikely to happen before morning. El Mahroug threw a strop about having to spend a night in jail, but that wasn't unusual. Police were, however, worried that she would be too cold in the skimpy clothes she had on, so they took her to the flat she said she had been staying in so she could collect something warmer. Her flatmate – who they suspected was working as a prostitute – happened to be in. She, too, kicked up a fuss, and started making phone calls. But it was when the police took El Mahroug back to the station and locked her in her cell for the night that things took an unusual turn. Station commander Vincenzo Indolfi got a phone call, and the prime minister was on the other end of the line.[69]

Silvio Berlusconi insisted there was nothing strange about his interrupting a trip to Paris to intervene personally in the case of an alleged petty thief back home. 'I am a person with a heart, and so I take an interest in people's problems,' he protested when asked about the incident.[70] But he went rather further than that. 'The caller said something like: "Is it true that you have detained this person? Then make the necessary checks and see what to do,"' said Indolfi.[71] Berlusconi told the commander that El Mahroug was a relative of the Egyptian president, Hosni Mubarak – accounts differ as to whether he claimed she was his niece or granddaughter – and if he and his colleagues didn't handle things correctly, they could end up with a serious diplomatic incident on their hands.

She was nothing of the sort. She wasn't even Egyptian – she came from Morocco, some three thousand kilometres away – but Berlusconi was never very good at all that racial stuff, greeting the election of Barack Obama two years previously by joking about how 'tanned' he was. For his part the prime minister claimed to have honestly believed El Mahroug's claims about Mubarak – he'd even brought her up in conversation with the Egyptian leader during a summit earlier in the month, resulting in what aides described as 'a rather confused conversation' – and only realized a few days later that 'everything she told me was a load of balls.'[72] But it didn't convince Annamaria Fiorillo, the magistrate who had given strict instructions that El Mahroug only be released when a place had been found for her in care. 'If she's Mubarak's granddaughter then I'm Queen Nefertiti of the Nile,' she snorted – but by then it was too late.[73] The seventeen-year-old had been discharged from the police station at around 2 a.m., in the company of twenty-five-year-old Nicole Minetti.

Minetti's career encapsulates everything you need to know about Berlusconi's Italy. She started off as a showgirl on one of the TV stations the prime minister owned; all Italian telly, no matter what genre, is liberally sprinkled with girls in bikinis. Then she retrained as a dental hygienist. She caught Berlusconi's eye when she treated him after he had several teeth smashed by an attacker at a rally in 2009. They started sleeping together – she insists she 'felt a sentiment of true love' – and he promptly installed her as a candidate for his own party. By 2011 she had a seat in the regional council in Lombardy. She was also being investigated, along with two of the prime minister's other associates, on suspicion of aiding and abetting prostitution by providing young women for the 'bunga-bunga' parties he notoriously hosted at Villa Certosa in Sardinia, at least some of which El Mahroug had attended (after lying about her age to secure an invitation).[74] El Mahroug claimed to have received €7,000 in cash from Berlusconi, an expensive necklace and even a car for her services, which she has always insisted (though a court begged to differ) did not involve sex with the prime minister.[75] But her presence alone provided more than enough motive for both Minetti and Berlusconi to want to get Karima El Mahroug out of police custody, quick smart.

El Mahroug did not shy from talking about how the prime minister had generously rewarded her. 'I felt like Cinderella,' she simpered in one of the interviews she subsequently gave.[76] But she wasn't Cinderella. Nor was she 'Ruby the Heartstealer', the nickname given to her by her male clients (and adopted by the eager media), who invariably prefer to think of a woman's participation in the sex industry as something voluntary and occasionally romantic rather than exploitative and often gross. El Mahroug had been a child runaway, who by her own account had been raped at the age of nine by two of her uncles and physically abused by her own father. When she went to Villa Certosa in February 2010, she was still seventeen, a minor, and if the seventy-four-year-old Berlusconi had had sex with her – as a number of witnesses at his subsequent trial testified he had – then it was a criminal offence under Italian law.

If Berlusconi had abused his office by intervening to spring her from the cells, then that was another criminal offence. And both could be added to the welter of charges the prime minister was facing – for corruption, bribery and tax offences. 'I am without a doubt the person who has been the most persecuted in the entire history of the world and the history of man,' he wailed histrionically in October 2009, after being stripped of his immunity from prosecution as an elected official.[77] This get-out-of-jail-free card had been one of his main reasons for going into politics in the first place. He'd been trailed by claims of massive corruption in his business career, and most of his efforts since getting into government had been devoted to trying to maintain and even extend the immunity perk. (He preferred to call it 'reforming the justice system'.) When it looked like he would face trial over the bunga-bunga parties and wiretaps of Minetti's phones were forming a major part of the prosecution case, he even tried to push a law outlawing the use of interception evidence through the Italian parliament. It failed.

What was needed, rather than desperate back-covering, was some statesmanlike behaviour – and that was exactly what Berlusconi didn't provide. 'It's better to be passionate about beautiful girls than to be gay,' he grinned when the news about El Mahroug broke, a comment that his own minister for equal opportunities – another former showgirl – felt compelled to denounce.[78] Even El Mahroug managed a more mature take than the prime minister, despite being nearly six decades years his junior: 'He is an institution, he should behave that way…. He can't expect discretion from people he doesn't know.'[79]

Berlusconi's status as the dirty old man of Europe had been well established the previous year, when his wife announced she wanted a divorce after he presented a glamour model with a diamond necklace at her eighteenth birthday party (he had missed his own daughters' coming-of-age celebrations). 'I cannot remain with a man who consorts with minors,' Veronica Lario announced in an open letter to the press.[80] Although polls showed the PM's priapism played well with some male Italian voters, the latest revelations prompted women's groups to lead a million-strong march demanding his resignation.

More revelations were coming. One prostitute claimed the bunga-bunga parties had been kept supplied with marijuana flown in on the PM's official plane. Police raided a gated apartment complex where he was rumoured to keep a harem of young women on call, and found large amounts of cash and expensive jewellery. El Mahroug's mobile phone records showed that she had been present at Berlusconi's villa at the same time as Russian leader Vladimir Putin, although no one could prove the two had met.

The case involving El Mahroug came to court in the summer of 2013, by which time Berlusconi had long since left the prime minister's office – though not as a result of any the multiple criminal charges he was facing; he had simply lost his parliamentary majority in the midst of fractious negotiations over an austerity package imposed by the EU after the financial crisis. He had previously been found guilty of tax fraud over a business deal in the nineties, but his prison sentence was commuted to community service. Two other cases for tax evasion and bribery had expired under the statute of limitations before they could make their way through Italy's labyrinthine legal system. Now the court ruled that Berlusconi had had sex with El Mahroug on no fewer than thirteen separate occasions, and abused his office with the phone call to the police station: he was sentenced to seven years in jail. A year later the appeal court overturned both convictions and acquitted him: though it didn't deny he had slept with the teenager, it ruled that there was no proof he knew she was underage at the time.

At time of writing, three years later, related cases were still ongoing. Italian prosecutors were seeking charges against dozens of young female witnesses in the trial for perjury, and although Berlusconi had admitted to paying them large amounts of cash, he insisted he did so out of his natural generosity rather than to persuade them to lie in court. El Mahroug – who at the height of the scandal announced she was marrying a nightclub owner in his forties – was one of the women on the list. She continued to maintain that she never had sex with the prime minister. 'It is the first time in my life that a man has not tried to take me to bed,' she told *La Repubblica*. 'He behaved like a father, I swear.'[81]

3

FINANCIAL FIBBING

There is a peculiar statistical anomaly that, just as we all impossibly believe ourselves to be better-than-average drivers, most of us assume our own income is somewhere close to average, if not on the low side. It allows us to go on simultaneously resenting both 'the rich' and the taxman, who must surely be helping himself to a bit more of our pay packet than everyone else's.

There has certainly always been a tendency among politicians to consider themselves badly paid. Oddly, it seems particularly prevalent in the sort of MPs who think other public servants, like social workers and nurses, ought to practise restraint in their salary demands and consider the virtue of their work as its own reward. But even those who like to make much of their own humility can seem to lack an awareness of how they compare to their constituents. Labour leader Jeremy Corbyn, who in 2016 was earning £137,000 a year, has the sort of pension after thirty-four years' service in Westminster that I am journalistically obliged to describe as 'gold-plated'. He also owned a home in one of

London's most expensive boroughs. Yet he blithely announced: 'I don't consider myself highbrow or wealthy'.[1]

He and every single one of his parliamentary colleagues, are. An MP's basic salary in 2016 was £74,962, nearly three times the national average.[2] The perks of the job aren't bad, either. But the company they keep doesn't help to keep them grounded. Civil service rates ensure that MPs' most senior advisers are considerably better paid than they are, and there is a surfeit of millionaires and billionaires keen to lobby them at every turn. New Labour made partying with celebrities into a political virtue, with Blair and his freebie-fan wife spending so much time in the holiday homes of fading pop stars.

When the coalition was assembled, twenty-three out of the twenty-nine incoming ministers were estimated to be millionaires, largely thanks to inherited wealth or property investments. After Theresa May assumed the mantle of leadership, having declared that her administration would be dedicated to everyone who was 'Just About Managing', she promptly selected as one of their representatives at the top table Boris Johnson, the man who described the £250,000 he got for moonlighting for the *Daily Telegraph* as 'chicken feed'.[3]

The precarious nature of a political career probably doesn't help either. When your statutory notice period is exactly as long as it takes the returning officer to finish a sentence, a nest egg is going to seem rather desirable. But what is perhaps unique to politicians is that they get to make their own rules. As this chapter will demonstrate, that means they can build in sufficient loopholes, ambiguities and get-out clauses to allow them to claim to be operating within both the letter and the spirit of the law – right up until the moment they get caught doing something that really doesn't add up.

* * * * *

> '**I think I can reasonably claim a respite from the burdens of responsibility and the glare of publicity which inevitably surrounds a Minister and, inexcusably, engulfs the private life even of his family.**'

Home Secretary Reginald Maudling,
resignation letter, 18 July 1972

At least Reginald Maudling was honest about his motivations. He had spent fourteen years in Parliament, all but two of them in ministerial office, and had failed to succeed Harold Macmillan as Conservative leader. The party's defeat in 1964 was the perfect opportunity for him to concentrate on 'building up a little pot of money for my old age', as he put it.[4] He would have been the first to admit that he hadn't shown much skill in that area as chancellor of the exchequer – he left a note for his successor at the Treasury, Jim Callaghan, which read 'Good luck, old cock – Sorry to leave it in such a mess.'[5] But both he and his wife, Beryl, had expensive tastes, and now it was time to start making some cash in order to fund them.

Not that Maudling intended to stand down from the Commons to do so. It was terribly agreeable representing Chipping Barnet, and the position did tend to open doors. The salary wasn't up to much – £3,250 a year, not even three times the average white-collar wage of £1,220 – but any MP worth his salt could bump that up significantly.[6] After all, there was no obligation on parliamentarians to declare any outside earnings. Maudling's civil servants might have issued mild protests about his role as a 'Lloyd's Name' – an underwriter of one of the biggest players in the insurance market

– when he also had ministerial responsibility for the sector as president of the Board of Trade, but he had brushed their concerns aside. Now that he was a mere backbencher, no one was going to be bothered about what he got up to – not least because he was prepared to be very imaginative when it came to disguising how he was remunerated.

First he took a consultancy with the Peachey Property Corporation, which was worth £5,000 a year.[7] Taking that as a salary would mean handing over a big chunk of his earnings to the Treasury, and Maudling knew from the inside that they would only waste it. Far better for Peachey to buy the freehold of his large country house, and lease it back to him at a peppercorn rent: that way he got all the financial benefits without having to trouble the taxman. Then a very successful architect and developer offered him a seat on the board of one of his companies. Maudling accepted it in return for an unusual pay deal that took care of both Beryl, who received an £8,000 annual covenant for the ballet theatre she was trying to establish in East Grinstead, and his son Martin, who got a job as a director of a related company straight out of university.[8] All three of them also took shares in the developer's businesses. In return Maudling was only too happy to make speeches in the Commons that aided the developer's building projects. Finally Maudling went international, taking a job as president of the Real Estate Fund of America. He got twenty-five thousand shares in the company for his efforts.[9]

My god, he knew how to pick them. The Peachey Property Corporation was chaired by Sir Eric Miller, who shot himself in 1977 while under investigation by the fraud squad over large sums of money that had gone missing from the company. The architect was John Poulson, whose success in landing public sector building contracts was down to the fact he had bribed local politicians on an epic scale; he ended up being sent to prison for seven years in

1973 by a judge who called him 'an "incalculably evil" man'.[10] The Real Estate Fund of America was the first of the three to explode, in 1970. Its founder, Jerome Hoffman, was indicted in the US on thirty-two charges of fraud and arrested in Rome. He was convicted on a single count in 1972 and sentenced to two years in prison. Maudling, tipped off by a *Sunday Times* exposé of Hoffman's previous fraudulent business, had jumped ship the year before.[11] But when the full extent of his financial interests emerged, more than one journalist was moved to paraphrase Oscar Wilde: to be associated with one conman may be regarded as a misfortune, two looks like carelessness, but three?

It all caught up with Maudling in 1972, when Poulson's business empire collapsed into bankruptcy and police started trawling through his web of contacts. By then Maudling was back in government, and installed as home secretary, which meant he was technically in charge of an investigation that was inevitably going to have to look into himself. He handed in his resignation to the prime minister on 18 July, getting a gushing reply from Ted Heath. 'I profoundly regret your going now,' he assured Maudling, 'and I hope that it will not be long before you are able to resume your position in the public life of this country.'[12] The *Daily Express* praised Maudling's honour in standing down despite no evidence (yet) that he had done anything wrong: 'a gesture without parallel in recent politics'.[13] *The Sun*'s front page declared it a 'tragedy' for 'the man who could have been Premier'.[14]

No one picked up on the paragraph Maudling included in his resignation letter having a pop at the press for 'inexcusably' invading his family's privacy. The chutzpah was incredible. Father, mother and son were in it up to their necks, and it wasn't as if they had limited their links to the professional. Reggie and Beryl liked to show off the swimming pool that had been put in for free at their Hertfordshire home by Poulson (it leaked), and were regular dinner guests at Eric Miller's house, where they nibbled on caviar, gauchely served on baked potatoes. Miller once presented Beryl with a silver chess set worth £2,750 as a gift.[15] Martin Maudling went to work for Miller on his father's recommendation too: one of his jobs was apparently to hand round a cigar box at the end of business lunches so the guests could help themselves to the contents – not Havanas, but hand-rolled fifty pound notes.[16]

It would, however, take a long time for these niceties to come out. In addition, the sheer scale of Poulson's corruption – two other MPs, one Tory and one Labour, had also been on retainers, not to mention dozens of local politicians and public servants – and the strong links between Miller and Labour leader Harold Wilson tended to draw attention away from Maudling. The most serious charges against Maudling, over the parliamentary interventions he had made on Poulson's behalf, did not emerge until 1974. They prompted the creation of the Register of Members' Financial Interests, which obliged MPs to 'disclose any relevant pecuniary interest or benefit of whatever nature, whether direct or indirect, that he may have had, may have or may be expecting to have' when conducting parliamentary business – or at least come up with clever ways not to.[17]

It took a further three years for a specially convened select committee to rule that Maudling had not only indulged in 'conduct inconsistent with the standards which the House is entitled to expect from its members', but written a resignation letter which was 'lacking in frankness'.[18] By then he was well on his way to drinking himself into an early grave. He started in the mornings on a mixture of gin and sweet vermouth. He could afford it.

> 'Mr Hamilton has given him an absolute assurance that he had no financial relationship with Mr Greer, and the president [of the Board of Trade] has accepted this.'

*Cabinet Office, memo on response of Neil Hamilton
to Secretary of State for Trade and Industry, 20 October 1994*

The tip-off that led to the disgrace of our current subject, Neil Hamilton, in the cash-for-questions affair, came from Mohamed Al-Fayed, the owner of Harrods. The tip-off that led to the downfall of Jonathan Aitken, which we will study in the next chapter, also came from Fayed. So too did the tip-off that led the *Sunday Times* to offer a number of backbenchers cash to ask parliamentary questions in the summer of 1994. Two snapped at the bait: one, David Tredinnick, gulped it down whole, then angrily claimed he 'did not expect to receive a cheque... I refused to accept a cheque', only for the paper to release a recording of him asking for a cheque to be sent to his home address. He was suspended from Parliament for a month.[19] For a while Mohamed Fayed was the biggest source of tip-offs in town.

This poses a problem, since Fayed is one of the world's most egregious liars. He is a man incapable of telling the truth even about his name or date of birth – he added the honorific 'Al' to the surname on his passport in 1970, knocking a few years off his age at the same time.[20] His wild lies about the death of Princess Diana, backed up with legal threats, prevented her inquest from being heard for an entire decade, at which point he lied that the delay was down to a conspiracy to keep him from discovering the truth.[21] He's a man – and don't take my word for it, these are the words of a team appointed by the Department of Trade and Industry (DTI) to conduct an exhaustive, year-long inspection of his businesses and the various claims he had made about his career – whose lies 'created a new fact: that lies were the truth and that the truth was a lie.'[22]

Trouble was, as such a man, Mohamed Fayed tended to surround himself with scoundrels and liars too. And sometimes – when it suited his own interests – he told the truth about them. He only told the truth about Neil Hamilton after the MP had outlived his usefulness and, in the businessman's view, betrayed him. And his disclosures, when they came, painted himself in just as bad a light as the politician, because for every corrupted MP there is also a corrupter, and Fayed admitted to enthusiastically corrupting not just Hamilton but, both personally and with the help of lobbyist Ian Greer, several other MPs too. He did so, he claimed, because Greer had informed him that, when it came to the Parliament of Great Britain, you 'rent an MP just like you rent a London taxi.'[23]

It began with the titanic struggle between Fayed and Roland 'Tiny' Rowland, a business mogul with equal enthusiasm for immorality, palm-greasing and feuds, over control of department store chain House of Fraser and its flagship, Harrods, during the early eighties. Fayed and his two brothers won the battle in 1984 with a £615 million cash bid. Rowland immediately devoted all his resources – which extended into every part of the globe and included a national newspaper, the *Observer* – to exposing the Fayed siblings as fibbing about the sources of their cash. The Fayeds claimed it was inherited wealth from their ancestral business empire in Egypt. The DTI inspectors would subsequently conclude that such claims were 'completely bogus'; the Fayeds' father had actually been a primary teacher turned school inspector.[24] Mohamed had built up his fortune, and the illusion of an even bigger one, through a series of dubious associations with powerful and wealthy men: Saudi arms dealer Adnan Khashoggi, Haitian dictator François 'Papa Doc' Duvalier, and the Sultan of Brunei (it was his money Rowland was convinced had been used for the House of Fraser deal).[25]

Tiny Rowland wanted more than newspaper exposés. Vowing to 'never forgive or forget', he strained every sinew towards forcing a government inquiry into the purchase.[26] Fayed became equally obsessed with preventing such an outcome, pursuing his vendetta with the same obsessive determination he would bring to his quest a decade later to convince the world that someone – *anyone* – other than his own drunken security boss was to blame for the deaths of his son and Princess Diana.

Enter Ian Greer, whose eponymous lobbying company kept several MPs on its books, paying them both for 'consultancy' on behalf of clients, and with 'introduction fees' for any potential customers the politicians could push in their direction.[27] Sometimes these would be declared to Parliament, sometimes not: a star performer, Michael Grylls, declared one payment on the Register of Members' Interests when he had actually received at least three, belatedly added another when it was exposed in print and was later found to have 'seriously misled' the authorities when it turned out he had actually banked at least six or seven.[28]

In 1985 Fayed agreed to pay £25,000 a year to Ian Greer Associates for lobbying services.[29] Before long he got his first result: the lobbyist wrote to say, 'I have spoken to Neil Hamilton MP, Vice-Chairman of the Conservative Party's Trade and Industry Committee, who has agreed to table a question'.[30]

Hamilton, elected as MP for Tatton in 1983, was way out on the right wing of the Tory party, a member of the Monday Club, who attacked the BBC for broadcasting a concert on behalf of the imprisoned Nelson Mandela and described the African National Congress as a 'typical terrorist organisation'.[31] Hamilton was not especially bright, talented or charismatic, and his preference for brightly coloured bow ties was not enough to make him the 'bit of a character' he obviously yearned to be. However, he was greedy and, having signed up to 'consult' for Greer's company as soon as he won his seat, quite happy to attack Rowland in the Commons on Fayed's behalf. The MP fired off questions about the ownership of the *Observer*, which Rowland was turning into his own demented propaganda sheet, even publishing special midweek editions of the Sunday title when he gathered sufficient dirt on the Harrods boss. Hamilton also pushed for a meeting with the trade secretary, Paul Channon, to complain about Rowland's persecution of Fayed. But after Rowland started pushing dodgy claims that Prime Minister Margaret Thatcher's son, Mark, had been recruited to help Fayed in the run-up to the 1987 General Election, Channon could no longer resist the political pressure, and he launched an official investigation into the House of Fraser purchase.

So much for the 'official' side of things. Fayed also claimed that during 1987 he started personally handing over brown envelopes filled with extra wads of both fifty-pound notes and Harrods gift vouchers to Hamilton after 'he came to me and complained that he wasn't getting enough from Greer alone.'[32] Hamilton certainly stepped up his efforts at this stage. He fired off a letter of complaint, on official House of Commons notepaper, about Rowland's business practices to the head of the London Stock Exchange, not forgetting to point out that he was 'Vice-Chairman of the Conservative Trade and Industry Committee', and personally visited new trade and industry secretary, Lord Young, to try to persuade him either to cut the House of Fraser inquiry short or launch a reciprocal one into Rowland's own businesses.[33]

That September Hamilton got a spectacular reward: an all-expenses-paid trip to the Paris Ritz, which Fayed owned, along with his wife, Christine. The couple certainly ensured that all expenses meant *all* expenses. They requested five nights in the hotel, which would have cost up to £3,000 for the room alone, stayed for six and dined in the most expensive in-house restaurant every night. The bill for their vintage Bollinger and lobster (the latter, Hamilton would later protest, was only a starter-sized portion), all their other meals (including afternoon tea) and their enthusiastic use of the minibar came to over £2,000, which Hamilton signed and left for Fayed to pay. Bear in mind, these are 1987 prices. 'I felt that he was abusing my hospitality,' grumbled Fayed, a man who used to press expensive gifts on every visitor to his office, sometimes smuggling them into the boot of their car in the valeted car park if they demurred.[34] Greer, too, later complained that Christine was always asking him for upgrades and extra freebies on the jaunts he organized for the couple, to the point where 'my patience was wearing thin.'[35] When the Hamiltons rang the Ritz to request an extra free stay on the way back from their subsequent holiday elsewhere in France, Fayed ordered staff to pretend that the hotel was full.

Hamilton did at least up his efforts, sending an OTT letter to Lord Young ahead of Fayed's first appointment with the DTI inspectors to say that the exercise was 'such a monstrous injustice… a twentieth-century Spanish Inquisition'.[36] He wrote an equally ridiculous letter to his paymaster, assuring him that 'everyone knows the Fayeds to be among the world's most significant businessmen.'[37] He tabled question after question in an attempt to cast doubt on the inquiry.

But it was not enough for the Harrods owner. Nothing ever could be. 'I want processions in Parliament!' he bellowed at Greer.[38] Fayed had a habit of demanding the impossible, then accusing those who failed to achieve it of betraying him. Alas, that was exactly Hamilton's fate. In 1992, long after the inspectors had ruled that Mohamed and his brothers had 'dishonestly represented their origins, their wealth, their business interests', the MP was promoted to a junior ministerial role at the DTI.[39] Fayed, who then was attempting to get the European Court of Human Rights to overturn the report's conclusions, assumed it was time to call in his favours. But while Hamilton was quite happy to carry on dealing with any number of other Greer clients in his new job without declaring any interest, the court action put Fayed in direct opposition to the department he now represented. The minister had no choice but to reject his former benefactor, U-turn on everything he had said from the backbenches and announce publicly that the inquiry was 'independent… a carefully considered and thorough investigation'.[40] Fayed's conclusion was blunt: 'The Government have shat on me.'[41] Now he had to get his revenge.

His weapon of choice was an odd one: the *Guardian*, whose editor, Peter Preston, he invited to Harrods for a series of meetings in 1993. In the book a team of *Guardian* journalists subsequently published about the cash-for-questions affair, they claim Preston 'put on the biggest pair of kid gloves he could find, and carried a very long spoon' before dealing with Fayed, but he was unable to resist the story he had to offer.[42] The problem was standing it up: Fayed changed the details with every telling, and he was surrounded by less loquacious aides who refused to hand over vital evidence and worried about Fayed incriminating himself. The meetings dragged on inconclusively for nearly eighteen months until the verdict from the Court of Human Rights came through – against Fayed – and he was finally ready to go on the record. 'TORY MPS WERE PAID TO PLANT QUESTIONS SAYS HARRODS CHIEF' roared the *Guardian*'s front page on 20 October 1994.[43]

It didn't come as a surprise in Downing Street. Fayed had been spouting off to so many people that Number 10 already knew what he was saying. The previous month, Hamilton and Tim Smith, another of the MPs recruited to Fayed's cause, had been pulled in for questioning by the cabinet secretary, Robin Butler. Smith had admitted everything, and resigned from his own junior ministerial position on the morning of the *Guardian* splash. Hamilton bluffed it out. He denied any misbehaviour, gave misleading accounts of the Ritz stay and his acquaintanceship with Fayed, and instructed London's fiercest libel lawyers, Peter Carter-Ruck and Partners, to rain a blizzard of writs down on the paper. (Greer, who was equally guilty, did the same.) Finally he took a call from his boss, Trade and Industry Secretary Michael Heseltine, who asked him the key questions again: had he ever taken any money from Fayed, and had he had a financial relationship with Ian Greer's company? Hamilton answered no to both, so he was allowed to keep his job.[44]

He lasted five days. On 25 October he was summoned to face the bad-cop/bad-cop/bad-cop combo of Butler, Heseltine and the chief whip. They informed him that further revelations – about undeclared payments from lobbyists for the South African regime and Mobil Oil – meant he had no choice but to resign. (In the later, unsuccessful libel case Hamilton brought against Fayed, barrister George Carman said that the £10,000 he got from Mobil alone 'establishes corruption on the part of a Member of Parliament'.[45]) There was also the problem of Hamilton attending the annual general meeting of a firm he had previously been a non-executive director of after becoming a minister, not least because the company had since collapsed and was under investigation by his own department. Once again, greed had been Hamilton's undoing: he protested he had only gone to the meeting 'for a good lunch'.[46]

Beleaguered Prime Minister John Major, shaken by a series of scandals in the previous few months, announced that he was setting up a committee 'to examine current concerns about standards of conduct of all holders of public office'.[47] Lord Nolan, the judge who chaired it, would conclude that the register of interests set up after the Maudling scandal was not fit for the job in its present form:

'such opaque descriptions are routinely being entered so there is disclosure in appearance but not in practice.'[48]

But if the prime minister thought the announcement of an inquiry would end this particular scandal, he was sorely mistaken: Hamilton hung around like a bad smell for the last three years of his administration – and beyond. Some of this was due to Hamilton's dogged insistence that he had done nothing wrong, but a great deal of it was down to the determination of some of his colleagues to prevent anyone proving he had. It didn't help that Mrs Thatcher, a Hamilton fan, kept popping up to offer her support. Right-wing fans banded together to fund his various legal actions. One of Major's whips, David Willetts, who was meant to be scrupulously disinterested, unwisely put suggestions in writing as to how an inquiry by the Select Committee on Members' Interests could be blocked, along with a note saying Hamilton 'wants our advice'.[49] When the memo later became public, he tried, even more unwisely, to pretend it meant the MP was 'in want of' advice, rather than the plain English meaning of those words that anyone born after the Victorian era would recognize.[50] There was even an effort to have the libel case against the *Guardian* heard not at the High Court but by Parliament under obscure mediaeval statutes. But the wide-ranging claims made by Greer and Hamilton in their libel suits meant that embarrassing details kept emerging as lawyers trawled through documents. They included accounts that clearly showed payments from Greer to Hamilton, as well as descriptions of shopping expeditions taken by Christine after which bills for paintings and garden furniture were sent directly to the very lobbyist with whom her husband claimed to have had no financial relationship.[51]

Hamilton and Greer abandoned their libel case just a week before it was due to go to trial. It seemed they had become aware of just how much evidence the *Guardian* had amassed against them. 'We trust you won't be running the story in your newspaper,' the MPs' lawyers optimistically faxed the broadsheet's editors on the day they pulled their case out of the courts.[52] They got their answer in the form of the next morning's front page: a photo of Hamilton staring balefully above the headline: 'A LIAR AND A CHEAT.'[53]

Still, Hamilton wouldn't go away. He continued to loudly insist he had only abandoned the libel case for lack of money, and that every accusation against him was a stinking lie. Even when he was forced to admit taking two separate payments from Greer, he anticipated Bill Clinton by claiming this didn't amount to a 'financial relationship'.[54] Hauled in front of Sir Gordon Downey, the parliamentary commissioner for standards, he whined: 'I did not mention the commission payments when I spoke to Mr Heseltine.... I knew that if there were to be another cause for adverse media comment against me... it could be used as a very big stick with which to beat me and to cause my resignation to take place.'[55] Psychologists could have a field day with the use of the passive voice in that phrasing. Hamilton seemed as incapable of accepting responsibility for his own plight as he was of paying for his own dinners.

Downey was having none of it. 'He knew that he had had a financial relationship with Mr Greer, and he deliberately decided not to disclose the existence of that relationship to Mr Heseltine,' the commissioner determined. He followed this up with some magnificent legalese: 'There appears to be validity in the allegation that the relevant statements by Mr Hamilton were, in varying degrees, untruthful.'[56] The verdict on Fayed's direct 'brown envelope' payments came later from the jury in another libel trial. Despite being warned by the judge that the Harrods owner's 'appreciation of what is fact and what is fiction and what is truth and what is fantasy is warped', and they should treat his evidence accordingly, the jury unanimously ruled that 'on the balance of probabilities...

Mr Al-Fayed has established on highly convincing evidence that Mr Hamilton was corrupt'.[57]

Of course by then the Hamiltons – very much a double act now – had fought, and lost, the 1997 General Election. The other parties managed to turn the campaign into the last thing John Major wanted, a referendum on sleaze, by standing aside in Tatton and letting squeaky clean former BBC correspondent Martin Bell stand as an independent. A televised ambush on the campaign trail saw Christine bark, 'Do you accept that my husband is innocent?' in the voice that launched a thousand cheap reality TV show and panto appearances.[58]

Two decades later Hamilton made an unlikely return to politics, getting himself elected as a Welsh assembly member for UKIP in 2016. So popular does he remain that a source close to party leader Nigel Farage said at the time of his selection as a candidate: 'every time someone tries to flush the s[hit] down the toilet he keeps coming back up.'[59]

> 'I think most people who have dealt with me think that I am a pretty straight sort of guy.'

Tony Blair,
interview, BBC On the Record, 16 November 1997

Before Lord Nolan had even finished his stint overseeing the new committee on standards in public life, the Labour Party and its bright shiny new leader were making political capital out of what he wouldn't look at. 'In the light of the concern expressed even in Government circles about the funding of political parties, is not the right, fair and honourable thing to do to widen the remit of the Nolan committee so that the funding of all political parties could be looked at in a proper and impartial manner?' demanded Tony Blair at Prime Minister's Questions on 21 May 1996. Across the dispatch boxes John Major, horribly aware that he would have to fight an election campaign within the year and would be unable to do so without the generous funds of anonymous businesspeople which traditionally flowed towards the Tory party, could only splutter, 'I do not believe that that is the right way to proceed,' and try to divert the exchange onto Labour's bankrolling by the trade unions.[60] It was a bit of a non-starter. The trade unions hated Tony Blair nearly as much as he hated them, and were zipping their wallets shut as fast as they could.

Fast-forward a year and swap ends. 'New' Labour was now in power and enjoying a lengthy honeymoon, with what felt like the whole country entertaining an uncharacteristic optimism that the bad old days of sleaze were over and everything was going to be cool in Britannia. The prime minister even felt confident enough to make a declaration in his party conference speech at the end of September: 'I can announce to you we are going to bring forward a Bill to ban foreign donations to political parties and to compel all parties to make contributions above £5,000 public. And we will ask the Nolan Committee to look at the wider question of Party funding. At the next election all political parties will at last compete on a level playing field.'[61]

Just over a month later the roof fell in. Tessa Jowell, the public health minister, declared that the outlawing of tobacco advertising and sponsorship in sport – something Labour had promised in their manifesto, and pledged to implement in their first Queen's Speech just a few months before – should make an exemption for Formula One, on the grounds that the motor racing business might move overseas and take up to 200,000 jobs with it.[62] Both Jowell and her boss, Health Secretary Frank Dobson, had previously argued vociferously for an outright ban; journalists smelt a rat.[63] The first suspect was Jowell herself, or rather her husband David Mills, who had been involved with the F1 team run by the Benetton family (he had a thing about rich Italians, becoming disastrously tangled with Silvio Berlusconi later on).[64] But Jowell was only obeying orders. Blair had instructed Dobson to push for the F1 exemption two weeks earlier, after personally entertaining at Number 10 the F1 owner Bernie Ecclestone; Max Mosley, the head of the motor sports governing body Fédération Internationale de l'Automobile; and their political lobbyist David Ward.[65] In keeping with Blair's relaxed, 'call me Tony', government-from-the-sofa style, no official minute of the meeting had been taken. So no one can say for sure whether or not the subject of donations came up. But Blair knew full well that the Labour Party's 'high value donors unit' were at the time actively soliciting cash from Ecclestone – and, more to the point, that they had already accepted no less than £1 million from him that January, to add to their election war chest.[66]

Ecclestone does like throwing large amounts of money around – in 2014, apparently oblivious to any irony, he paid a German court

£60 million to drop bribery charges against him – but why the tycoon decided to hand over so much money to Labour seemed a bit of a mystery, even to him. 'I thought Blair had the same ideas as me, that he was anti-European and anti-Common Market,' he later told the *Sunday Telegraph*, which suggests he needed to watch the news more carefully.[67] Mosley, who had moved on from supporting his fascist father Oswald's Union Movement in the 1960s to New Labour in the 1990s, claimed he had teased his colleague into making the donation when he noted how much money he would save thanks to the party's pledge not to raise income tax. Labour would be obliged to declare the cash, like they did with all donations over £5,000, but because it fell into the 1997 accounting period, the rules said they wouldn't have to do so until way off in September 1998.[68] And that, Blair and his closest advisers swiftly decided, was how they wanted things to stay. Instead of coming clean about the donation and denying it had anything to do with the change in policy, they would sit tight, despite the journalists sniffing around. Gordon Brown 'got him to agree that unless we were absolutely clear the press had the story itself, we should hold fire, and let it dribble out,' wrote Downing Street spin doctor Alastair Campbell in his diary. He agreed to the plan despite personally thinking 'we were just waiting around for a car crash to happen.'[69] Labour press officer David Hill would subsequently confess: 'My job… was to try to throw everyone off the scent.... I did not say to journalists that Ecclestone had *not* given us any money, although I know I did say everything but that.'[70] Ecclestone agreed: 'If someone puts me up against the wall with a machine gun, I will not confirm or deny anything.'[71]

In the meantime Blair and Co. sent a confidential letter to Sir Patrick Neill, Lord Nolan's successor as commissioner on standards in public life, about the donation – and the possibility of a second one – so that if journalists *did* stumble across the truth, they would be able to produce correspondence to show they were doing the right thing. Except they couldn't even bring themselves to be honest in covering their backs. The letter was written in Downing Street, but sent in the name of the Labour Party's general secretary, further blurring the very lines between party and government that they were supposedly highlighting. And the letter failed to describe the gobsmacking scale of the January donation; it simply said it was 'substantial'. Neill, not unreasonably, assumed that meant something around the one-hundred-thousand mark, not ten times as much. Yet still he came back with the last response Labour wanted: not only should they refuse any further donations, but they should give back the first one, to avoid 'even the appearance of undue influence on policy'.[72]

By that point, however, things had got considerably worse in the bunker. Gordon Brown, who had been party to the whole thing and knew every detail, was questioned on the BBC's *Today* programme about whether or not Ecclestone had donated any money, and panicked. He replied, 'You'll have to wait and see, like I'll have to wait and see when the list is published. I've not been told and I certainly don't know what the true position is.'[73] According to Andrew Rawnsley, the most informed historian of the Blair–Brown period, the chancellor came storming back to the Treasury 'in a red mist which staggered even those who had long endured his titanic tempers. Brown raged at his staff: "I lied. I lied. My credibility will be in shreds. If this gets out, I'll be destroyed."'[74] His spokesman later denied this version of events.

The following afternoon Ecclestone, who was getting heartily sick of being badgered by the press, confirmed he had given the party a cool million. The wangling over the second donation dribbled out twenty-four hours later. 'Day after day we were forced to reveal more and more, look like we had more and more to hide,' grumbled Campbell to his diary. 'It was a disaster.'[75]

Any chance of making the argument that the donation had had no influence on the policy change – which Blair insists to this day was the case – was long gone. It was as if the whole top tier of the government had been so paralysed by the fear of how bad the donation would look, they failed to realize it would look even worse to be caught hiding it.

Now that the worst had happened, they all refused to take responsibility. 'TB… went straight into head-in-sand mode,' wrote Campbell. 'There was a problem with his mindset, in that he was thinking he could do no wrong, and that people would therefore not assume he could do any wrong on issues like this. But in part because of the way we had handled it, it looked like he had done something wrong. We had made a big mistake in not going up-front, but he would not admit it.'[76] Brown's spin team were going round falsely briefing journalists that he had been 'out of the loop' on the whole thing. The rest of the cabinet, who really hadn't known what was going on, were refusing to defend the government; Jeremy Paxman sneered that 'no ministerial bottom' could be found for the empty chair in the *Newsnight* studio.[77] The only person who was happy was John Major, who, having barely been heard of since being swept out of office in May, was now making loud noises about 'hypocrisy on a very grand scale'.[78]

Eventually Campbell persuaded the prime minister, who had begun to convince himself that the scandal might end his premiership before it had even got going, that he needed to kill the story by 'taking a kicking' on live TV.[79] John Humphrys, one of the BBC's most ferocious attack dogs, was invited down to Chequers on Sunday morning to administer it. But even at this point, Blair could neither bring himself to say sorry properly – 'It hasn't been handled well, and for that I take full responsibility, and I apologize for that' – nor to give an honest explanation. 'Before any journalist had been in touch, anything to do with donations and Mr Ecclestone, we had informed his people that we couldn't accept further donations,' he told Humphrys. 'What about the original donation? We decided to seek the advice of Sir Patrick Neill. We did so on the Friday.'[80] This was nonsense. The letter to Neill had specifically been about whether they were allowed to accept a second donation, and didn't ask anything about the first. Even Blair's most sympathetic biographer, John Rentoul, admits bluntly: 'this was simply untrue.'[81] Loyal sidekick Peter Mandelson offered his own euphemism for how the team handled the whole thing in his memoirs: 'we got into trouble over the chain of events.'[82]

Blair felt the objective truth was not as important as his own self-belief. 'I hope that people know me well enough and realize the type of person I am, to realize that I would never do anything to harm the country or anything improper,' he simpered as the interview drew towards a close. 'I think most people who have dealt with me, think I'm a pretty straight sort of guy and I am.'[83]

Indeed, most people did give him the benefit of the doubt. Well, it was early days.

'I confirm this form has been completed by myself or at my dictation and that the information given is true to the best of my knowledge and belief and all material information as explained above has been disclosed.'

Peter Mandelson,
signed declaration on mortgage application, 30 August 1996

Odd fish, Peter Mandelson. Feted – admittedly largely by himself – as a PR genius, able to spin any story so it showed Labour in a good light, or strangle an unfavourable one at birth. And yet at the height of his powers it was almost impossible to find anyone with anything nice to say about him, and when the media spotlight moved in his own direction, you could guarantee he would bungle things so badly the story would run for days. When political journalist Matthew Parris blurted out on air that 'Peter Mandelson is certainly gay' – it was a secret everyone already knew.[84] Further, Mandelson was in a settled long-term relationship, the happiest he had ever been, and so secure in his Hartlepool constituency that the local paper ran the headline: 'WHO CARES IF OUR MP IS GAY?' Somehow he still managed to cackhandedly escalate the remark into a rolling scandal of media censorship by demanding action from the BBC's director-general and chairman of governors, and then trying to claim he hadn't done anything of the sort.

It was exactly the same with his house-hunting. Instead of upgrading from his 'small flat in not-yet-up-and-coming Clerkenwell' to somewhere a little bit bigger that he could afford on an MP's salary – a salary which, by the by, received an unprecedented boost in 1996 from £34,000 to £43,000[85] – he had to have an entire house in Notting Hill, that even he admitted 'I obviously could not afford.'[86] When writing about it in an allegedly contrite mood in his memoirs over a decade later, he claimed he had only been looking for 'a real home of my own, a place I could be proud of, with a desk on which to spread out my papers, shelves filled with my books', as if such facilities did not exist anywhere outside London W11.[87] He spent £475,000 on the house, enough to buy an entire street in his constituency, and invited Lord Snowdon round to take a photo portrait with him reclining in a chair that was captioned as costing £1,800.[88]

So how had Mandelson afforded a house that cost more than ten times his pay packet? He got a friend to help out. Geoffrey Robinson was the Labour MP for Coventry and a millionaire businessman. He was also a close political ally of Gordon Brown, with whom Mandelson had horribly fallen out a couple of years earlier – another thing you'd think might have set off some alarm bells. By his own account, the younger MP pretty much threw himself at Robinson's mercy when they met for dinner at his penthouse flat in Park Lane (at least he could afford his domicile). Robinson recounted that Mandelson

> initiated the discussion of his financial circumstances and of his flat. He told me how miserable he felt there. From what he told me it was a dingy place…. What I heard from Peter was a *cri de coeur*. He dedicated himself to New Labour but the salary was modest. He worked arduous long hours and had nothing to show for it, not even a decent flat where he could relax and entertain his friends. I asked what he had in mind. He replied, 'Oh, a place in Notting Hill is what I would really like. But it's too expensive and there is no one to help me!'[89]

Who wouldn't take pity at such a sob story? Robinson – who, after the election the next year, would take the ironic government job of paymaster general – promptly agreed to lend his colleague £373,000.[90] Take a second to think about that. Three hundred and seventy-three thousand pounds. How heavily would a debt of those proportions hang over your entire existence? Just how obligated would you feel to a friend to whom you owed that much money?

Apparently, it didn't bother Mandelson, who famously said his party was 'intensely relaxed about people getting filthy rich' and obviously included himself in that.[91] He didn't bother to enter the loan in the Register of Members' Interests, which had recently been beefed up following several Conservative scandals. He also didn't tell the Britannia Building Society, from whom he obtained a mortgage for most of the rest of the purchase cost. When both he and Robinson were made government ministers after the next year's election, and he was specifically asked, *in writing*, by his principal private secretary if he held 'any outside positions we should be considering and (very important) any major financial interests we should be aware of', he didn't declare it then either.[92] 'I regarded the loan as private rather than secret, something that was between us and had nothing to do with our political or public lives,' he primly writes in his memoirs.[93] All the while Tony Blair was boasting about how 'we will observe the highest standards of propriety in government' in line with a strict new code of conduct for ministers, which required them to 'scrupulously avoid any danger of an actual or apparent conflict of interest between their ministerial position and their private financial interests'.[94]

What should happen next, but an apparent conflict of interest popped up! Long-buried scandals from Robinson's business career began to re-emerge. They were particularly eye-catching as they involved not only spectacular crook (and former Labour MP) Robert Maxwell, but also a dead Belgian millionaire with the magnificent name of Madame Bourgeois. The government department charged with investigating Robinson's affairs was the DTI – now led by Peter Mandelson. He did declare that the two of them were friends, which meant his civil servants took steps to insulate him from the inquiries – but he still didn't think the fact that he owed Robinson (and I'm sorry to go on about this, but really) *three hundred and seventy-three thousand pounds* was worth mentioning.

The set-up finally came out as a result of the toxic infighting that dominated the top of New Labour. The short version is that someone in Brown's circle leaked the existence of the loan to a sympathetic journalist, Paul Routledge, though it then took a longer-than-expected route onto the front pages by way of a misdirected set of page proofs of his book, and thus first appeared in the *Guardian* rather than his own paper, the *Mirror.* Blair's reaction when his right-hand man confessed all was to repeatedly ask: 'How could you *do* this? What were you *thinking?*'[95] Alastair Campbell's was apparently more succinct: 'you stupid cunt.'[96]

To make everything worse, the news broke just before Christmas 1998. The lack of other news as everyone shut down for the holidays meant this story dominated everything. Mandelson wanted to bluff it out; at first Blair thought he might get away with it, and even Brown offered his support. 'My sense was that Gordon wanted to damage rather than destroy me,' reckoned the sacrificial victim.[97] But on 23 December journalists started asking questions about exactly what Mandelson had and hadn't declared on his mortgage form, which pushed the arrangement into the realm of potential criminal offences – and Blair told him he had to go.[98] To celebrate, *The Sun* went with a truly disturbing Christmas Eve photomontage of the former minister and a stuffed – geddit? – turkey.

'At the time I was certain Peter had to resign,' wrote Blair in his memoirs many years later. 'Now I am not so sure.' With the arrogance of hindsight he puts the whole thing down to a 'media frenzy'.[99] But it was not until January 1999 that Britannia announced it would not be pursuing the former minister-without-portfolio-but-with-a-really-nice-sitting-room for fraud.

Robinson claimed in his own memoir the following year that 'Britannia was subsequently inundated by requests from other customers for similar treatment. I am told that extra staff were temporarily required to handle the situation.'[100] That's probably a fanciful story that he used to comfort himself for the fact that he, too, was obliged to resign as a minister. Unlike Mandelson, he never made it back into the cabinet.

> '[Ashcroft] committed to becoming resident by the next financial year in order properly to fulfil his responsibilities in the House of Lords. This decision will cost him (and benefit the Treasury) tens of millions a year in tax, yet he considers it worthwhile.'

William Hague,
letter to the prime minister, 23 May 1999

In 1999, something that was still quite rare happened: the Political Honours Scrutiny Committee rejected a billionaire businessman from the list of people being put forward for peerages before it was sent to the Queen. The businessman in question, Michael Ashcroft, was not, they ruled, a 'fit and proper person' to serve in the House of Lords.[101] It wasn't because the Conservative Party treasurer had blatantly only been put up for the award by opposition leader William Hague because he was bunging shedloads of cash at the party. The committee could hardly object to that: they had passed Labour's chief fundraiser Michael Levy for a lordship two years previously without so much as a squeak. The real problem with Ashcroft was that he just wasn't British enough.

All right, he was born in Sussex, and he had a house in Westminster, which was handy for Tory party HQ, but his main home in Florida was more than four thousand miles away. Most of his companies lived offshore too. He was so strongly identified with the Central American country of Belize that he actually served as its ambassador to the UN, as well as owning the nation's main bank, half of its shipping register and a significant chunk of its sole telecommunications company. To maintain his tax exile status he could spend only ninety days a year in Britain. Even some of the hereditary peers whom the government were in the process of kicking out of the House of Lords managed to turn up and sit on the red benches more often than that.

These circumstances, and the bad publicity about Ashcroft's business dealings which ensued as a result of his rejection, made him so manifestly and evidently unsuitable for a peerage that William Hague... waited exactly a year, and then nominated him again. 'I am deeply indebted to William that he pursued the issue of my peerage so vigorously,' Ashcroft wrote a few years later.[102]

> The honours committee came back to this second nomination with the same response. 'Our primary reservations in respect to Mr Ashcroft... were that, though proposed as a Working Peer he would be unable to fulfil that function until he became a permanent resident of the UK – and so, in his case also, a UK tax payer. It seemed to us that without such assurances, the appointment of anyone, and of Mr Ashcroft in particular, to a seat in Parliament would give rise to highly critical and damaging publicity.'[103]

Ashcroft agreed to move. He wrote a memo to Hague on 23 March 2000 that appeared to clear the matter up once and for all:

> I hereby give you my clear and unequivocal assurance that I have decided to take up permanent residence in the UK again before the end of this calendar year. I have given my advisers instructions to make arrangement to give effect to this decision and I will instruct them forthwith to do so within this calendar year. I hereby firmly agree that I will not seek to be introduced to the House of Lords until I have taken up residency in the

United Kingdom…. These are my solemn and binding undertakings to you.[104]

Pretty emphatic declarations. But if you looked carefully, the memo didn't actually specify anything about the second half of the committee's requirements – that bit about 'also a UK tax payer'.

Over the next few months, in a lengthy and confidential exchange of correspondence between the committee, the official responsible for the admin surrounding new peers (that's the Clerk of the Crown in Chancery, fact fans), and the Conservative chief whip, James Arbuthnot, it became obvious that Ashcroft had no intention of fulfilling that requirement. The committee suggested that tax forms 'IR P86 (Arrival in the UK) and IR DOM 1 (Domicile) would seem to be significant in discharging the assurance he gave.'[105] The party replied that he was quite happy to hand over the first, but not the second: 'Mr Ashcroft does not believe that his domicile for tax purposes is relevant to the question of his Peerage, having undertaken to be resident in the UK.'[106]

At this point we need to take a brief but thrilling excursion into the world of tax law. The first big thing you need to understand is that residence is not the same thing as domicile. And the second big thing is that if – as Ashcroft was and remained – you are non-domiciled in the UK, you are not what most of us would understand as being 'a UK tax payer'. 'Non-dom' status – enjoyed by such other vocal patriots as Viscount Rothermere, owner of the *Daily Mail*, and Zac Goldsmith (until he decided to run as an MP) – is achieved by pleading either your father's past residence or your own intended future one as evidence that you don't really live where you seem to, and it gets you out of paying tax in the UK on any money you make abroad. You do pay tax on profits you make within the UK – but if, as in Ashcroft's case, the bulk of your businesses are based overseas (or you can arrange things so that they appear to be), you need not trouble the UK taxman at all.

The committee were 'somewhat concerned' by the prospect of Ashcroft continuing to enjoy this considerable perk. 'In their view the undertaking given by Mr Ashcroft did involve domicile as well as residence as defined by the Inland Revenue.'[107] The Conservatives, however, were firm on Ashcroft's behalf: 'Mr Arbuthnot does not believe that the question of domicile is or can be relevant to the fulfilment of the undertaking.'[108]

Thus, from the moment that the new Baron Ashcroft, of Chichester in the County of West Sussex – he'd thought better of his first proposed title, Baron Ashcroft, of Belize – took his place on the Conservative benches in October 2000 until the moment in July 2010 that he had to give up his status thanks to a change in the rules, he got to have his say on the laws of Britain whilst shielding most of his income from the exchequer that paid for them. In 2004 he even gave Belize as his 'location of main residence' in the Lords' expenses register, which, frankly, was just taking the piss.[109] After years of refusing to answer questions about where he really lived and paid tax ('Hell is more likely to freeze over,' his spokesman said in 2007[110]), and just ahead of the truth being flushed out by a Freedom of Information (FOI) request, he finally admitted being a non-dom in the run-up to the 2010 General Election, which he was once again helping to bankroll for the Tories. He had given the party over £8 million during the previous decade.[111] In the same period, it was estimated that he had, quite legally, avoided £127 million in tax thanks to his status.[112]

Conservative leader David Cameron claimed it had all come as news to him. William Hague – long since deposed as party leader but still on the front bench – claimed he had only recently found out too. 'Over the last few months I knew about that and of course I was keen to support him then in making his position public.'[113]

A few weeks later the Cabinet Office released the correspondence regarding the peerage negotiations a decade earlier. It concluded with the following letter from Hague's chief whip, dated 12 July 2000: 'I confirm that I agree with your understanding of the position, and that the Leader of the Opposition is satisfied that the action adequately meets the terms of Michael Ashcroft's undertaking to take up permanent residence in the UK.'[114]

Incidentally, you might think that one of the biggest lies in politics is the pretence that making donations to political parties is *not* a sure-fire way to buy yourself a place in House of Lords. But, thanks to the diligent efforts of the Metropolitan Police and Crown Prosecution Service in 2006 and 2007, which involved arresting several senior Number 10 aides and even questioning the prime minister in Downing Street, we know that this is not the case. 'There is… substantial and reliable evidence that there were proper reasons for the inclusion of all those whose names appeared on the… working peers list,' the CPS ruled. 'The available evidence is not sufficient to enable an overwhelming inference to be drawn, such as to afford a realistic prospect of convicting any person for any offence contrary to Section 1 of the 1925 [Honours (Prevention of Abuses)] Act.'[115]

It is pure coincidence that so many big-league donors, in the decades before the investigation and the years that followed, have ended up taking ermine on behalf of their respective parties. Who would have thought it?

'It is all within the claims policy and that's why I'm angry about this because not only has it been very stressful for me and my family, it gives the incredibly misleading impression that somehow we've been dodgy, that we've been fraudulent or we've been corrupt. Nothing is further from the truth. I've done everything by the rules.'

Margaret Moran,
BBC Politics, 11 May 2009

The expenses scandal was a long time coming. As far back as 1983, an official report by the Senior Salaries Review Body recommended a 31 per cent pay rise, which would bring MPs' salaries to a level comparable with that of senior civil servants. A jump from £14,150 to £19,000 a year was completely unacceptable to Mrs Thatcher, who was forcing pay restraint on the rest of the public sector and had made a show of her own parsimony by refusing the £10,000 extra salary on offer to her as prime minister. Instead, Parliament was forced to agree to a fudge: pay went up by 5.5 per cent, which gave MPs only an extra £800 a year, but the various allowances that were available to them to cover accommodation, office costs, travel and the like were all significantly boosted.[116] An MP who entered the Commons that same year noted that 'an unspoken pact arose: pay would not rise… but a regime bordering on total self-assessment was allowed on expenses. The abuses were clear and indefensible, yet also entirely explicable.'[117]

Unfortunately, when that MP – a youngster by the name of Tony Blair – became prime minister in 1997, he allowed the situation not only to continue but to bloat. Not that it was up to him. Extraordinarily, until 2010 MPs were the only workforce in the country who got to decide on their own rewards: although the government of the day could make its views very firmly known, salaries and allowances were a matter for Parliament itself to decide. The turkeys were very unlikely to vote for Christmas, but they rarely missed a chance to vote for more stuffing.

Even before the epic and blatant abuse, there was no possible justification for some of the rules. Why should MPs with constituencies classed as 'outer London', like Brent North, Leyton and Romford – all less than an hour's commute from Parliament – get subsidized second homes in the centre of town? Why should taxpayers pay £25 on 'subsistence', with no receipts required, for every night that MPs spent in the capital – did they not bother to eat when they were at home in the bosom of their families? How many inner tubes would they have to get through to justify claiming twenty pence per mile when they travelled by bicycle? Why did they need a resettlement grant *and* a winding-up allowance for when voters kicked them out of office? And why did the so-called 'John Lewis List' used by Commons officials allow them to splash out as much as £10,000 on new kitchens for their second homes, and £750 on a TV or stereo?[118] The perfectly reasonable proposition that the public should pay for the staff and office equipment that MPs genuinely needed to perform their public service had tipped over into the assumption that MPs should be allowed to claim for almost everything they spent, over and above their quite generous salaries. What on earth did they think the rest of us spent our wages on?

They knew it was indefensible. And so they tried desperately to keep it secret. When campaigners used the Freedom of Information

Act – the single piece of legislation that Blair said he most regretted introducing – to try to wrench the details of MPs' expenses out of them, the Commons authorities went all the way to the High Court to protest that such a move would be 'unlawfully intrusive'.[119] When judges ordered them to release the information anyway, they insisted on removing so much personal data that the information which eventually saw the light of day was practically useless. It was yet another of those cases where politicians, fearing how bad something might make them look, put themselves in a situation that made it look much, much worse. In May 2009 a whistle-blower sold the unredacted information – a disk containing around 1.5 million documents – to the *Daily Telegraph*, which set a team to going through it with a fine-tooth comb, cross-referencing the documents with public records to uncover exactly what was going on. Even then the politicians did not give up, taking to the airwaves to bluster about 'stolen information' and 'a breach of the Official Secrets Act'.[120]

What were they trying to hide? The most common practice the *Telegraph* discovered was 'flipping', which involved MPs nominating either their London or constituency property as their second home, claiming the costs of doing it up and furnishing it from public funds, and then swapping the designations around so they could do the same for their other residence.[121] Sometimes they would go on to sell the freshly refurbished 'second home', but tell the taxman it was their primary residence so as to avoid having to pay capital gains tax on the profits. (It goes without saying that the rules entitled them to claim back mortgage interest for second homes while also keeping any and all proceeds from a sale for themselves.) Sometimes they did this more than once – cabinet minister Hazel Blears claimed for three different 'second homes' in the space of one year, as well as billing the public for hotel stays in between. Her constituents in Salford and Eccles were so furious that there were protests in the streets. She tried to make amends by going on TV and waving about a cheque made out to HMRC for £13,332 to cover the missing tax, only to prompt more public resentment for the ease with which she could rustle up such a sum.[122]

But Blears was the tip of the proverbial iceberg. No fewer than 232 MPs were revealed to have flipped their residences since the 2005 election. Among them were Chancellor of the Exchequer Alistair Darling, Secretary of State for Transport Geoff Hoon and Conservative frontbenchers Michael Gove and John Bercow, the last of whom became speaker of the Commons in the wake of the expenses scandal. One pair of husband and wife MPs, Tories Julie Kirkbride and Andrew MacKay, went further than flipping, indulging instead in 'double-dipping': he said their London house was their second home, while she said her constituency flat was. This allowed them to claim over £100,000 in expenses from taxpayers between them. They were not the only ones keeping things in the family: Labour's Ian Gibson claimed £80,000 in mortgage interest for a London flat in which he spent a few nights a week while his daughter and her partner lived there full-time; he later sold it to them for around half the market value.[123]

Parliament's insistence on removing all address details from the data they proposed to publish would have ensured that no one ever found out about such scandals had the whistle-blower not gone to the press. Another common scam which the *Telegraph* uncovered was for MPs to tell the parliamentary authorities that one residence was their second home, and then tell the local authorities that the other one was: that way you could get your council tax paid in full on one property and get a discount on the other. This was not against any rules. In another open invitation to cheating, the fees office did not require receipts for any expenses under £250. The newspaper's investigation team found themselves looking at an awful lot of vague claims that came in at around the £249 mark.[124] Some MPs were quite happy to bung in fully itemized receipts for the finest furniture expenses could buy: Michael Gove and his journalist wife, Sarah Vine, kitted out their homes in Notting Hill and Surrey from the high-class store run by their friend Samantha Cameron's mother: a cabinet costing £493 here, a £432 chair there. Their bed sheets were pure Egyptian cotton from The White Company.[125] When the *Telegraph* approached Gove for his excuses, he was one of the few MPs to respond with a lawyer's letter threatening 'appropriate steps to defend his reputation'.[126]

He was far from the only big spender. Other household necessities billed to taxpayers included repairs to a burst pipe under Oliver Letwin's tennis court;[127] servicing to Alan Duncan's ride-on lawn-mower;[128] half the £29,000 of repairs to Sir Gerald Kaufman's Regent's Park home he insisted were needed to prevent him 'living in a slum';[129] fixing the boiler for Michael Ancram's swimming pool;[130] mowing and rolling two paddocks on David Davis's property;[131] trimming the hedges around Sir Michael Spicer's helipad;[132] paying a forester to 'carry out annual maintenance programme to approx 500 trees within the grounds' of Anthony Steen's mansion;[133] and, most notoriously, clearing Douglas Hogg's moat.[134] Hogg, a former cabinet minister, protested that he had not specifically claimed for the cost of the dredging at his Lincolnshire manor house; rather, he had submitted a full set of expenses for running his estate to the Commons fees office to demonstrate that they should let him claim the full possible amount without having to supply specific receipts. The list included staffing costs for his full-time gardener, housekeeper, £4,000 spending on 'machines and fuel' and £650 for 'general repairs, stable etc.'[135]

Astonishingly, all of these were within the rules as they stood – even if the fees office sometimes quibbled over one or two of the amounts, or turned down items like Sir Peter Viggers' notorious

£1,600 'floating duck island'.[136] But such open-handedness was not enough for some MPs. Tory husband and wife Sir Nicholas and Ann Winterton, who had paid off the mortgage on their London flat, transferred the ownership to a trust controlled by their children, and then between them claimed £120,000 of public money to rent it back. When the parliamentary commissioner for standards ruled that this was unacceptable, the couple moved out rather than meet the bills from their own pockets.[137] Fellow Conservative Derek Conway was ordered to repay £17,000 he had paid to his two sons out of his staffing allowance after the authorities discovered that one of them had been given an 'unnecessarily high salary' while the other had actually been a full-time student in Newcastle during the period he was supposedly turning up to work in Westminster.[138]

Labour MP Elliot Morley continued to claim £800 a month to pay off a mortgage on a house in his constituency even after it had been repaid in full. He would later be jailed for false accounting.[139] His Labour colleague David Chaytor went to prison for claiming back rent he had never paid on a flat he owned himself and a cottage that belonged to his mother. He had faked tenancy agreements for the benefit of the fees office.[140] Yet another Labour backbencher, Margaret Moran, had flipped between no fewer than three different residences, one of which was neither in London nor her Luton constituency but one hundred miles away, near Southampton. She had demanded – and received – £22,000 of taxpayers' cash to treat dry rot there, but refused to answer any questions about it because she claimed to be 'entitled to a family life'. She later faced twenty-one charges of forgery and false accounting over £60,000 of fake claims. Having been found unfit to face trial she was given a supervision order requiring her to undergo mental health treatment.[141]

Former Europe minister Denis MacShane was jailed for submitting 'deliberately... misleading and deceptive invoices'.[142] Two other

Labour MPs, Jim Devine and Eric Illsley, and two Conservative peers, Lord Taylor of Warwick and Lord Hanningfield, also went to prison.[143] Dozens and dozens of MPs agreed to stand down rather than face the voters at the next election. The entire pay and expenses system was taken out of parliamentarians' control and handed over to an independent body, which massively tightened the rules about what could be claimed for. Eventually, 392 MPs were ordered to pay back a total of £1.3 million.[144]

No political scandal in my lifetime has caused the level of righteous public anger this one did. The cross-party, across-the-board scale of the offences was a rare justification for that most tedious of pub-bore arguments: 'They're all the same.' At *Private Eye*, the magazine I have worked at since 1997, we received piles of correspondence from readers apoplectic with their elected representatives: one voter had taken the trouble of going through a constituency mail-out that had been posted through his letterbox, scrawling 'THIEF' on every single photo of his MP, and sending it on to us. For the first time ever, the BBC's *Question Time* audience only submitted questions about a single topic; they also booed every single politician on the panel as they were introduced.[145] Labour backbencher Diane Abbott complained that the public wanted 'dead MPs hanging from lamp-posts';[146] excitable Tory Nadine Dorries claimed that at Westminster, 'Everyone fears a suicide. If someone isn't seen, offices are called and checked.'[147]

So ingrained had their entitlement become that it took many politicians a long time to understand why. They showed an astonishing tin ear to public opinion in the early days of the scandal. Commons speaker Michael Martin continued to fulminate against the press right up until he became the first occupant of the post to be forced out of office for more than three hundred years. He called in the police to investigate the leak. The Met admirably announced that going after the mole would not be in the public interest, but that an investigation into some MPs' behaviour definitely would be.[148] Prime Minister Gordon Brown came up with the genius idea of replacing all expenses with a daily Commons attendance allowance and unilaterally announced it in a bizarre YouTube video in which his unconvincing grin could not disguise the fact he was essentially proposing to bribe MPs to turn up and do the job they were already paid to do.[149] Even as the scale of the scandal became apparent he could not bring himself to issue a proper apology for the system he and his predecessors had presided over for decades: instead he offered a general one 'on behalf of politicians, on behalf of all parties, for what has happened in the events of the last few days'.[150]

The only one who seemed to really get it was the leader of the opposition. From the outset, Cameron was straight up about 'just how bad this is. The public are really angry and we have to start by saying, look, this system that we had, that we used... was wrong, and we're sorry about it.'[151] He was the first to launch disciplinary procedures against his own MPs, the first to bring in rules on their claims that were stricter than Parliament's own and the first to order repayments. He even wrote out a cheque for the £680 he had himself claimed for repairs which included stripping wisteria from the chimney of his constituency cottage in the Cotswolds.[152]

One reason he came over so well during the crisis was that he had recruited a very special adviser to help out with any situation that had the potential to embarrass the Conservative Party – one Andy Coulson, former editor of the *News of the World*. Ring any bells?

4

GAMBLERS' CONCEITS

There are several personality traits that are required to go into politics. A fairly big ego. Being able to think on your feet. A high boredom threshold. Clubbability. Willingness to compromise. A peculiar propensity – unique to politicians, this one, I think – for putting on slogan T-shirts over formalwear and not thinking you look silly. A slight sense of public duty. And in many cases, a massive capacity for self-destruction.

Maybe it's the nature of such an all-or-nothing profession, where you can go from literally ruling the country to claiming Jobseekers' Allowance in the blink of a ballot box. Maybe it's the pressure of being on your best behaviour and so much in the public eye. Maybe it's a reaction to the responsibility. But again and again, certain politicians prove themselves unable to resist playing with fire. Not just in the usual, bit-on-the-side, hand-in-the-till methods displayed in previous chapters, but in spectacular, baroque, logic-defying ways. They find inventive ways to deliberately magnify manageable risks beyond all proportion, constructing great tottering edifices of deceit where there was no need to build anything at all.

Like villains in bad detective dramas, they just can't help scattering clues as to their real identity – to the extent where you begin to wonder if they aren't all secretly desperate to be found out.

* * * * *

'These investigations… have, at my direction, had the total cooperation of the – not only the White House – but also of all agencies of the Government…. I can say categorically that his investigation indicates that no one in the White House Staff, no one in this Administration, presently employed, was involved in this very bizarre incident.'

Richard Nixon,
news conference, San Clemente, California, 29 August 1972

The weirdest thing about Watergate was how unnecessary it all was. President Nixon's approval ratings were on the up in 1972: they peaked for the year, at 62 per cent, just a fortnight before the burglary of the Democratic National Committee (DNC) headquarters. He would go on to win his second election that November by a landslide. Yet the sitting president's ego was so fragile that he saw plots and potential disaster on all sides. He was determined to strike first, strike hardest and do anything – absolutely anything – to ensure he remained on top. 'I was paranoiac, or almost a basket case,' he would admit later, years after his resignation.[1]

With the help of a ragbag of close advisers whose lack of morality and grip on reality rivalled his own, he came up with a series of 'black ops' aimed at his enemies, both real and imagined. Like a group of primary-school bullies who are having a particularly hard time at home, they drew up an 'Opponents List, Political Enemies Project' and launched demented campaigns against those on it. Over two hundred names graced it – not just politicians, but also academics, celebrities (people like Barbra Streisand, Andy Warhol and Bill Cosby) and quite a number of journalists whose coverage had displeased the president.[2] The tax authorities were encouraged to subject them to extreme inspections. A 'Special Investigations Unit' was set up to look into those the president deemed especially threatening. He ordered its staff get their hands on a set of documents which he thought would make his Democratic opponents look bad, even if they had to 'break in' to a Washington think tank and 'blow the safe' to do so.[3] This was not a subtle or sly suggestion: he made it in a White House meeting in the presence of Attorney General John Mitchell, the country's top law enforcement officer, who raised no objection.

Encouraged, more junior members of the special unit went on a spree, breaking into a psychoanalyst's office where a suspected leaker was a patient to try and steal his medical records, and planning a similar raid on the National Archives. They also ran surveillance on opponents and illegally tapped their phones. Proposals to lure senior Democrats into 'honeytraps' and photograph them with prostitutes, sabotage the air conditioning at their party convention and even kidnap anti-Vietnam War demonstrators and hold them in Mexico so they couldn't embarrass the president were forwarded to Mitchell. He ruled them out – but not on legal grounds; he was simply worried that such escapades might be a bit expensive. When White House counsel John Dean objected that such plans were 'incredible, unnecessary and very unwise…. We don't need bugging, muggings and prostitutes and kidnappers', the president's chief of staff, H. R. 'Bob' Haldeman, simply removed Dean from the list of people who were told about them.[4]

The intrigues unravelled thanks to a particularly alert security guard at the Watergate complex dialling 911 on 17 June 1972. Watergate consisted of several blocks of luxury apartments, offices and a hotel named for its site where the Chesapeake and Ohio Canal flowed into the Potomac River. (Take a moment to reflect on the depressing thought that if another scandal were to occur there now, the media would undoubtedly dub it 'Watergategate'.) One of the offices belonged to the DNC, and it was there that police arrived to find five intruders attempting to fit a bug to the phone of the party's national chairman, Larry O'Brien. It wasn't even the first time they'd broken in. They'd had to return because the first set of wiretaps they had fitted weren't working properly.

It didn't take long to trace the intruders back towards Nixon. One was the security coordinator of the Committee for the Re-Election of the President (CRP, or, as his enemies preferred to dub it, CREEP); another was carrying a notebook containing the phone number of E. Howard Hunt, a former CIA man and thriller writer who might have baulked at putting such an obvious clue in one of his own books. Hunt had been seconded from Nixon's Special Investigations Unit to the CRP earlier in the year, which gave Nixon the get-out clause he used when questioned about the burglary not long afterwards: 'no one in this Administration, presently employed, was involved'.[5]

Thus, with the indictment of all five burglars for wiretapping and theft, and a trial scheduled for after the election, the issue might have been tabled – if not for those pesky tapes. Because Richard Milhous Nixon, the man who honestly believed that 'When the president does it, that means it is *not* illegal', personally provided all the evidence that prosecutors needed to bring him down.[6]

Two years into his presidency, and unknown to all but a handful of his closest staff and the secret servicemen charged with operating them, he had installed a recording system in the Oval Office and the other rooms he used most in the White House. Voice-activated microphones picked up every sound, and reel-to-reel tape recorders in the basement captured them for posterity – in theory, for the purpose of compiling the president's future memoirs. There were five microphones in Nixon's desk alone. And despite being fully aware of the system – it was, he said, 'my best insurance against... others, even people close to me [who] would turn against me' – he had had plenty of conversations in which he referred to the activities of his black ops team within their hearing.[7] Even more extraordinarily, he continued to use the recording system after the arrests, fully incriminating himself in the conspiracy to cover up the truth about the burglary.

'The FBI is not under control... and... their investigation is now leading into some productive areas,' Haldeman warned the president six days after the arrests, as the recorders whirred away. 'And it goes in some directions we don't want it to go.' Nixon helpfully clarified: 'You open that scab there's a hell of a lot of things and that we just feel that it would be very detrimental to have this thing go any further.' Between them, in a recording that would subsequently become known as the 'smoking gun' tape, they hatched a plot to get the CIA to intervene with their rival agency and, in the president's words, 'say that we wish for the country, don't go any further into this case, period!'[8] After the burglars went to jail in 1973 – and the president had been safely re-elected – Nixon continued to shoot off about the need to keep on bribing them to stay silent: 'you could get a million dollars. And you could get it in cash. I know where it could be gotten.'[9]

For months, a special Senate committee – with which Nixon and his staff refused to cooperate on the grounds of 'executive privilege' – had been investigating suspect presidential campaign activities before they finally stumbled across this archival goldmine. On 13 July 1973, Haldeman's former deputy Alexander Butterfield was called before the committee and asked if recordings were ever made of the president's conversations. 'I was hoping you fellows wouldn't ask me about that, I've wondered what I would say,' he replied awkwardly. 'Well, yes. There's a recording system in the President's office.'[10] The next day a stunned committee staffer phoned Bob Woodward, a member of the *Washington Post* team who had been following the money to the heart of the conspiracy, to tell him: 'Nixon bugged himself.'[11]

It took months to prise the tapes out of the president's sweaty paws. The committee requested them; Nixon refused. The committee issued a subpoena; Nixon refused. The special prosecutor appointed by Elliot Richardson – who had become attorney general after Mitchell left to head up CRP in the spring of 1972 – asked the Supreme Court to order Nixon to hand the tapes over; Nixon ordered Richardson to sack the special prosecutor. Richardson refused, and resigned instead. His deputy wouldn't comply either, so the president fired him too. Nixon eventually found someone willing to fire the prosecutor, but by then nearly half a million telegrams of protest were flooding into the White House and there were open calls for the president's impeachment. In October 1973, Nixon agreed to hand over transcripts of the recordings; the Supreme Court ruled that he must make the actual tapes available by the following summer.

Despite a mysterious gap of eighteen and a half minutes during one crucial discussion, the tapes provided more than enough evidence to implicate Nixon in a cover-up. Not only that, but the full horror of the president's psyche was revealed: in private he was a ranting, foul-mouthed racist and anti-Semitic drunk. After listening to some of the recordings, Nixon's spiritual mentor, Reverend Billy Graham, burst into tears and threw up. The president became such a pariah that the British prime minister, Harold Wilson, ordered the Foreign Office to 'take any measures open to us to ensure that Mr Nixon did not come to London'.[12]

Nixon, who had gradually fired more and more members of his inner circle as they became implicated in the scandal, himself finally resigned as president on 9 August 1974. Vice President Gerald Ford took over and granted his predecessor a 'full, free, and absolute pardon'.[13] Ford hadn't been Nixon's first, or even second, choice for the job – his VP candidate in both the 1968 and 1972 elections had been Spiro Agnew. But, in a considerable scandal of his own, he had been forced to resign from office the previous autumn after admitting tax evasion relating to the massive bribes he had taken as governor of Maryland.

The American people really had been spoiled for choice that year.

> 'I wish, with all the emphasis which I can command, to deny that I was at any time engaged in any homosexual relationship with Norman Scott whatsoever, or that I was, at any time, a party to any homosexual familiarity with him.'

Jeremy Thorpe,
statement to police, 3 June 1978

Whether or not former Liberal leader Jeremy Thorpe had been in a gay relationship with Norman Scott was never the most important issue. His trial at the Old Bailey, at which the jury took an incredible fifty-two hours to come up with a verdict of 'not guilty', was concerned with whether he had been part of a farcical conspiracy to murder Scott, along with a fruit-machine manufacturer, the owner of a carpet warehouse and an airline pilot who only succeeded in shooting Scott's pet dog. Yet the full extent of Thorpe's sex life, and the extraordinary risks he took not only with Scott but with other lovers too, finally emerged after his death in 2014, thanks to the diligent work of his biographer Michael Bloch, who agreed to sit on his manuscript for nearly a quarter of a century to comply with Thorpe's 'urgent insistence that it should not appear in his lifetime'.[14]

Jeremy Thorpe married twice, first to Caroline Allpass, who he told colleagues he hoped would provide 'at least 5%' boost in the opinion polls, and, following Caroline's tragic death in a car accident, to Marion Lascelles, Countess of Harewood – a union that he boasted was 'practically marrying into the Royal Family'.[15] At the same time, he enjoyed a promiscuous gay sex life that he made little effort to hide, regularly introducing his conquests to colleagues and friends merely as youngsters from less fortunate backgrounds to whom he was acting as a kind of mentor. When he achieved celebrity as a television interviewer, he shocked colleagues with his approaches to handsome strangers on filming trips. His deliberately old-fashioned style of dress which he described as his 'trademark' soon made him instantly recognizable around the country, but he continued to haunt notorious gay pick-up joints in London's Piccadilly. And after his election as an MP in 1959, he regularly used House of Commons notepaper to write romantic notes to other men – one of them, to a lover in San Francisco, was intercepted by the FBI, who tipped off the Foreign Office.

When Princess Margaret got engaged to Antony Armstrong-Jones in 1960, Thorpe even used a parliamentary postcard to complain to a friend that it was 'a pity... I rather hoped to marry the one and seduce the other.'[16] He claimed to have pulled policemen guarding Parliament and footmen attending at Buckingham Palace receptions, and by the time he was elected as Liberal leader in 1967 he was being blackmailed by a rent boy he had met on the King's Road in Chelsea, a situation he could hardly complain about given that he had picked him up by asking, 'Do you know who I am?'[17] A scorned ex-boyfriend once turned up in the public gallery of the Commons shouting that Thorpe had jilted him. A man he had made an unsuccessful pass at provided full details not just to Thorpe's own constituency association but to his local Conservative rivals too – just ahead of the 1966 election campaign. As Norman Scott put it in his evidence at the Old Bailey, 'Jeremy Thorpe lives on a knife-edge of danger!'[18]

Thorpe first met Norman Scott at the Oxfordshire stables of a horse trainer friend in the summer of 1960. Scott, who was working there as a groom, was twenty and, as Thorpe told a friend, looked 'simply heaven'.[19] The MP told the groom that if he ever needed help or happened to find himself in London, he could always get in touch with him via the House of Commons. Scott wasn't a constituent – Thorpe's seat was in North Devon – but then that wasn't exactly the sort of help either man had in mind. Despite this being their first and so far only meeting, Scott almost immediately started claiming an intimate, and sometimes a sexual, relationship with Thorpe to anyone who would listen, and offered as evidence a number of letters he had stolen from his trainer boss, who conveniently also had the first name Norman. It quickly became apparent that Scott was quite an unstable stable lad, and the following year he spent several months under compulsory detention in a psychiatric clinic being treated for what he later admitted were 'delusions'.[20] When he got out, he took Thorpe up on his invitation.

Thorpe was so delighted to see Scott that he took him home to meet his mother. By Scott's account this was the night they first had sex, though the details of the event changed on the many, many occasions he subsequently shared them. Thorpe did, however, give Scott cash to set himself up in a flat in London and write letters authorizing him to order clothes on Thorpe's account at his tailor and shirt maker, actions which he later claimed were merely evidence of a 'close, even affectionate relationship' rather than anything else.[21]

The two men continued to see each other regularly for more than a year, despite increasing evidence of Scott's unreliability. When police wanted to interview Scott about a stolen coat, Thorpe insisted they come to his office at the House of Commons to do so and told them that he was 'more or less a guardian' to Scott, since he had 'lost both parents'[22] – which, unfortunately for Thorpe, was one of Scott's numerous tall tales. Scott was not, as he claimed, an orphan who had been cheated out of an inheritance from his famous architect father after he died in a South American plane crash, *or* the illegitimate son of the Earl of Eldon, but a bloke from Bexleyheath whose parents were both still alive. Perhaps it shouldn't have come as a surprise when Scott was dismissed from two jobs Thorpe had managed to wangle for him.

Soon they had fallen out to such an extent that Scott told a friend he was going to get a gun, kill Thorpe and commit suicide. The friend was so alarmed that she called the police, and that was how in December 1962 Norman Scott came to make the first official complaint about what he called 'my homosexual relations with Jeremy Thorpe' – which, in that year, were still a criminal offence.[23]

Scott would spout off about those relations in public many times over the next seventeen years, to the decreasing shock of anyone listening. In this first case, Scott's obvious flakiness as a witness meant that nothing was done other than to pass a report up to the assistant commissioner of the Met and on to Devon and Cornwall police, but biographer Michael Bloch reckons that by 1960 Thorpe's sexual preferences were 'fairly common knowledge' in his constituency, and were mostly regarded 'merely as another of his many eccentricities'.[24]

In 1965, after Thorpe's attempt to pack Scott off to Switzerland ended in a huge row, Scott wrote to Thorpe's mother to tell her about their affair; she simply passed the letter on to her son. But that was also the year in which Thorpe's ill-advised dalliance became a full-scale cover-up. He arranged a meeting with Home Secretary Frank Soskice to discuss what he branded as nonsensical claims made by Scott to the police. Soskice assured Thorpe there was unlikely to be any further trouble so long as he avoided any more contact with the person Soskice charmingly referred to as 'the creature'.[25] To be on the safe side, Thorpe dispatched a fellow Liberal MP, Peter Bessell, to Ireland, where Scott was then living with another lover, to try to silence him with the promise of regular payments. This was not a clever move. It would cost him a lot of money over the years, have no effect in silencing Scott (who by this point was blaming his ex for his inability to hold down a job and everything else that had gone wrong with his life) and ensure that the gossipy Bessell passed the gory details on to a number of political colleagues.

Thorpe took the precaution of telling Caroline about Scott before he married her in 1968, though he maintained Scott was just a lunatic with a grievance rather than one of many men who had actually shared his bed. (He was seeing a twenty-two-year-old Buckingham Palace servant and continuing to pick up rent boys on the side even during their engagement.) Caroline apparently declared that it wouldn't bother her even if Scott's claims were true, and coped admirably when in 1969 the young man phoned their constituency home ranting about the loss of his National Insurance card, a regular obsession of his.

But still Thorpe felt he could not rest easy. According to Bessell, Thorpe first brought up the subject of permanently doing away with Scott in 1968, ironically telling him it would be 'no worse than shooting a sick dog'.[26] Another Liberal, party treasurer David Holmes, was brought into discussions about the possibility of killing the young man and dropping his body down a disused tin mine in Cornwall. Both Bessell and Holmes said they thought these were more fantasies by Thorpe than a concrete plan.

A further six years would pass before the attack that would eventually land Thorpe and Holmes in the dock at the Old Bailey (with Peter Bessell appearing as a prosecution witness). In the meantime Scott blurted more details of his sex life with Thorpe and the payoffs he had subsequently received to officials at the Department of Social Security, several social workers, a vicar, the doctor treating him for depression, the coroner conducting an inquest into the death of one of his friends, the Liberal chief whip David Steel, an internal party inquiry set up to investigate his claims from which he fled in tears, Devon and Cornwall police, a freelance journalist who touted the story round Fleet Street, and Thorpe's Conservative opponent in the 1974 election – among others. In 1972 Scott moved to a cottage in Thorpe's constituency and started telling anyone who would listen about their now decade-old dalliance. He even turned up at Thorpe's home in a 'totally hysterical' state, which Thorpe's new wife, Marion, dealt with in the most British way possible: she just said, 'I don't think he'll see you,' and then politely offered to help him reverse out of the driveway because he couldn't manage it by himself.[27]

'Everybody in the constituency knew about him and it didn't make any difference because they thought he was a nut,' David Holmes told the *News of the World* many years later. 'In the end [that's] the tragedy of the whole thing, because Jeremy needn't have reacted.'[28]

But react he did. First he got Holmes to broker the purchase, for £2,500, of a cache of incriminating letters between Bessell and Scott regarding the retainer he had been paying and burned them.[29] Since they were not the only copies, and Holmes's use of a cheque provided a paper chain linking him to the transaction, this was perhaps his worst move yet. Then Holmes, along with the aforementioned fruit-machine maker and carpet merchant, came up with what they maintained was only ever a plot to 'frighten' Scott into shutting up. (The jury accepted this explanation.) Thorpe himself claimed he had no idea any of this was going on. But he did personally arrange for £10,000 of a donation from a wealthy Liberal supporter to be paid through a backchannel at around the same time, supposedly to keep some 'irregular' expenses off the books. The figure tallied with the amount an amateur hitman, Andrew Newton, later claimed he had been paid to shoot Scott.[30]

Famously, Newton failed. He came up with a bizarre cover story designed to appeal to Scott's paranoia, approaching him in Barnstaple in October 1975 to tell him his life was in danger from an assassin who was on his way from, of all places, Canada. Several days later he picked Scott up, along with Scott's Great Dane, Rinka, and drove the pair of them to Porlock, where he deposited them in a hotel bar for several hours. Finally he returned to collect them, drove to a remote lay-by on Exmoor, pulled out an ancient and unreliable Mauser he had borrowed from an old school friend who collected antique weapons, and shot… Rinka. Scott testified that Newton then started swearing loudly, 'seemed to be having difficulty with the gun', and drove off shouting, in top cartoon villain style, 'I'll get you.'[31]

It didn't take the police long to trace Newton, and even less time after that to find the gun, which he had hidden in his mother's shed. Charged with 'possession of a firearm with intent to endanger life', he came up with the story that Scott had been blackmailing him over some compromising photos; he also had made an arrangement with Holmes to keep Holmes's and Thorpe's names out of things in return for £5,000. Newton kept his word and was jailed for two years the following March.[32]

It was all undone by another trial entirely, that of Norman Scott for social security fraud. 'I am being hounded all the time by people just because of my sexual relationship with Jeremy Thorpe,' he announced to a stunned magistrates' court in January 1976.[33] Thorpe issued his only response through his solicitors. 'It is well over twelve year since I last saw or spoke to Mr Scott. There is no truth in Mr Scott's allegations,' it read.[34] But it was open knowledge in the Liberal Party that various go-betweens had been in operation during those twelve years, and Thorpe's rival for the party's leadership, Cyril Smith, was only too happy to say so to journalists. When Bessell tried to claim he had merely been handing over reams of his own cash to Scott out of charity, Smith exploded to the *Daily Mirror* that 'someone is telling bloody lies.'[35] When the paper revealed Holmes's £2,500 purchase of Scott's letters a few days later, Smith announced: 'I have not been told everything known about the affair, even by members of my own party.'[36] There is, you will note, a certain dark irony in Smith being the final exposer of Thorpe's dishonesty about his sexual activities.

Thorpe tried to fight on, lying through his teeth to the *Sunday Times* that 'the existence of a homosexual relationship' and the idea that he 'was acquainted with or involved in a correspondence between Scott and Bessell and that I knew of, or was involved in, the purchase of the letters' were both 'totally false'.[37] This prompted Bessell – who had lost his seat and was in severe financial trouble – to sell his story to the *Daily Mail*, which printed it under the splash, 'I Told Lies to Protect Thorpe'. More bills which Thorpe had paid on Scott's behalf during the period also emerged, along with an extremely embarrassing letter dating from 1961 which the MP had signed off 'yours affectionately – Jeremy – I miss you'. In the body of the letter, Thorpe assured Scott that 'Bunnies *can* (and *will*) go to France!' – a phrase that was hard to spin as heterosexual banter.[38]

Thorpe finally resigned as Liberal leader in May 1976, complaining of a 'campaign of denigration' and a 'sustained witch hunt' by the press. 'You will know that from the very beginning I have strenuously denied the so-called Scott allegations and I categorically repeat those denials today,' he thundered.[39] His lawyers started threatening journalists with the archaic, but terrifying, offence of criminal libel, which could see them put in prison. However, Thorpe's determination to blame others for his own bad behaviour had managed to transform one loose cannon into three: Norman Scott, Peter Bessell and, when he was released from prison, Andrew

Newton too. 'I WAS HIRED TO KILL SCOTT' was the headline on his story when he sold it to the *Evening News* the following October.

The case for conspiracy to murder finally came to trial in May 1979, after Thorpe successfully managed to get it postponed until after the general election, at which he had lost his seat. It was most notable for the extraordinary summing-up by the judge, Sir Joseph Cantley, in which he described Scott as a 'hysterical, warped personality, an accomplished sponger… a crook, a fraud… a whiner, a parasite', and generally implied he would quite like to have bumped him off himself.[40] But with three prosecution witnesses – Scott, Bessell and Newton – forced to admit they had lied about the case in the past, it was not difficult for Thorpe's barrister, a young George Carman, to pick holes in their evidence. Thorpe walked from court a free man, but his career was over. He had finally slipped off the knife-edge on which he had balanced for so long.

'The meeting took place and terminated at around 9.45 so as to allow sufficient time for me to catch a train from Waterloo in order that I would reach my home to take a call from the United States at approximately 4pm Californian time. I told Mr Archer that I would advise him of the outcome of the call as it concerned the matters under discussion.... I arrived home at approximately 11.20pm, took the call from the United States and telephoned Mr Archer.'

Ted Francis,
letter to lawyers of Jeffrey Archer, 22 January 1987

Jeffrey Archer: where to start?

All right, deep breath. By the time Jeffrey Archer committed perjury in a libel trial he had brought against the *Daily Star* in 1987, he had accomplished quite a few things. He had allowed people to think he had attended prestigious public school Wellington College in Berkshire rather than the less well-known Wellington School in Somerset. He had falsely claimed to have done a two-year degree course at the University of California. He had transmuted a twelve-month diploma course at the Oxford Department of Education into three years of full participation in the Union and Athletics Club of the university, as if he were an undergraduate, despite having a mere three O levels to his name. He had got himself elected to the Greater London Council for the Conservatives and persuaded colleagues to let him cream off 10 per cent of their expenses claims in return for his filling out their forms for them. He had worked as a fundraiser for the United Nations Association, been caught faking expense claims and left with a ringing reference from the chairman, 'he should be in a remand home!'[41] He had been elected in 1969, at twenty-nine, as MP for Louth and repeatedly claimed to be the youngest member of the House of Commons despite the very famous election of twenty-one-year-old Bernadette Devlin the very same year. He had edged up to the verge of bankruptcy due to a dodgy investment and been forced to resign his parliamentary seat. He had written an international bestseller. He had been appointed deputy chairman of the Conservative Party by Mrs Thatcher, and started claiming a close personal relationship with the prime minister which was not borne out by her appointments diary. He had installed a mistress, Andrina Colquhoun, in the London penthouse where he lived during the week while keeping his wife, Mary, in their Cambridge home. And all the while he was constantly adapting and renewing his life story and CV to fit whomever he happened to be trying to impress at the time.

Then, in October 1986, the *News of the World* splashed with the scrupulously phrased headline 'TORY BOSS ARCHER PAYS VICE GIRL'. Beneath it the paper detailed several conversations Archer had had with a prostitute, Monica Coghlan, and how he had sent his friend Michael Stacpoole to Victoria station to try to give her an envelope stuffed with fifty-pound notes and told her to 'go abroad as quickly as you can'.[42] What the story carefully didn't say, despite the fact that one of Coghlan's other clients had come to the paper claiming it and Coghlan had subsequently confirmed it, was that Archer had had sex with her. He denied having done so in the pair's recorded conversations, and when the paper put the allegation to him directly. (He did say, off the record, that 'a lot of what you have got is true. I accept that totally.... I would beg you not to print it.'[43]) But that didn't really matter, because his bizarre behaviour in trying to bribe the woman – rather than simply saying 'publish and be damned' – made for a very good story indeed.

Unfortunately the *Daily Star* was not nearly so clever, and followed up with a story headlined 'VICE GIRL MONICA TALKS ABOUT ARCHER', even though Coghlan had done nothing of the sort – at least not to them. They had only spoken to her nephew, and repeated his claims that she had definitely had sex with the politician and added that most of her clients 'demand a specialized field of sexual perversion'.[44] Archer, who was known for his regular threats to sue journalists and his attempts to frighten them off by appealing to their bosses (as he had tried and failed to do in this case with *News of the World* owner Rupert Murdoch), issued writs against both papers. He asked to have the case against the *Star*, which he knew had very little in the way of evidence against him, heard first.

It was a cunning move. The two tabloids were forced, unprecedentedly, to pool their resources and work together. The *Star* lost their case, with the jury awarding damages of £500,000 – at that time, a record – to Archer.[45] Now the *News of the World* felt obliged to settle too. Much of the credit for the victory has been attributed to the raging horn that judge Sir Bernard Caulfield had for Mrs Archer. When he summed up for the jury, Caulfield rhapsodized about her performance in the witness box:

> Your vision of her will probably never disappear. Has she elegance? Has she fragrance? Would she have, without the strain of this trial, radiance? What is she like in physical features, in presentation, in appearance? How would she appeal? Has she had a happy married life?... Is she right when she says to you – you may think with delicacy – 'Jeffrey and I lead a full life'?... Is he in need of cold, unloving, rubber-insulated sex in a seedy hotel

round about a quarter to one on a Tuesday morning after an evening at the Caprice?[46]

Poor Monica Coghlan – who became a prostitute after being sexually assaulted as a teenager, who spent time in prison, who left her two-year-old son to be looked after by relatives in Rochdale while she earned money in London, who never tried to tout her story to the tabloids in the first place: she never stood a chance against this.

Archer could prove he visited Le Caprice, one of London's flashiest restaurants, on the night of 8 September 1986. But what happened 'after an evening at the Caprice' was the real issue, and Archer had been far from honest about that. He said he had sat in the restaurant's bar with a friend, Terence Baker, until around 1 a.m., and then given him a lift home. Baker testified that this was true, but he later admitted to friends that he had been lying about the lift, raising questions about the politician's alibi for the relevant period.[47] Conveniently, Baker had died in 1991, which left Archer's alibi intact. But like the scrupulous plotter of fiction he was, Archer had taken care to cover all his bases. Because it wasn't initially clear to him whether he needed an alibi for the early hours of the Tuesday or the Wednesday, he had phoned up another friend, TV producer Ted Francis, and told him, 'I want you to have had dinner with me here on 9 September.'[48]

Archer explained this subterfuge by telling Francis that he had actually been seeing his mistress, Colquhoun, that night, and he didn't want Mary (or indeed, everyone in the High Court) to find out. Francis thought that sounded reasonable, so he wrote a letter to his friend's legal team giving the details he requested.[49] In gratitude, Archer invested £12,000 in a project Francis was working on. (He promised £25,000, but he was never very good at keeping his word.) For good measure, he gave £24,000 to

Michael Stacpoole, the intermediary who had taken the cash to Coghlan. The money was to be used to finance a jaunt out of the country so that Stacpoole couldn't be called as a witness at the trial.[50] (Years later Stacpoole would admit to the BBC that 'I knew of two occasions when he went with prostitutes.') Another prostitute, Dorrett Douglas, later told how she had been paid for sex by Archer in his London flat, and noticed that the bookshelves were almost entirely filled with Jeffrey Archer books. (Of course they were.) 'I'm storing them for Jeffrey Archer who lives upstairs,' he smugly told her.[51]

But, thorough storyteller that he was, Archer was determined to dot all the i's and cross all the t's. He set about faking evidence to back up his obliging friends' stories. He gave his secretary, Angie Peppiatt, a new desk diary before the trial along with a list of engagements he wanted to pretend he had had on the relevant days, so she could write them in, in her own handwriting. This was presented as evidence in court. In deference to Archer's privacy, all but the 'relevant' eight days' worth of pages were carefully bound up; this was fortunate as the remainder were completely blank. He had not considered that Peppiatt, who thought 'Jeffrey was as guilty as hell', might keep hold of the original diary and the list he gave her. She did. But she would not share the real evidence for another twelve years.

Archer, meanwhile, had carried on in much the same way as before: he had launched a massive charity concert to raise funds for displaced Kurds in Iraq, through which he claimed to have raised more than Live Aid, then expressed himself bewildered by how little of the £57 million had made its way to the intended recipients. He received a life peerage from his friend John Major. And he purchased a large number of shares in Anglia Television shortly after Mary, a director of the company, learned a takeover was in the offing, making a tidy profit for a friend – without his wife's knowledge. After the DTI launched an investigation into their possible insider trading, he admitted that he had made a 'grave error' while repeatedly changing his story about what exactly had happened.[52] Despite this indiscretion, in 1999 he was adopted as Conservative candidate to be the first Mayor of London despite rampant evidence of his unsuitability for the position. When journalists brought up the many, many scandals in his past, he furiously threatened them: 'you wait until I'm Mayor, that's when I'll show how tough I am... all the writs will go out on May 6th.'[53]

The prospect of his old pal having real political power was too much for Ted Francis, who spilled the beans to Archer's old nemesis, the *News of the World*. As if to prove he had learned nothing in the ensuing decade, Archer fell for exactly the same trick of taped telephone calls as he had with Monica Coghlan. 'We have got to be careful, Ted,' the paper recorded him saying. 'We don't want to go to court of law with this.'[54] Fronted up by the paper's editor ahead of publication, Archer could only say, 'oh well, thank God I never committed perjury.'[55] Except, as it turned out, he had.

Archer was sacked as mayoral candidate before the *News of the World* even hit the streets. Soon afterwards he was stripped of the Conservative whip in the Lords and informed by party leader William Hague, 'This is the end of politics for Jeffrey Archer.'[56] Two years later, in 2001, a jury at the Old Bailey found him guilty of perjury and perverting the course of justice over his fake alibi, fake diary, fake affidavits and fake evidence during the libel trial. Francis, whose evidence had never actually been used in the 1987 trial, was cleared of perverting the course of justice.

Archer was sentenced to four years in prison. Obviously he managed to get a series of bestselling books out of his time inside, because, well, he's Jeffrey Archer. But by this time even his former friends had recognized the real man behind the carefully contrived image. As Michael Stacpoole, who had carried the cash to Coghlan all those years before, told the BBC after his trial: 'Archer does what the hell he wants to do.... How long has he lied for? How many times have people helped this man out with lies – I mean he has lied and lied and lied.'[57]

'The article alleges that the Prime Minister had an adulterous relationship….These charges are wholly untrue and damaging and distressing to the Prime Minister and his family for reasons that are self-evident. The Prime Minister is not prepared to leave these serious libels unchallenged.'

Biddle & Co., letter sent on instructions of John Major, 17 August 1993

If there was one thing everyone could agree on, it was that John Major was not a very interesting man. *Spitting Image* thought he was so dull that his puppet was entirely grey. So it was something of a surprise when, in October 1992, a magazine called *Scallywag* claimed that before becoming prime minister, he had had a torrid affair behind his wife Norma's back.

The story might have been surprising, but it turning up in *Scallywag* was less so: the magazine was notorious for printing any political rumour that came its way, regarding juiciness as a mark of authenticity rather than a reason for caution. The rag was edited by a former *News of the World* hack, Simon Regan, who rarely let the minor matter of checking facts or searching for evidence get in the way of what he regarded as the real journalistic business: heavy drinking. His managing editor, Angus James (who also went by the name Angus Wilson), defined the magazine's editorial approach thus: 'We're confident enough that the stories are true, but part of the reason we're publishing is to flush out more information.'[58]

This Major tale was, however, taken seriously enough to be picked up the following January as a three-thousand-word cover story in the *New Statesman*, although the left-wing weekly took care to point out that there wasn't a 'shred of evidence' that it was true. Editor Steve Platt maintained that the story was 'not about whether the Prime Minister has had an affair', but rather about 'the anatomy and persistence of the rumours and the role of gossip and innuendo'.[59] That didn't cut much ice with Major. As soon as the *New Statesman* appeared on newsstands he interrupted a diplomatic trip to India to announce that both he and the woman in question – one Clare Latimer, a caterer who had served up main courses, but definitely not bits on the side, for Major at Number 11 Downing Street when he was chancellor – were suing both magazines.

The prime minister demanded not only an apology for 'a serious and unpleasant libel', but 'payment of a substantial sum as compensation and to vindicate his reputation', something that was more problematic for both publications.[60] The *New Statesman* sold about 25,000 copies and had only just returned to profit after years of losses. As for *Scallywag*, it was edited from a pub, and had been dumped as an investment by the publishers of the *Sunday Sport* because they thought it was too dodgy; Regan was bankrupt and had been living in a caravan until it burned down the previous year. When the action finally made it to court, Latimer took pity on the scandal sheet and pulled out. 'When I saw the state of them I realised I couldn't take any money from them. If you saw how they looked you'd see they don't have two pennies to rub together.'[61] Major's case against *Scallywag* petered out when it became clear that they had no cash and were not taking it seriously anyway. But both Major and Latimer extracted substantial amounts of cash from the *New Statesman*: £1,000 in damages, but substantial legal costs which the magazine said were enough to take it 'very close to bankruptcy'.[62]

And they got a further £60,000 from the printers, distributors and even the newsagent chains that sold both magazines.

One of the many parliamentary colleagues offering the prime minister support in the libel battle was Edwina Currie, briefly and notoriously a junior health minister under Mrs Thatcher. 'I hope he takes them to the cleaners,' she told the *Daily Mirror* on 29 January 1993.[63] She knew what she was talking about. Two years earlier she had successfully sued the *Observer* for libel over a 1989 interview in which the actress Charlotte Rampling described a politician she played in the film *Paris by Night* as 'an Edwina Currie figure'.[64] It wasn't so much that the character ends up murdering someone that Currie had objected to, but rather the fact that she neglects her husband and children to have an affair. She wrote to the paper to complain primly that she had been married to the same man for seventeen years and did not have a lover. When they printed a clarification that the article 'was not intended to imply that a character in the film was based on' her, her avaricious lawyer Peter Carter-Ruck announced this was 'quite insufficient' and issued a writ.[65] 'I thought it was outrageous,' Currie told the High Court, claiming that the Rampling character's behaviour was 'directly antagonistic and opposite' to her own. 'It upset me very much.'[66] Her husband Ray followed her into the witness box to testify that 'the security and privacy of her home life is very, very important to her.'[67] The jury awarded Currie £5,000: once again the legal costs were much higher, pushing the *Observer*'s total bill up to around £150,000.

'Newspapers must be careful about what they say about public figures and their personal lives,' Currie crowed after the verdict. 'I have shrugged off most of the junk written about me over the years. This was different because it referred to my marriage and family life.'[68]

And that was the end of it. Both Major and Currie faded into the past with their political careers. Then one Saturday morning in September 2002, the nation woke to the horrendous image of them at it like rabbits. 'He may have been grey to the world, but he was a very exciting lover,' she wrote in her soon-to-be-published diaries, serialized exclusively in *The Times*, 'on good form, both talking and everything else – I am very lucky'. At the end of one marathon session, she told him, 'That was some going.' On another occasion, it was 'unexpectedly spectacularly good, for such a long time'.[69] Their affair, which had begun with her seducing him in her office, had lasted from 1984 to 1988, a period which saw him rise from backbencher to chief secretary to the Treasury, including his tenure as a government whip. Currie told *The Times*: 'Part of the fun was the thought that there John was sitting in the whip's office, sometimes discussing other people's affairs and keeping very quiet about his own.'[70]

It does, of course, take two to tango, but it has to be said that Currie didn't come out of the whole thing very well. She referred to Major as 'Mr B' throughout the diaries, not for any cutesy, pet-name reasons but because he was the alternative 'Man B' in her life. Ray, who she had dumped in 1997, was derided throughout as being dull and useless. All that Major would say when asked about the affair, then and forever after, was that his wife knew all about it and it was 'the one event in my life of which I am most ashamed'.[71] In response, Currie crassly declared: 'he was not very ashamed of it at the time, I can tell you.'[72]

However, on one subject – Major's campaign, announced at the 1993 Conservative conference, as a 'return to those old core values' – she did have something interesting to say. Recalling how it had led to the fall of so many of his ministers, his ex-mistress told *The Times*:

Back to Basics was absolute humbug, wasn't it?... It was very cruel to people who were otherwise excellent ministers, who didn't deserve to have the magnifying glass turned on their lives at that time by their own leader.... It was pompous and facetious and stupid. What should have been triggered in his mind was, 'We're all human, and, boy, don't I know it?'[73]

Major would subsequently insist that he never meant his 'basics' to include sexual morality, but his spin doctors had told journalists at the conference that the speech was a declaration of 'war on permissiveness', and he explicitly included 'traditional teaching' and 'respect for the family' in the list of values he wanted to return to.[74] It was certainly Major who accepted the resignation letters from a string of ministers caught with their pants down over the following several years – something that must have caused him an odd bat-squeak of conscience along the way.

Or perhaps not. After the Currie diaries were published, Clare Latimer was understandably somewhat bitter about being thrust into the headlines when she had done nothing wrong. 'John did nothing to clear my name, made no public statements about the scandal or my good reputation,' she recalled. 'I can see now that had he said, "I am not having an affair with Clare Latimer", then the question could have been asked, "Well who are you having an affair with?"... He used me to get away with the Edwina affair. He never spoke to me again.'[75]

'I have done nothing wrong. If it falls to me to start a fight to cut out the cancer of bent and twisted journalism in our country with the simple sword of truth and the trusty shield of British fair play, so be it. I am ready for the fight.'

Jonathan Aitken, press conference,
Conservative Central Office, 10 April 1995

No one listening to Jonathan Aitken that afternoon could have been in any doubt about how vehemently the chief secretary to the Treasury denied the claims in the day's *Guardian*. He was 'shocked and disgusted' by their 'outrageous falsehoods'. 'I have no hesitation in stating categorically that these allegations are wicked lies. I have today issued a writ for defamation against the *Guardian*, its Editor-in-Chief and the journalist who wrote the story,' he declared to a crowd that included the journalist in question, David Pallister, feeling decidedly awkward. 'The total picture of the *Guardian*'s report is one of deliberate misrepresentations, falsehoods and lies. It is clearly part of the paper's long campaign of sustained attempts to discredit me.'[76]

Next came the peroration, with its magnificently mixed metaphors, sword and shield pressed into oncological service specifically to recall Aitken's great-uncle Lord Beaverbrook, owner of the *Daily Express*, every edition of which was mantled by the armed figure of 'The Crusader'. (Beaverbrook, you might remember from chapter 1, was one of the press barons who had been so ready to lie on behalf of Winston Churchill.) Aitken himself was the author of an admiring biography of Richard Nixon. The clues really were all there.

Aitken's speech wasn't actually aimed at the *Guardian* at all. His target was ITV, whose *World in Action* programme was due to repeat and expand upon the paper's claims at 8:30 that evening. The morning's newsprint could be dismissed as the partisan ravings of a left-leaning broadsheet with a limited circulation; a prime-time documentary on one of what for most people were still only four TV channels would do a lot more damage. He was determined to scare them out of broadcasting.

He failed. The producers of the programme even managed to add Aitken's bravura performance in time to slam the re-edited tape into the output machine at exactly 8:31 p.m. A rewritten voiceover was appended live. The programme's production company, Granada, were the next to receive writs. This too failed to deter journalists, and more stories about Aitken piled up in the broadsheets and tabloids. Eventually the minister announced that he would be stepping down from the cabinet in order to devote himself to full-time suing: 'I expect to be heavily engaged in preparing for legal battles with my adversaries in the media…. I need to give my full commitment to fighting my current and possible future libel actions.'[77]

What were the claims about Aitken? Well, there were plenty.[78] He had worked for decades as a fixer for Prince Muhammad bin Fahd, a son of the King of Saudi Arabia, and been lavishly rewarded by him for arranging deals on luxury cars, a private jet and a string of London properties. Yet Aitken had failed to declare this clearly in the Register of Members' Interests, even when in 1992 he was appointed as minister for defence procurement. Since the UK conducted an enormous amount of arms trading with the Saudis, his fixing was a blatant conflict of interest. Aitken had also been a director of a company owned by a Lebanese businessman involved in arms deals before going on to oversee such deals for the government, something he again failed to declare, as was legally required, in the official records of other companies he was a director of. He had also been on the board of another arms company which had sold guns to Singapore that ultimately ended up in Iran, a country Britain had barred itself from selling weapons to. He ran his parliamentary office out of the HQ of a company owned by Prince Muhammad's business manager, Said Ayas, claiming a publicly funded 'secretarial allowance' while his administrative staff were on the company payroll. He served as the frontman for the Inglewood health farm in Berkshire, which had been secretly purchased through a Panamanian company by the Saudi royal family. He asked staff there if they would provide prostitutes for wealthy Arab guests. (Aitken was particularly cross about this one, claiming in the witness box that his twelve-year-old son had read it and asked him, 'What is a pimp, Daddy?' – even though the *Guardian* hadn't used the word.[79]) For good measure, the *Mirror* had piled in with claims about Aitken's own sex life and how he liked to be spanked by dominatrices. But for various reasons, Aitken's libel trial, which kicked off in June 1997, ended up hinging entirely on who had paid his hotel bill for a weekend in Paris four years previously.

The answer was Said Ayas, on behalf of Prince Muhammad, who was also staying in Paris that weekend and with whom Aitken had a meeting on Saturday, 18 September 1993. Because he was determined to hide the extent of his personal contacts with the Saudi prince – and because he had already failed to declare the hospitality, as he was obliged to do under the ministerial code of conduct – Aitken lied and claimed instead that 'the hotel bill was paid by my wife, with money given to her by me for this purpose.'[80] Since his wife Lolicia had not actually been anywhere near Paris on the weekend in question, he was then forced to pile lie upon lie, until the whole teetering tower of falsehood came crashing down at the trial, taking his entire career with it.

First Aitken was obliged to pretend that Lolicia had arrived at the Ritz from dropping off their daughter Victoria at her Swiss boarding school on the Sunday morning, two days after he had himself checked in. He was helped by a letter he managed to get from the Ritz management saying the cashier remembered the bill being paid by 'a brunette lady of European aspect'.[81] (This was not quite as much help as he might have liked, given that Lolicia was blonde.) Then it emerged that this payment only accounted for half the bill, obliging Aitken to come up with another cock and bull story. He claimed that Ayas's nephew, who had also been staying at the hotel, had accidentally paid for the other half – you know, the sort of thing that happens all the time in top hotels – but he had sent him a cheque to cover the cost once he realized the mistake. Ayas helped out by claiming to have personally witnessed Lolicia paying the bill, and threatening to sue the *Guardian* if they suggested he had picked it up himself. Unfortunately for Aitken, Ayas then fell out with Prince Muhammad, who accused him of stealing £25 million, and was unable to testify at the libel trial because he was under house arrest back in Saudi Arabia.

Still, Aitken carried on stacking up the lies. The *Guardian*'s barrister George Carman challenged him with Ritz phone records showing a call from his room to a Swiss hotel where Lolicia had been staying at 10:15 a.m. on the Sunday, despite his claim that she had joined him in Paris 'late to mid-morning' that same day. He smoothly lied that his wife was on the road at the time and he was on the phone with his mother-in-law. Since he hadn't mentioned anything about his mother-in-law being in Switzerland before this point, he got his seventeen-year-old daughter Victoria to sign a witness statement claiming that 'my mother was not there but my grandmother was there', and, for good measure, detailing how 'on Thursday 16th September my mother and I drove to Dover where we caught the ferry to Calais and the train to Paris.'[82] He had drafted every word of it.

It was only when the trial was well under way – and things were not looking good for the *Guardian* – that the paper's team managed to turn up some killer evidence: British Airways ticket records which showed Lolicia and Victoria flying directly from Heathrow to Geneva on the Friday, and Lolicia returning on the same route alone. They also had a car hire receipt that showed Lolicia dropping off a vehicle at Geneva airport at 6:25 p.m. on the Sunday.[83] By her husband's sworn account, she was meant to be some five hundred miles away in Paris at the time.

Carman had the pleasure of passing these newly sworn witness statements up to the judge and suggesting 'it might be very important for your Lordship to read it immediately.' Having done so, Justice Oliver Popplewell murmured to Aitken's legal team: 'no doubt you will want to consider the position overnight.'[84]

Aitken had thought he had covered his tracks: he had refused to hand over records for the family's American Express cards, which would have given away Lolicia's movements, and checked with a friend who was a senior director at BA, who assured him the company would have long since destroyed records of passengers from 1993. When the statement from the airline arrived, his 'heart sank, my head pounded, my confidence exploded into tiny pieces like flying shrapnel. I knew at once that I had lost the libel case and that with it I had lost my whole world.'[85] And how.

Aitken had already lost his parliamentary seat in the Labour landslide of 1997; now he was forced to abandon his libel case and pay legal bills for both sides amounting to several million pounds. He declared bankruptcy as a result. Lolicia announced she was leaving him. He was forced to step down from the Privy Council. Victoria was arrested over her false witness statement, which her father described as his 'worst and most shameful mistake'.[86] Although she was not charged, he was, and on 19 January 1999 he pleaded guilty to perjury and conspiracy to pervert the course of justice. He was jailed for eighteen months.

The collapse of his house of cards is detailed in *Pride and Perjury*, the tear-jerking, self-serving memoir Aitken published after he was released and had got God in a big way. He blames his appalling behaviour on 'something troubling me in that interior province of life which religious people call "the soul" or "the spiritual dimension."' While he was happy to hold his hands up to what was actually proved in court – 'telling a lie about the relatively unimportant matter of who paid my £900 Ritz Hotel bill seemed to me to be a necessary small one in self-defence against much greater falsehoods' – he continued to deny all the other accusations that were at issue in the trial. The only reason he was meeting Prince Muhammad that weekend was apparently to discuss 'one or two defence and security issues which were on my agenda as Defence Minister'. He fails to explain why, in that case, he tried so desperately to keep it a secret rather than inviting officials along to take minutes.[87]

Nor, while wallowing soppily in the redemptive love of his children – he even quotes a school essay in which his son describes him as 'inspirational' – does Aitken find space in its 369 pages to record that he had also attempted to exploit his other daughter, Alexandra, in the trial. He had claimed that the *World in Action* crew had 'stampeded' them both outside the family home and made her cry – only for the recording of the incident to be shown in court, revealing Alexandra wasn't even there.[88]

5

SINS OF SPIN

We tend to think of political spin as the invention of New Labour, something that arrived in Downing Street on 2 May 1997 along with the crowd – carefully compiled from the most photogenic workers at Labour HQ and their families – that waved Union Jacks behind Tony Blair as 'Things Can Only Get Better' played. (The original plan had been to have Labour Party banners, but it was overruled by civil servants.) But the idea that spin is the invention of New Labour is itself nothing but spin.

It was spin fifty years earlier when a young Harold Wilson started waving around a pipe to make himself look older, and then realized that if he made a bit of theatre out of lighting it, that would give him extra time to find a way out of answering difficult questions. It was spin in the seventies when Gordon Reece ordered Margaret Thatcher to ditch the pearls and pussy bows and undergo elocution lessons to make her seem more human (just imagine what she must have been like before). It was spin when Boris Johnson started deliberately buying clothes that don't fit and ruffling up his hair before he went in front of TV cameras. And it was spin when

David Cameron refused, very rudely, to honour the dress code at a friend's wedding, just in case photographers snapped him wearing a morning suit and looking like the posh boy he was desperately pretending not to be.

Of course, spin is not merely about the presentation of people: it is about how to sell a story, how to assemble (or dissemble) information to put forward the version of events that you want people to believe is true. It is about polishing up policies, dazzling with statistics, finding a case study that fits your needs – and ensuring that your version of reality is robust enough to hold together for the ever-diminishing period before the media get bored and move on. If you're lucky, it works. If you're unlucky, your efforts become the story. If you're really unlucky, the reporters refuse to move on at all – Alastair Campbell, the ultimate spin doctor, was often claimed to have a 'golden rule' that if a scandal was strung out over more than a week, the figure at the centre of it was doomed. Like many other things attributed to him, he now says he never uttered such words.

And if you're incredibly unlucky, people remember your disastrous efforts decades later, long after whatever policy it was you were trying to push has faded from memory.

* * * * *

> 'Eight years ago in a respectable street in Wolverhampton a house was sold to a Negro. Now only one white, a woman old-age pensioner, lives there. This is her story.'

Enoch Powell, speech,
Birmingham, 20 April 1968

'I am going to make a speech,' Enoch Powell, then shadow secretary of state for defence, told his friend Clem Jones as he asked Clem and his wife, Marjorie, to babysit his two daughters that Saturday. 'It is going to go up and fizz like a rocket.'[1]

He wasn't wrong. Powell's talk to members of the Conservative Political Centre at the Midland Hotel, Birmingham, was notorious. It was known as the 'Rivers of Blood' speech, though that was actually a misquotation. What Powell, a classical scholar, said was that when he considered the future results of immigration from Commonwealth nations, he was 'filled with foreboding; like the Roman, I seem to see "the River Tiber foaming with much blood".'[2] But then Powell got it wrong too. He was quoting from Book VI of the *Aeneid*, specifically the sybil's prophecy about Aeneas's return to Italy, and the sybil wasn't a Roman at all. Until the last minute Powell had planned to deliver the quote in the original Latin, but he realized 'that's pedantic.'[3]

The classical allusions may have been fairly unusual, but much of the rest of the speech – which Conservative leader Edward Heath denounced as 'racialist in tone and liable to exacerbate racial tension' as he sacked Powell from the shadow cabinet the following day – is tediously familiar.[4] Having quoted the prophecy of 'a middle-aged, quite ordinary working man' in his constituency who complained that 'in 15 or 20 years' time the black man will have the whip hand over the white man', the MP delivered his argument – still beloved by people who never stop talking about immigration – that people were being prevented from talking about immigration. 'I can already hear the chorus of execration,' Powell whined. 'How dare I say such a horrible thing? How dare I stir up trouble and inflame feelings by repeating such a conversation? The answer is that I do not have the right not to do so…. What he is saying, thousands and hundreds of thousands are saying and thinking'.[5]

For the longest section of his infamous speech, however, Powell concentrated on just one of his purported hundreds of thousands. His subject was another constituent, a pensioner who, he claimed, was now the only white resident of her Wolverhampton street, where she rented out rooms to lodgers:

> With growing fear, she saw one house after another taken over. The quiet street became a place of noise and confusion. Regretfully, her white tenants moved out…. Immigrant families have tried to rent rooms in her house, but she always refused…. She went to apply for a rate reduction and was seen by a young girl…. When she said the only people she could get were Negroes, the girl said, 'Racial prejudice won't get you anywhere in this country.' So she went home.[6]

Lest anyone be in any doubt, Powell was arguing vehemently *in favour* of the old lady's right to be a racist. Proposed anti-discrimination laws, he told the crowd, 'mean that the immigrant and his descendants should be elevated into a privileged or special class'. Such legislation would 'give the stranger, the disgruntled and the agent provocateur the power to pillory them for their private actions.' You wouldn't even be allowed to practise bigotry in your own business!

He continued with his constituent's story:

> She is becoming afraid to go out. Windows are
> broken. She finds excreta pushed through her letter box.
> When she goes to the shops, she is followed by children,
> charming, wide-grinning piccaninnies. They cannot
> speak English, but one word they know. 'Racialist,' they
> chant. When the new Race Relations Bill is passed, this
> woman is convinced she will go to prison. And is she
> so wrong? I begin to wonder.[7]

It was incredibly strong stuff, much worse than the rhetorical flourish that everyone remembers. But don't be downhearted: this was far from acceptable even in its own time. Though only one person in the audience present apparently showed 'any sign of annoyance', Powell's words caused an instant media firestorm.[8] On Monday, *The Times* denounced it as 'AN EVIL SPEECH'. The coverage finished forever the friendship between Powell's family and the Joneses, with Marjorie handing Enoch's kids back on the doorstep and telling him: 'I don't think we shall be seeing each other again for a very long time.'[9]

There is no evidence that any of Powell's story was true. He hadn't even spoken to the woman he was talking about. Powell's biographer Simon Heffer says the MP's information came from 'a letter to him from a woman in Northumberland', more than two hundred miles from his own constituency.[10] And despite scores of journalists from both local and national titles scouring Wolverhampton top to bottom, no one was able to find anyone who matched the old lady's description. Powell's former friend Clem Jones, who edited the *Wolverhampton Express & Star*, never found her, and suspected the whole thing was just one of 'many myths about the immigrant population doing the rounds, some of which ended up in Powell's constituency correspondence'.[11]

'You were dealing with dynamite. Didn't you have a *fantastic* duty to check that story to find if it was true?' demanded interviewer David Frost the following year. 'I haven't the slightest doubt that is as true as it is typical,' replied a stony-faced Powell. He could only say that he had 'verified the source from which I had that information.' Frost persisted: 'Do you know the lady?' Powell replied, still stony-faced: 'I have never agreed to answer any question whatever which could lead to the identification either of the source or of the case and I'm not going to do so.'[12] He kept his word right up to his death in 1998.

It took some serious detective work by the BBC in 2007 to track down the only suspect who fitted the 'special combination of features' outlined by Powell in his speech. Druscilla Cotterill owned one of the seven terraced houses on Brighton Place, Wolverhampton, where she had previously taken in lodgers; she was sixty-one in 1968; and a large majority of immigrants had moved into the street around that time. But not all of the other white residents had fled – another family stayed until they died – and in plenty of other respects, she sounded nothing like Enoch's pensioner. 'She would never give in to any sort of prejudiced behaviour,' local resident Lance Dunkley, a West Indian, insisted to the BBC. 'You had a child and you were working, you couldn't find a childminder, she would step in and say, "I'll do it for you," free of cost. You couldn't class her as a racist.' He wasn't alone in his assessment. 'No, I didn't find that with her,' confirmed neighbour Roderick Foster. 'If she did have a problem, we weren't aware of it,' said Carol Antonio, who grew up in the street. The last two did admit that, as kids, 'We did tease her quite a bit,' but they were adamant that the only incident when dog excrement was put through a letter box involved 'a black family at number 6'.[13]

Either Powell or his mysterious Northumberland correspondent seems to have spiced the story up beyond all recognition in the telling. If Powell was responsible, it was not his first offence. In a speech two months earlier he had announced that 'only this week a colleague of mine in the House of Commons was dumbfounded when I told him of a constituent whose little daughter was now the only white child in her class at school.'[14] It was only after five days of investigating that the Wolverhampton Education Committee were able to establish and announce that this was because so many children had been off sick on a particular day.

Maybe that was one of the reasons why Powell remained so insistent that he would never reveal any more details of the letter. 'He had a very strong view that anyone who wrote to him, wrote to him in confidence, and that should not be broken,' his long-serving private secretary told the BBC in 2007.[15] Five years later Powell's widow Pam provided another explanation that was just as convincing. 'The letter most certainly did exist. I did see it, but I don't know where it went.... I saw that letter and probably put it somewhere so safe that we could never find it again. Whatever happened to it I don't know, I wish I did; we all turned the place upside down and we couldn't find it.'[16]

> 'This monstrous brutality is but the latest act in Colonel Gaddafi's reign of terror. The evidence is now conclusive that the terrorist bombing of La Belle discotheque was planned and executed under the direct orders of the Libyan regime.'

Ronald Reagan,
address to the nation, 14 April 1986

The most useful thing any government can have is an enemy, some foreign power that every ill and misfortune can be blamed upon. It doesn't much matter if the foreign power is actually responsible – look at George W. Bush's attempts to associate Saddam Hussein with the 9/11 attacks; what matters is that the foreigner can be portrayed as a convincing baddie. And if the figure is prepared to play along with the pretence – because it also suits his (or her) purposes to pretend that it is your imperialist regime that is the baddie in this black-and-white game of realpolitik – then all the better.

There is not the space here – probably not the space in all the pages of this book – to do full justice to the story of Colonel Muammar Gaddafi's flip-flopping relationship with the US, and by extension Britain. We'll instead have to make do with a brief chronology. In the mid-1980s Gaddafi was public enemy number one, blamed for events his regime was behind – the 1984 shooting of WPC Yvonne Fletcher by a gunman inside the Libyan embassy in London – and events it was not – simultaneous grenade and rifle attacks on Rome and Vienna airports in 1985 which were the work of a rogue Palestinian faction – as well as events whose true perpetrators remain unclear more than three decades later. In many cases Gaddafi was only too happy to drop hints that he might be involved: the Rome and Vienna attacks were, he declared, 'heroic acts'. Sometimes he would go so far as to stump up reparations: families of victims of the 1989 Lockerbie bombing got more than $1.5 billion in compensation though Libya refused to accept responsibility for the attack. In other cases, Ronald Reagan's White House were happy to pin the blame on their favourite bogeyman even when there was very little evidence for his involvement, or even for any plots existing. Such was the situation in 1981, when news broke that US interceptions had revealed a Libyan 'hit squad' was on its way to Washington to assassinate the president. The government leak came complete with sketches of the squad's supposed members. In the words of the journalist who was selected to receive the leak, it all 'turned out to be phoney'.[17]

In 1987, while Reagan was still the sitting president, Robert Oakley, a diplomat who served as director of the State Department's office of combating terrorism and had a seat on Reagan's National Security Council, admitted to the BBC in an interview that Gaddafi's regime had been selected as a 'soft target' for a show of strength against terrorism. 'There were less downside consequences, if you will. There's less Arab support for Gaddafi. We figured there would be less Soviet support for Gaddafi.'[18] After Italian authorities announced that they had found no evidence of Libyan involvement but plenty of 'clear implications of a Syria connection' in the airport attacks, the US State Department simply dismissed the findings, and Reagan announced they had 'irrefutable evidence' of Gaddafi being behind both atrocities.[19] At the time, Syria was under the rule of Hafez al-Assad (father of Bashar), who was considered a key US partner in the Middle East, since he was standing strong against an Islamic uprising like the one that had toppled the Iranian regime a couple of years earlier. America needed a different enemy.

Just a few months after the airport attacks, on 5 April 1986, a bomb exploded in West Berlin's La Belle discotheque, a favourite haunt of US servicemen. The bomb killed an American soldier and a Turkish woman and injured hundreds of others. Within two days Reagan announced that Gaddafi was 'definitely a suspect'; within ten days he confirmed in a televised address that it was definitely him. 'Our evidence is direct, it is precise, it is irrefutable,' he informed the American people.[20] It was anything but that. In fact, it primarily consisted of some intercepted messages from the Libyan capital, Tripoli, to the country's embassies ahead of the attack, which the Israelis, no friends of the Gaddafi regime, had dismissed as 'wild rhetoric'.[21] But as the president noted in his address, the evidence didn't really matter: 'Several weeks ago… I warned Colonel Gaddafi we would hold his regime accountable for any new terrorist attacks launched against American citizens.' He had ordered US planes – flying from a base in the UK, chosen as much to bind another country into the operation as for logistical reasons – to bomb targets in Tripoli in retaliation.

Naturally, Gaddafi played his part, appearing on Libyan TV from the ruins of his house to claim that his wife had been badly injured in the attack and that his adopted daughter Hana had been killed. (Despite him producing a child's body for the cameras, it was later reported that Hana had lived to adulthood; there were also suggestions she never existed.) The US hardly helped gather allies to their cause by boasting that they had targeted sites that had a 'full terrorist connection' with 'precision bombing' – before it turned out they had hit the French embassy in Tripoli and a residential area more than two miles from the military base they were aiming for.[22]

Initially, the investigations into who had been responsible for the La Belle bombing pointed in a different direction. That November two Jordanians were convicted of another terror attack in Berlin, conducted a week earlier using the same kind of explosives; they confessed to working for the Syrian government, then recanted, and German police announced they didn't have enough evidence to charge them with the disco bombing too. The trail went cold until the Berlin Wall fell four years later. Evidence from the Stasi secret police archives provided enough evidence for a Libyan who had worked at the country's embassy in East Berlin to be charged. He was put on trial in 1997 along with two of his former colleagues, a Palestinian and a German, and the latter's wife and sister, who it was claimed had carried the bomb onto the dance floor after it was brought across the border in a diplomatic pouch. The sister was acquitted and the others convicted, but the proceedings were described as 'murky'.[23] Judge Peter Marhofer complained about the unwillingness of the German and US secret services to fully share intelligence, even a decade after the events. In November 2001 he finally concluded that while 'Libya bears at the very least a considerable part of the responsibility for the attack', there was no evidence Gaddafi himself had personally been involved, as Reagan had asserted.[24]

By then, the colonel himself was well on the way to being rehabilitated in the international community. He had agreed to surrender two Libyan suspects for trial in Europe over the Lockerbie bombing, which killed 259 airline passengers and crew over the Scottish town just before Christmas 1988. The investigation into that atrocity had also swerved sharply away from Syria around the time it became necessary to keep that country onside during the first Gulf War; some very dubious evidence presented at the subsequent trial was not enough to convict one of the men, and the other, Abdelbaset al-Megrahi, continued to vehemently (and convincingly) protest his innocence right up until he was released on compassionate grounds in 2009 – an act of mercy which prevented any further evidence being presented at appeal.[25] And although Gaddafi discomfited the British and Scottish governments by turning al-Megrahi's return into a hero's welcome, Reagan's 'most dangerous man in the world' somehow seemed to have been completely transformed into one of our best friends. Having installed Saddam Hussein in the top spot Gaddafi once occupied, US President George W. Bush pointedly left Libya off his list of countries in the 'axis of evil' who were providing arms to terrorists in his State of the Union Address in 2002. Again, there was no evidence of Saddam doing anything of the sort, and plenty concerning Gaddafi. (To name but one, the colonel had been sending guns to the IRA throughout the Troubles.)

Two years later, as the wars in Iraq and Afghanistan dragged on, the president's right-hand man, Tony Blair, travelled to Tripoli to be photographed shaking hands with the Libyan leader in the desert tent he liked to do business in. Gaddafi had said he fully intended to get rid of his country's 'weapons of mass destruction' – which was handy because it meant Blair could say they had found some WMDs somewhere – and was fully on board with the global fight against al-Qaeda.[26] He was duly rewarded with the lifting of sanctions, which allowed him to start doing serious business with the West for the first time in decades – including welcoming BP back into his oil-rich lands and sending his son to London to study (or at least pick up a PhD from a university that received a £1.5 million donation from his family). 'The relationship between Britain and Libya has been completely transformed in these last few years,' enthused Blair in 2007, after another desert love-in. 'We now have very strong co-operation on counter-terrorism and defence.'[27]

This new-found friendliness with the West did not, however, stop Gaddafi from brutalizing his people, who had seen all internal dissent ruthlessly crushed since he had seized power in a military coup in 1969. And when they finally rose up against him in 2011 as part of the Arab Spring and the country erupted into civil war,

America and Britain flip-flopped again. 'It is time for Gaddafi to go – now, without further violence or delay,' announced Secretary of State Hillary Clinton.[28] 'This behaviour cannot be allowed to stand,' declared Prime Minister David Cameron. 'It is quite clear to me that someone who I have never supported, whose regime I have never supported… is clearly behaving in a totally and utterly unacceptable way'.[29] Both countries committed to a NATO-led military intervention in March of that year; it proved just as disastrous as the one in Iraq. Five years on, Libya had two rival parliaments and three governments, but the real power had devolved to well over a thousand armed militias, each under distinct leadership. ISIS had also established a serious power base in the country.

'Libya is a mess,' admitted Barack Obama in April 2016.[30] He was the eighth US president to try to deal with Gaddafi, and he was also the last: the Libyan leader was cornered in an underground drain by a mob of his former subjects in October 2011 and beaten, shot and bayoneted to death. A crowd queued up to pose for selfies with his body afterwards.

> 'So on the fiftieth anniversary of the NHS this Government will now make the biggest ever investment in its future, giving the NHS for the first time for decades the long-term resources it needs. Under the last Government the increase for the last three years was seven billion. For the coming three years, I am announcing an increase in health service funding of a total of twenty-one billion.'

Gordon Brown,
House of Commons, 14 July 1998

One of New Labour's tactics to take power in 1997 involved convincing the public that they would not be as profligate as their party predecessors by pledging to stick to the spending targets set by the Conservatives for the first two years they were in government. Another was promising to give health and education the generous funding they said had for so long been denied them. It was very difficult to reconcile these two things, and when Gordon Brown announced a £21 billion infusion of cash for the NHS in the summer of 1998, it came as a huge and welcome surprise.[31] 'This settlement is far better than we had dared hope,' the head of the NHS Confederation told the BBC. 'All our expectations had been around a figure of £10 billion to 12 billion. To have received £21 billion is beyond our wildest dreams.' The director of the Institute of Health Services Management hailed a 'massive injection of new cash in a desperately threadbare NHS'.[32]

It all seemed too good to be true, and it was. Brown was doing the sort of counting that earns you a big red cross on your maths homework, and quite possibly a 'see me'. Health services spending in England that year stood at £37 billion; by the end of the three-year period covered by the spending review it would rise to £46 billion – a simple increase of £9 billion. But that wasn't how things worked under the chancellor's alternative maths. The 1999 budget was £3 billion higher than the 1998 one; the 2000 budget was £6 billion higher; and the 2001 budget was £9 billion higher. Add 3 + 6 + 9 and you get 18 – which, when added to an extra £2.8 billion for health in Scotland and Wales, rounded up to 21. Yes, it involved counting some of the money twice, and some of it thrice, not to mention the fact that none of it was coming just yet, because there was still another year to go on New Labour's spending guarantees. But the vagueness of the term 'a total of...' covered a multitude of mathematical sins, and in the meantime he could bask in headlines like 'CASH GIFT STUNS NHS' (*Guardian*), 'BROWN GOES ON A SUMMER SPREE' (*Daily Mail*), 'GOLDEN BROWN' and 'BROWN PUMPS £21BN INTO THE NHS' (both BBC News).[33]

The Treasury select committee spotted the deceit. Just a fortnight later they reported that 'Assessing the extent of the increase in real resources going in to key departments over the next three years has been complicated by "presentational" issues' and further that 'it is clear that as a percentage of GDP (a useful measure of real resources being spent) expenditure on the NHS is set to rise from 4.4 per cent in 1998–99 to 4.7 per cent in 2001–02.... There is thus no cash bonanza of the type which newspaper headlines might suggest'.[34] This didn't sound quite as sexy as a multi-billion-pound giveaway, and the media continued to cite the £21 billion sum for years to come.

Brown continued his creative approach to accounting throughout his ten years at the Treasury, never announcing a spending commitment once if he could announce it several times. Debts, meanwhile, weren't counted at all, if he could help it. The private finance initiative (PFI) – inherited from the Tories but massively expanded and exploited by Brown – allowed him to farm out public building projects such as schools and hospitals to the private sector; in return the private companies would receive ever-increasing payments from the public purse for decades to come. The rules – *his* rules – said such commitments could be kept 'off balance sheet' and not counted as part of the public debt.[35] That helped with another of Brown's arbitrary rules, a pledge to keep debt below 40 per cent of GDP in order to demonstrate what a responsible fellow he was.[36]

Following the 2008 financial crisis, when the size of the debt became a major political problem, the Institute for Fiscal Studies calculated that if you included PFI debts in the total, the debt would swell to nearly twice its official size.[37] Suddenly, Brown was less keen on doubling-up his numbers.

'When we are dealing with these problems, let's talk fact, not fiction.'

Alan Milburn,
BBC Radio 4 Today, 22 January 2002

By the time Labour had settled into their second term in office, their constantly whirring spin machine seemed to have been accepted as a routine part of the game of political reporting. Whitehall press officers would put out a story, and journalists would set about testing and teasing each aspect of it to see which would be the first to fall down. The teams would sometimes swap ends, and the government's shock troops would devote themselves to demolishing the details of a front-page scoop that showed the Court of King Blair in a bad light. No one emerged much the wiser from any of it, but there were only a few casualties – the odd special adviser here, a political correspondent deafened by an Alastair Campbell earbashing there. Then, suddenly, it all got considerably darker.

The first victim was a ninety-four-year-old woman called Rose Addis who had had a fall and cut her head quite badly. She was found by one of the care workers who visited regularly at her North London flat; the carer called an ambulance, which took Addis to the accident and emergency department at the Whittington Hospital. It was there that Addis's daughter Zena Gold, herself in her seventies, found her two days later – still in the clothes she had been brought in wearing, and with dried blood caked in her hair and on her face. 'I went absolutely ballistic,' Gold said. She 'asked why she hadn't been moved to a ward. The nurses said they didn't have any beds.'[38]

The hospital denied this, saying there had been beds available but doctors had chosen to keep her mother in the A&E department so she could 'be kept under observation'. They also said that it was standard practice not to wash a patient's hair immediately after they had suffered head wounds, lest the wound open up again. They said they had tried to change Addis's clothes and clean her up, but she had 'refused' their help and been 'most particular about whom she will allow to care for her'. She was, they said, understandably, 'confused and agitated' after her accident.[39]

What took this beyond the bounds of a horrible trauma for Mrs Addis was the family's decision to tell not just the papers but their MP about it. Their MP happened to be the leader of the opposition, Iain Duncan Smith, and he promptly laid the whole thing at Blair's feet at Prime Minister's Questions. 'Mrs. Addis's daughter also said to me: "If my poor mother had been a dog she would have been treated better",' the Tory leader roared. 'Will the Prime Minister now apologise to Mrs. Addis for her treatment…?'[40]

The prime minister was not in the mood to do anything of the sort. Instead, he went on the attack. 'The idea that one elderly woman's care was the big political story for the entire country was ridiculous,' chief spin doctor Alastair Campbell noted in his diary. 'If we were not careful we would be into a new season of personal case histories presented as the big picture… we agreed we had to get the doctors at the Whittington Hospital out there.'[41]

The clinical director of the Whittington, James Malone-Lee, was only too happy to oblige, going on various BBC programmes to throw blame firmly back onto his ninety-year-old patient. 'She would not allow the nursing staff who were on duty in the A&E department at the time to change her. She refused.'[42] At the end of his long day of interviews (Campbell applauded the appearances as 'excellent'), Malone-Lee went further on *Newsnight*: 'She had a particular reservation about some of the nurses who were on duty,' he said. 'I'm not going to develop that much further. I have discussed it with my colleagues and it's an area of health care that's often a problem to us. It causes a great degree of distress to the staff. It is a sensitive issue.'[43]

What was being implied was that Addis was a nasty old racist who had actively resisted treatment from certain staff. Spinners for the health secretary, Alan Milburn, who himself had dismissed the family's version of events as a 'fiction' – were forced to deny that they were actively pushing this line. This innuendo was something her family would not stand for. 'My grandmother has two social carers from Hackney social services who are both from ethnic minorities. She absolutely adores them and they love her,' stormed her grandson Jason Gold to the *Evening Standard*. 'She has absolutely no problem with them.'[44] The chief executive of the Whittington, Trevor Campbell Davis – Malone-Lee's boss – hastily withdrew any hint of accusation. 'I would not want the hospital ever to give the impression that there was any racist overtone that might be seen as a slur on the family.'[45]

Things were about to get even more churned up. Malone-Lee was exposed as a Labour Party activist, although he insisted he had 'been wearing my clinician's hat at all times when I have spoken during this recent episode, not a Labour Party hat'.[46] Campbell's deputy Tom Kelly was upbraided for revealing confidential medical details about Addis and two other patients in a briefing to journalists. 'It was a tactical error because it allowed the Tory papers to make it a "Labour dirty tricks" story, rather than being about IDS getting his facts wrong,' complained Campbell.[47] In fact, Iain Duncan Smith, the hospital and Addis's family between them had already put most of the details in the public domain. Only one thing was painfully obvious: none of this had been the fault, intention or desire of

Rose Addis, who was still recuperating on the Whittington ward to which she had eventually been moved.

She was merely one of the many ordinary people who were to feel the full force of the Whitehall attack dogs, their teeth sharpened on the harder necks of professional politicos. A few months later Dan Corry, a special adviser at the Department of Transport, was caught attempting to dig up dirt on survivors of the Paddington rail crash, which had killed thirty-one people and injured more than five hundred. In particular Corry wanted to identify any 'political affiliations' ahead of a meeting with Stephen Byers at which it was suspected the survivors might criticize the minister.[48] Another of Byers' advisers, Jo Moore, was forced out in a storm of publicity over an email in which she had urged colleagues to take advantage of the 9/11 attacks as 'a good day to "bury" bad news'.[49]

The manic whirligig at the centre of Whitehall, epitomized by the increasingly unstable figure of Alastair Campbell, was beginning to spin out of control.[50] And in the summer of 2003, when it caught up an unassuming weapons expert at the Ministry of Defence, Dr David Kelly, and forced him to face public pressure that was too much for anyone to bear, the machine finally exploded.

'We all know the stories about the Human Rights Act. The violent drug dealer who cannot be sent home because his daughter – for whom he pays no maintenance – lives here. The robber who cannot be removed because he has a girlfriend. The illegal immigrant who cannot be deported because – and I am not making this up – he had a pet cat. This is why I remain of the view that the Human Rights Act needs to go.'

Theresa May, Conservative Party Conference,
Manchester, 4 October 2011

It is a rule that is very rarely broken. Perhaps we could call it 'Littlejohn's Law'. If anyone, particularly anyone who hails from the same end of the political spectrum as that particular *Daily Mail* columnist, prefaces a statement with words along the line of 'you couldn't make it up', you can be almost certain someone did.

That was certainly true of the moment when Home Secretary Theresa May put on her best pub-bore act at the Conservative conference in 2011 to cite various reasons why 'human rights' were – *nudge, nudge* – more like 'human wrongs', if you know what I'm saying, eh, squire? Among her reasons was – and she really *was* making this up – a cat.[51]

It took but a handful of minutes for judges at the Royal Courts of Justice in London to shoot her down in flames. 'This was a case in which the Home Office conceded that they had mistakenly failed to apply their own policy – applying at that time to that appellant

– for dealing with unmarried partners of people settled in the UK', came the stern announcement. 'That was the basis for the decision to uphold the original tribunal decision – the cat had nothing to do with the decision.'[52]

Indeed, the published judgments in case number IA/14578/2008 of the Asylum and Immigration Tribunal make it clear that the man in question had actually been allowed leave to stay in Britain due to the misapplication of 'a withdrawn policy, DP3/96, which no longer applied at the date of decision'.[53] He was a Bolivian national who had come to the UK as a student, met his partner, been living with her for four years, had outstayed his visa and was now seeking leave to remain in the country. Unlike the two other examples that May had lumped him in with, there was no suggestion that he had committed any criminal offences during his time here.

He had, however, been helping to care for his partner's father, whose state of ill health prevented the couple from moving together to Bolivia. They did own a cat – but that was only one of a host of pieces of evidence they had offered to prove they were in a long-term relationship, along with bank statements, diaries and sworn statements from their friends. 'The evidence concerning the joint acquisition of Maya (the cat) by the appellant and his partner reinforces my conclusion on the strength and quality of the family life that appellant and his partner enjoy,' noted Judge James Devittie, who had no doubt at all that their relationship was genuine.[54] Problem was, when the case was referred to the upper tier of the tribunal, Judge Judith Gleeson had done what no judge should ever do: she tried to make a joke about it. 'The Immigration Judge's determination is upheld,' she wrote in the last paragraph of her ruling. 'The cat… need no longer fear having to adapt to Bolivian mice.'[55]

On such flights of fancy do reputations rest. After the unprovoked assault on Maya the cat, May the human found herself caught up in a catfight of her own. A cabinet colleague, Lord Chancellor Ken Clarke, pooh-poohed her call to rip up legislation on such flimsy grounds and informed the party conference that the case 'certainly has nothing to do with the Human Rights Act and nothing to do with the European Convention on Human Rights'.[56]

After taking over as prime minister in the summer of 2016, May declared that she intended to scrap both of them – once she had got Brexit out of the way (Clarke was already long gone). Until then, however, both pieces of legislation remain. A bit like Maya and her owner.

'The benefit cap sets a strong incentive for people to move into work and even before the cap comes in we are seeing thousands of people seeking help and moving off benefits…. Already we've seen 8,000 people who would have been affected by the cap move into jobs. This clearly demonstrates that the cap is having the desired impact.'

Iain Duncan Smith, Department of Work and Pensions press release, 12 April 2013

Iain Duncan Smith is a man driven by ideology. He has his beliefs, and he holds strongly to them even when evidence suggests quite different conclusions. For instance, he believed very sincerely that the judges of the Supreme Court, in ruling in January 2017 that Parliament must have a vote on the Brexit process, had 'stepped into new territory where they've actually told Parliament not just that they should do something but actually what they should do', despite the fact that the judgment made it explicit that they were doing nothing of the sort.[57] He also truly felt in his heart of hearts when filling out his *Who's Who* entry that he had studied at the University of Perugia, rather than the language school in the same town where he had failed to finish his exams.[58] He believed so strongly that he could get by 'if I had to' on the £53 per week that his department expected certain jobseekers to survive on, that he graciously declined all invitations to prove it by experiment. And he absolutely, unequivocally believed that his proposed benefit cap, which would limit the amount that any household or individual could receive in public handouts, no matter their circumstances, was going to be such a roaring success in pulling people out of poverty and into work that he released a bunch of figures to the media before it was even introduced proving it was already working.[59]

Except the figures didn't prove any such thing. The UK Statistics Authority, the official independent watchdog which keeps tabs on government figures, wrote to Duncan Smith on 9 May 2013 to point out his claim that eight thousand scroungers had already gone out and got jobs because of his initiative was 'unsupported by the official statistics' published by his department – and, in fact, that the civil servants who put together those statistics had explicitly warned that they could not be used as evidence of 'additional numbers entering work as a direct result'.[60] What's more, they noted that the numbers Duncan Smith had quoted 'do not comply fully with the principles of the Code of Practice [for Official Statistics], particularly in respect of accessibility to the sources of the data, information about the methodology and quality of the statistics, and the suggestion that the statistics were shared with the media in advance of their publication.'[61]

It wasn't his first offence with respect to statistics, and it wouldn't be his last. Less than a week before the watchdog had drawn Duncan Smith's attention to problems with figures relating to his flagship work programme, stating that 'the information published by the Department was unclear, and Parliament, the public, and the media were left confused as to the relevance and meaning of the information that did enter the public domain'.[62] In January 2012 they observed that his department had provided figures on 'the nationality of benefit claimants' which 'attracted wide media coverage and comment', but put them out as 'ad-hoc statistics' rather than official ones, which meant they didn't have to comply with the rules or highlight 'important caveats and weaknesses that need to be explained carefully and objectively to Parliament and the news media'.[63] In 2010 they had rebuked his department for 'serious deficiencies' in the way unemployment figures were presented;[64] the admonishment came in the same week Duncan Smith was forced to correct the parliamentary record after figures he quoted on local authority housing – which he had claimed came from the Office for National Statistics – turned out to have been plucked from the slightly less authoritative findaproperty.com website.[65] This lackadaisical approach to empirical evidence would continue throughout his six-year career at the DWP, culminating in 2015 when the department put out a leaflet in which named and photographed benefit claimants sang the praises of a hard-line approach to docking payments – only for it to emerge that they were actors, the department having been unable to find a single genuine enthusiast among the 5 million recipients of working-age benefits in the UK.[66]

But as usual, what mattered was what Iain Duncan Smith believed. When challenged about his dodgy benefit cap numbers, he replied: 'What the Statistics Authority said to us was that we couldn't say the number of people going back to work in the early days of the cap was directly linked, that we couldn't prove that was the case. But then again it also has to be admitted you can't *disprove* that.... I have a belief I am right.'[67]

6

CONTINENTAL DRIFT

The Brexit referendum campaign at times resembled a 'who can lie the loudest' competition. All was sound and fury as the idiots took turns blaring on the nightly news; grossly partisan papers enabled and amplified grotesque exaggerations, scare stories and blatant falsehoods in lieu of a genuine national debate. Some minds must have been changed, but most just calcified around long-held positions. And it ended, uniquely, with a winning side who seemed to be just as angry as the all-but-equally proportioned losers.

Yet spectacular dishonesty about the EU did not begin in 2016. Europe had long been the one subject about which it was somehow okay for journalists to make stuff up, thanks largely to an early nineties coterie who took their cue from the *Daily Telegraph*'s masterful Brussels correspondent Boris Johnson. A quarter of a century later, having carefully weighed up which option would play out best for his new political career, Johnson would return to finish the job, but he was far from the first charlatan to jump on the sceptics' bandwagon in the intervening years. The soaring success of UKIP as they split and then set the agenda for the Conservative Party was largely down to Nigel Farage's skill at influencing popular opinion with spurious statistics and wild, if heartfelt, claims. Yet mainstream politicians have never been entirely straightforward about Europe either. David Cameron's 'cast-iron promise' to hold a vote on the terms of the Treaty of Lisbon in 2007 turned out to be a very weak alloy indeed. That was no more than we should have expected. By then politicians had been breaking their word on the European subject for a good four decades.

Relations with our Continental neighbours have, right from the outset of this experiment in governance, been characterized by a common complaint: when it comes to Europe, the strength of one's argument comes from its passionate intensity, not its veracity. You go with your gut, not with your brain. And whichever side you put yourself on, there are always plenty of people who are happy to feed you exactly what you want – no matter how bad it might be for your digestion.

* * * * *

> 'There is no question of any erosion of essential national sovereignty; what is proposed is a sharing and an enlargement of individual national sovereignties in the economic interest.'

Government white paper,
'The United Kingdom and the European Communities', July 1971

It became an article of faith among Eurosceptics, stunned by the scale of their defeat in the referendum of 1975, that the British people had been 'tricked' into entering Europe without being made fully aware of the implications. 'The British people were led to believe that they were voting to stay part of a "Common Market" or free trade area,' blustered UKIP's Nigel Farage. It was 'very simply a step towards a far larger and, to me, more sinister goal: European economic and political union, the creation of a United States of Europe.'[1] MP Bill Cash insisted: 'All the European stuff before from 1972 was about trading, that sort of thing.'[2] And in announcing his timely conversion to Brexit campaigner ahead of the 2016 referendum, Boris Johnson claimed: 'it isn't we in this country who have changed. It is the European Union... the project has morphed and grown in such a way as to be unrecognisable.'[3]

Politicians had been making similar noises about any form of European grouping involving a subsuming of national identity since the very earliest days. Cabinet minutes from the Attlee era show his ministers were fretting that the integration of the coal and steel industries under the Schuman Plan 'appeared to involve some surrender of sovereignty',[4] and in 1962, when Harold Macmillan was leading the first unsuccessful attempt to get us into what was then the European Economic Community, his Labour counterpart Hugh Gaitskell warned that it would make us 'no more than a state… in the United States of Europe, such as Texas and California'.[5] Macmillan dismissed this outright: 'What nonsense!'[6]

It wasn't nonsense. The concept of an 'ever closer union' – one seen as so unacceptable to the British that David Cameron made its abandonment one of the 'red lines' in his renegotiations ahead of the 2016 referendum – was right there in the second line of the Treaty of Rome, which had established the European Economic Community in 1957. And that 'ever closer union' was not just a platitude. The Hague summit of 1969 specifically committed members to 'paving the way for a United Europe capable of assuming its responsibilities in the world of tomorrow'.[7] Two years later a committee led by Pierre Werner, the prime minister of Luxembourg, proposed a supranational body to take over decisions on economic policy for all members and suggested that 'the adoption of a sole currency… would confirm the irreversibility of the venture.'[8] The year he proposed for its introduction was 1980. It would be a further twenty-two years before the euro went into circulation.

This was fully comprehended back in London. Noted a Foreign Office report:

> the plan for economic and monetary union (EMU) has revolutionary long-term implications…. It could imply the ultimate creation of a European federal state with a single currency. All the basic instruments of national economic management… would ultimately be handed over to the central federal authorities…. The degree of freedom which would then be vested in national governments might indeed be somewhat less than the autonomy enjoyed by the constituent states of the US.[9]

Was Prime Minister Edward Heath, who had been fully committed to the European project from the outset and was now busy trying to negotiate our own entry, put off? Certainly not. They 'discussed the progress of the European Community towards economic and monetary union, and its implications for existing financial relationships,' runs the official communiqué of the summit he held with French president Georges Pompidou in May 1971. 'The Prime Minister reaffirmed the readiness of Britain to participate fully in a European spirit in this development.'[10]

There was, however, no mention of this 'European spirit' in the sixteen-page booklet distributed to every household in the UK that summer. Instead, it paraphrased a government white paper to assure the soon-to-be Europeans: 'There is no question of Britain losing essential national sovereignty; what is proposed is a sharing and an enlargement of individual national sovereignties in the economic interest.'[11] This was rather different to how a secret Foreign Office document drawn up that year put it:

> we shall be accepting an external legislature which
> regards itself as having direct powers of legislating with
> effect within the United Kingdom, even in derogation
> of United Kingdom statutes, and as having in certain
> fields exclusive legislative competence, so that our own
> legislature has none.... The loss of external sovereignty
> will however increase as the Community develops,
> according to the intention of the preamble to the Treaty
> of Rome 'to establish the foundations of an even closer
> union among the European peoples'.[12]

When, courtesy of Ted Heath's Labour successor, Harold Wilson, the UK eventually got a vote on the matter in 1975, the official leaflet encouraging Britons to vote to stay in quoted several of the other aims as laid out in the Treaty of Rome – but, funnily enough, not that one. The section, headed 'WILL PARLIAMENT LOSE ITS POWER?', noticeably ducked away from answering that question too. In its place it made the striking argument that 'in the modern world even the Super Powers like America and Russia do not have complete freedom of action.'[13] The British people voted 67 per cent to 33 per cent to stay in Europe.

Writing his memoirs in 2015, William Waldegrave, who was Heath's private secretary at the time of the referendum, was straightforward about the duplicity. 'If the "Yes" campaigners had said "This is what we want! A single great new nation of Europe to stand as equal with America and Russia", a majority of the British people might even have signed up to the European integration project,' wrote Waldegrave. 'Instead, they said "Nothing will really change. Britain will still be Britain. Just trust us." Because that was palpably false, Britain never committed itself to an honest and fundamental change.'[14]

'Now they've really gone bananas – Euro bosses ban too bendy ones.'

The Sun, 21 September 1994

Strictly speaking, it is true that EU rules do ban wholesalers from selling bananas which have a 'malformation or abnormal curvature' to shops. The regulation, number 2257/94, later superseded by number 1333/2011, also insisted that fruit should be 'intact, firm, sound [not rotting]... clean... free from pests [and] damage caused by pests, with the stalk intact, without bending, fungal damage or dessication, with pistils removed, free from malformation or abnormal curvature... free from bruises' and from damage inflicted by speed-chilling and damp – and not strange-smelling.[15] As such, the Eurocrats only really disadvantaged those of us who prefer our fruit stinky, rotten and unpalatable, and we could still take our chances with bananas graded 'class 2', which were allowed to have as many 'defects of shape' as we desired.

This regulation was one of thousands of such rules aimed at protecting consumers, the existence of which seem to come as a personal affront to the same sort of people who (I strongly suspect) are first at the supermarket customer service counter demanding their money back if they find so much as a blemish on their groceries. In 2016 it was new rules about the thickness of oven gloves that were particularly exercising Eurosceptics, who insisted on the inalienable right to spend money on kitchen accessories that would allow them to get badly burned. But the bananas – first 'straightened out' in the autumn of 1994 so as 'to ensure that we are not paying out for rubbish and [to stop] Euro-subsidies acting as an incentive to produce poor bananas' – just wouldn't go away.[16]

A few weeks before the 2016 referendum – apropros of nothing but a random heckle in the middle of a speech – Boris Johnson announced: 'It is absurd that we are told that you cannot sell bananas in bunches of more than two or three bananas…. This is not a matter for an international supranational body to dictate to the British people.'[17] Of course it wasn't, because as everyone who has ever been into a greengrocers or supermarket, or so much as glanced at a fruit bowl, knows, bananas were still being proffered in bunches of four, five and even more. The Remain campaign immediately dispatched staff to photograph bunches of bananas to prove the point. When Johnson's Leave colleague Iain Duncan Smith was challenged about the remark, he replied: 'I don't know, because I don't eat bananas.' He didn't rely on benefits, but that had never deterred him from banging on endlessly about them.

Johnson himself had form on this front. After being sacked from *The Times* in 1988 for making things up he had been taken on by the *Daily Telegraph* and sent to head up its Brussels bureau. There he became known for his, to put it charitably, 'imaginative' spin on stories about the antics of the European authorities. While campaigning for Brexit in 2016 he was still boasting of how 'I informed readers about euro-condoms and the great war against the British prawn cocktail flavour crisp', undeterred by the fact that both tales had been proved false a quarter of a century earlier.[18] (Condom regularization had to do with their safety testing, not size, as he had claimed, and the palaver over prawn flavouring came from the fact that a careless British official had left it off some paperwork, not any attempt to ban it.) 'He wasn't making things up, necessarily, just over-egging to a degree that was dishonest,' said his counterpart on the *Independent*, David Usborne.[19] Johnson described his approach to reporting on the EU: 'I was just chucking these rocks over the garden wall. I'd listen to this amazing crash from the greenhouse next door, over in England.'[20]

And his legacy was a long one. Days after Johnson went bananas over bananas, the *Daily Express* – which had allied itself uncritically to the Brexit cause when its proprietor donated more than a million pounds to UKIP – ran a list on its website of what it called 'Amazing things we get back if we leave the EU.' It stated as fact that you could no longer buy eggs by the dozen in the UK, and that jam could no longer be called 'jam', both thanks to European rules. Challenged by press watchdog IPSO, the *Express* stated that 'it was satisfied that the picture gallery and accompanying captions were accurate.'[21] IPSO thought otherwise and forced them to run a correction. Four months later the paper ran an almost identical list; this time it had straight bananas on it too.

> 'I went to Brussels with one objective: to protect Britain's national interest, and that is what I did…. I made it clear that if the eurozone countries wanted a treaty involving all 27 members of the European Union, we would insist on some safeguards for Britain to protect our own national interests…. frankly I have to tell the House that the choice was a treaty without proper safeguards or no treaty – and the right answer was no treaty.'

David Cameron,
House of Commons, 12 December 2011

When David Cameron stalked out of a Brussels meeting room at 4 a.m., and his officials began briefing that he had used the never-before-employed British veto to scupper the EU's fiscal compact treaty, the Eurosceptic papers were ecstatic. 'Mr Cameron resolutely defended British interests by rejecting demands for treaty change across the EU as part of a rescue plan for the single currency,' frothed the *Mail*.[22] 'CAMERON'S VETO CREATES NEW ERA FOR EUROPE,' hollered the *Telegraph*.[23] *The Sun* reported that he had 'blasted the bully-boys of Europe with a sensational Winston Churchill-style "Up Eurs".[24] Even BBC political editor Nick Robinson could barely contain his excitement: 'For years people have talked about a British veto. For years it has existed as a threat never used. Not any more. The consequences could scarcely be greater for Europe and for Britain's relationship with Europe.'[25]

So was that the end of the treaty, which was meant to create financial reforms to help the struggling eurozone? Er, no. Representatives of the other twenty-six countries simply carried on with their discussion, and agreed unanimously to press ahead with their plans, but called them something else, an 'Accord between the Euro Area Heads of State or Government'. The newly named accord had exactly the same language, with exactly the same lack of safeguards for the City of London, and it was signed at the same EU meeting by the same EU representatives, just with very slightly different proverbial hats on. They didn't even bother to move meeting rooms.

'We renamed it a veto to claim it was a veto,' one Downing Street aide told Tim Shipman, first and best historian of the referendum campaigns. Another told him: 'he never thought he was going to veto it. It was initially, "Oh fuck, what have we done?" Then the polls went up. It was a completely accidental triumph.'[26]

Not everyone was convinced.[27] 'The Prime Minister claims to have wielded a veto,' jeered opposition leader Ed Miliband in the Commons a few days later. 'Let me explain to him that a veto is supposed to stop something happening. It is not a veto when the thing you wanted to stop goes ahead without you. That is called losing. That is called being defeated. That is called letting Britain down.'[28]

All Cameron had actually done was remove Britain from the negotiating table and ensure that it didn't get a say any more. But by now an awful lot of people were beginning to think that as a position, that sounded just fine.

> 'I was astonished last week when Nick Clegg claimed that only 7 per cent of our laws are made in Brussels. He said it was there in the House of Commons library note and therefore was unequivocal. I've got the note with me, and on page one it says the British government estimates that around 50 per cent of UK legislation comes from Brussels. There are other estimates coming direct from the European Commission that over 70 per cent of our laws are made in Brussels.'

Nigel Farage,
TV debate with Nick Clegg, 2 April 2014

In a deliberately provocative speech in 1988, former president of the European Commission Jacques Delors predicted that 80 per cent of the laws affecting the economy and social policy in ten years' time would be made in Brussels. Thirteen years later Conservative think tank The Bow Group said it was 55 per cent. Campaign group Business for Britain put forward a precise-sounding 59.3 per cent a year after Farage and Clegg's ding-dong. In the summer of 2017, Donald Trump's favourite website, Breitbart, offered a 'definitive' 65 per cent.[29]

Perhaps the most damning statistic comes from the House of Commons briefing paper which both Clegg and Farage waved about during their TV debate in April 2014: it offers fifty-five pages of dense, numbers-heavy analysis, but warns that 'there is no totally accurate, rational or useful way of calculating the

percentage of national laws based on or influenced by the EU...
it is possible to justify any measure between 15% and 50% or
thereabouts.' The paper goes on to note that it isn't as if every bit
of legislation that Brussels had a hand in was *forced* on the UK:
'the degree of involvement varied from passing reference to explicit
implementation.'[30] Since the UK has, or – depending when you're
reading this – had, a voice in each and every institution in Brussels,
it's a certainty that our national government was actively pushing
for, and even instigating, some of the measures in question.

The picture is further muddied by the fact that there are two
different types of 'law' which the EU can impose: 1) directives,
which are given to national governments to impose through their
own legislation; and 2) regulations, which apply automatically
to all member countries. A lot of these laws cover topics that
are completely irrelevant to Britain, such as trading standards for
industries that don't exist here. You're welcome to have a go at
producing olive oil or tobacco in Britain, but it's not EU red tape
that will stand in your way; it's the weather.

As part of its sloganeering around Article 50, the clause that
enables any country to exit from the EU, Theresa May's government
proposed to sweep away the whole lot of them with a 'Great
Repeal Bill' which, they said, will make 'the UK an independent,
sovereign nation again'.[31] It will do away with every single obligation
contained in the 'acquis communautaire' applying to EU states. In
the same stroke, it will replace every single one with an identical
British version that is somehow magically free from the taint of
Brussels. In May's own words, 'The same rules and laws will apply
on the day after Brexit as they did before.'[32] The Eurocrats will
have been swapped for good old-fashioned Bureaucrats (the 'B'
obviously standing for British, even if it is a suspiciously French-
sounding word). And everything will apparently be better – even
though it is exactly the same.

'We know the bigger issue today is migration from within the EU. Immediate access to our welfare system. Paying benefits to families back home. Employment agencies signing people up from overseas and not recruiting here. Numbers that have increased faster than we in this country wanted.... Britain, I know you want this sorted, so I will go to Brussels, I will not take no for an answer, and – when it comes to free movement – I will get what Britain needs.'

David Cameron, speech,
Conservative Party Conference, Birmingham, 1 October 2014

The prime minister arrived at the party conference in 2014 fresh from a gamble that had paid off. He had allowed Scotland a referendum on independence, something the Scottish National Party had been pushing for since the seventies, and, despite things looking a bit dicey towards the end of the campaign, he had brought his side comfortably over the winning post. He was also starting to believe his own publicity materials: 'judge me by my record. I'm the first Prime Minister to veto a Treaty,' he boasted to the packed crowd. 'Around that table in Europe they know I say what I mean, and mean what I say.'[33] He had committed himself to staking everything on an in–out referendum, but only – and he couldn't stress this enough – after he had negotiated a spectacular new relationship between the UK and the EU.

At the heart of the new relationship between the UK and EU was the issue of immigration. Upstart UKIP had made the issue their own, and were using it to leech tens of thousands of supporters from Cameron's own party. The 2004 expansion of the EU to ten more countries, mostly from Eastern Europe, had seen an unprecedented influx of people into Britain. Shifting demographics were putting strains on services and labour markets; they were also creating resentments among those people who can't cope with hearing languages they don't understand on the bus or shops selling pickled things they haven't seen before. Now Cameron – undeterred by having pledged in 2010 to get net migration down to 'the tens of thousands' only to see it rocket to over 300,000 – was putting his political life on the line by promising to fix the immigration 'problem'.

It was recklessly ambitious. The 'Four Freedoms', guaranteeing the free movement of goods, capital, services and people between member states, had been a fundamental principle of the EU and its predecessor communities ever since the Treaty of Rome. They were pretty popular with the newest recruits to the club (the ones whose inhabitants were doing all that travelling westward), who were unlikely to agree to them being curtailed. This meant that Cameron had to concentrate all his persuasive powers on the single biggest hitter in the EU, German chancellor Angela Merkel. A charm offensive involving cosy chats and episodes of *Midsomer Murders* had failed to convince her to back him over the fiscal compact treaty, but he was convinced he stood a better chance this time around.

Once again, he was wrong. Merkel had grown up behind the wall in East Germany, and that experience had been formative to her political character in the same way Britain's island status has shaped generations of UK politicians. She was constitutionally incapable of putting up barriers where none needed to exist. 'Germany will not tamper with the fundamental principles of free movement in the EU,' she announced at a summit that same month, and just like that, the central plank of Cameron's negotiations was kicked away.[34] He tried pushing for what he called an 'emergency brake' – a temporary curb on the number of EU migrants the UK was obliged to admit – but Merkel wouldn't back that either, and no one in Whitehall could actually suggest any way of making it work. He was left with a mishmash of proposals about access to benefits that read like a weak compromise – for the very good reason that it was a weak compromise. Taking no for an answer was, it seems, an option after all.

> '£4,300 a year: Cost to UK Families if Britain leaves the EU.'

HM Government poster,
unveiled by George Osborne, 18 April 2016

A cynic is supposedly a person who knows the price of everything and the value of nothing. George Osborne, the chancellor of the exchequer from 2010 until his ignominious sacking in 2016, often came across as a man who didn't have any values at all but could slap a price on anything.

As one of the key figures of the Remain campaign, Osborne relentlessly concentrated on the numbers. In vain did Labour activist Will Straw, the supposed boss of the cross-party 'Stronger In' coalition, protest that making it all about money might work for the Tory audience Osborne was used to, but it wouldn't have the universal appeal that was needed to ensure they topped 50 per cent. Campaign analysts warned that people did not – could not – translate highfalutin concerns about the economy into an understanding of the direct impact on their own lives, say, in the cost of their shopping or whether or not they had a job. But it made no difference. Osborne's 'views were disseminated – it seemed at times – on tablets of stone,' wrote Tim Shipman in *All Out War*, his account of the campaigns.[35] 'Osborne was totally open about his plan: it was to follow exactly the same playbook… that had led to victory in the Scottish referendum and given the Conservatives their surprise majority in the general election the year before. The first leg of the strategy was to publish reports by the Treasury on the risks of leaving the EU.'[36]

These reports, unveiled early in the referendum campaign, did indeed look terrifying. One was two hundred pages of drastic figures like a 6.2 per cent drop in GDP, a 'black hole' of between £36 billion and £45 billion in public finances and rises in the basic tax rate of either 8p or 10p in the pound. It would be 'the most extraordinary self-inflicted wound' which would leave us all 'permanently poorer'.[37] And we'd be poorer by a specific amount, as emblazoned on the officious poster in front of which Osborne posed to deliver his report: '£4,300 a year: Cost to UK Families if Britain leaves the EU'.[38]

But hang on a second: was *every single family* going to lose exactly that much? Both the ones with six kids, and the ones with no kids at all? The same shortfall for Sir Alan and Lady Sugar and a single mum on benefits? Obviously not. The amount was apparently for an 'average household' – whatever that might be – but it swiftly emerged that Osborne's boffins had reached this sum by taking the (estimated) total loss of GDP by 2030 and dividing it by the number of households which existed in the UK... in 2015. Even without the temporal inconsistencies, the sum was meaningless. 'The government is confusing GDP per household with household income,' noted the BBC's 'Reality Check' service, which was shaking down every statistic from each side of the referendum. 'GDP is currently about £1.8tn a year – if you divide that by 27 million households you get £66,666. But average household income is about £44,000. They are clearly not the same thing.'[39] Leave campaigners, who had successfully managed to rebrand any warnings of possible consequences from Brexit as 'Project Fear' and 'talking down Britain', now gleefully rebranded the Treasury document as 'George's dodgy dossier'.[40] 'Our point is that people will be considerably worse off, and we simply changed it into something more understandable,' huffed Craig Oliver, chief spin doctor for both Downing Street and the

Remain campaign.[41] That they had also changed it into something risibly meaningless seemed to have passed him by.

But the chancellor wouldn't learn either. Two months later, just days from the vote, Osborne was back with more prophecies of doom, this time in the form of an 'emergency budget' that he claimed he would be forced to implement one week after a Leave vote, to plug a £30 billion 'black hole' which would apparently instantly open up in the nation's finances.[42]

In the intervening period, pollsters for the Remain campaign had found that the £4,300 number had fallen on stony ground because it had a 'spurious specificity'.[43] Despite his poor reception, Osborne was ready to barrage the public with yet another set of ridiculously precise numbers. He would have no choice, he said, but to put basic income tax up by 2p in the pound, raise the higher rate by 3p, and also raise inheritance tax – the last having totemic significance for the chancellor as he had turned it into a battle ground with Gordon Brown in the 2010 General Election. Alcohol and petrol prices would rise by 5 per cent. Budgets for policing and transport would be cut by 5 per cent, and spending on the NHS, previously ring-fenced, would have to be 'slashed'. All other manifesto commitments would also be abandoned. A full £15 billion would have to come out of government spending as a whole, because we would quite simply not be able to 'afford the size of the public services we have at the moment'.[44] In the Commons, his neighbour and closest political ally David Cameron joined in the finger-wagging: 'Nobody wants to have an emergency Budget. Nobody wants to have cuts in public services. Nobody wants to have tax increases…. We can avoid all of this by voting Remain next week.'[45]

It sounded like a threat, and that was exactly how the opposition portrayed it: not a proposed emergency budget but a proposed punishment budget. The Leave team were able to get their retaliation in early, because they had signed up to the mailing list for Stronger In's embargoed press releases. So, when Osborne unveiled his plans during the 8:10 a.m. interview slot on Radio 4's *Today* programme on 15 June 2016, he had already heard them being shot down – on the preceding news bulletin. No fewer than fifty-seven of his party's backbenchers had scrambled together to sign a round-robin letter saying they would refuse to vote for such a budget in the event of Brexit. As the day wore on, eight more names were added to the list, and leaders of other parties, including Labour's Jeremy Corbyn, piled in to say they wouldn't support it either.

When Britain voted to leave the EU on 23 June, the supermassive black hole that the chancellor had forecast failed to open up. On 27 June, three days after his BFF David Cameron announced he would be moving out of the house next door, Osborne broke cover. He told the country that the vote 'will have an impact on the economy and our public finances…. Given the delay in triggering Article 50 and the Prime Minister's decision to hand over to a successor, it is sensible that decisions on what that action should consist of should wait… for the new Prime Minister to be in place.'[46]

It will be a long time before we know exactly what the consequences of actual Brexit, as opposed to the vote for Brexit, will be. I suppose it's possible that in 2030 we'll all find ourselves staring dumbly at a deficit of precisely £4,300 in our joint bank accounts. But the immediate aftermath turned out not to be such a dire emergency after all.

> 'We send the EU £350 million a week
> let's fund our NHS instead'

Slogan,
Vote Leave campaign battle buses, 11 May 2016

The bus – probably the most famous red bus since the one Cliff Richard jumped on board for his *Summer Holiday* – was unveiled by Brexit's biggest hitter, Boris Johnson. He descended its steps for the first time in Truro while brandishing a Cornish pasty, a foodstuff that – ironically – owes its protected geographical indication status as one of the best of British products to Brussels bureaucrats. Over the next six weeks every other significant figure in the Vote Leave campaign – Michael Gove, Iain Duncan Smith, Gisela Stuart, Douglas Carswell, Andrea Leadsom, Priti Patel and a host of other members of Her Majesty's Government – made a point of positioning themselves in front of the unmissable white-on-red slogan. There was a second version of the message too, for those incapable of dividing by seven: 'We send the EU £50 million a day. Let's fund our NHS instead.'[47]

But whichever way you looked at the sums, we sent the EU nothing like that much money. According to the Office for National Statistics, the gross figure which the UK contributed to the EU was £19 billion a year, but thanks to the rebate which Mrs Thatcher negotiated in 1984 – something anti-EU campaigners were usually only too happy to bang on about – we only actually sent £15 billion.[48] (The name is misleading, as it wasn't so much a rebate as money that never got, er, 'bated' in the first place.) Since we were also one of the twenty-eight countries that the EU spent its budget on, in the form of regional funds, farm subsidies, academic grants and the like, plenty of money also flowed back in the opposite direction. So the actual sum which Britain handed over to the EU, never to be seen again, was more like £11 billion – or around £250 million a week.[49] But Dominic Cummings, the ruthless and bloody-minded head of the official Vote Leave campaign, publicized the bigger figure – and continued to do so even after the UK Statistics Authority said it was 'misleading and undermines trust'.[50] Even former Labour spin doctor Alastair Campbell, notorious for his bullheaded determination in pushing his own version of reality on the public, was gobsmacked: 'I can't remember campaigns where you mount the campaign based on a lie, and then when it's exposed, you just keep going'.[51] But that is exactly what Cummings did.

When he was hauled in front of the parliamentary Treasury committee to account for his figures on 20 April 2016, Cummings refused to concede any ground. 'Yes, that is debited from the UK.... That is exactly what the ONS [Office for National Statistics] says,' he sneered when it was pointed out that much of the cash never left our shores. 'If you do not like that then you should argue with the ONS, not with me.'[52]

No less an authority than Prime Minister David Cameron had described Cummings, a former special adviser to the education secretary, as a 'career psychopath'.[53] In the words of Steve Baker, a pro-Leave Tory MP, 'If you don't care about what collateral damage you sustain, he's the weapon of choice. He operates with the minimum of civilised restraint. He is a barbarian. Dominic has undoubted mastery of leadership and strategy and political warfare. But he will not let himself be held to account by anybody.'[54]

It was the same with that NHS logo, which appeared like an official stamp on the bus's side. The health secretary had already dispatched a letter to the Vote Leave campaign threatening legal action after they used it on leaflets without permission, but a Vote

Leave colleague told journalist Tim Shipman that Cummings was 'literally jumping around saying, "We're going to use the NHS logo and they're going to hate it!"'[55] The Remain campaigners were utterly outplayed. Their official pollster, Andrew Cooper, briefed his colleagues very early on that 'in a world where almost no facts are known and nothing sticks, a surprising number of people think it costs £350 million a week to stay in the EU and this money could be spent elsewhere if we left.'[56] His boss Craig Oliver despaired: 'This is absurd – does it mean I can make something up that suits me and assert it?'[57]

The answer to Oliver's question appeared to be yes, if you did it with enough chutzpah. That May Boris Johnson went to an aluminium processing plant to be filmed feeding an enormous cheque for £350 million into a furnace; when Sky News presented him with an identical one the following October and asked if he would sign it over to the NHS, he tutted that they were 'doing a pointless stunt'.[58]

Perhaps the weirdest thing about the whole affair is that the real figure was equally shocking: £250 million is still a stonking amount of money by any normal person's standards. It is considerably more than the highest jackpot ever won on the National Lottery (a mere £161 million). For all the protests from the Institute for Fiscal Studies that it represents less than a percentage point of GDP, both it and Cummings' preferred gross sum are the sort of numbers which register only as 'a hell of a lot of money'. It's not just those of us who don't have to count up anything higher than our monthly pay packet that are afflicted by this problem, by the way. I once had a conversation with a cabinet minister who was charged with giving collective approval to the sort of eleven-billion-pound headline announcements Gordon Brown liked to throw around as chancellor. She confessed that she and her colleagues found it all but impossible to get a proper grasp of the sums they were discussing. Even Cummings, hauled in front of the parliamentary committee, got his billions and millions muddled up at one point. Ultimately, this is exactly what the Vote Leave boss had counted on: that ongoing confusions about figures in the hundreds of millions would only serve to repeatedly emphasize that a hell of a lot of money – specifically *our* money – went to Europe. Everyone else, whether they liked it or not, played along with his game.

As for the idea of handing over all the cash to the NHS, that was a cynical piggyback on an institution often regarded as our 'national religion': the proposal didn't even make it as far as the small print. Vote Leave had also made promises to safeguard various groups, such as scientists and farmers, who were funded by the EU. If they took their 'fair' share of the supposed £350 million jackpot, there was clearly no way the full sum could also be given to the health service. Besides, Vote Leave were not in any position to make funding guarantees: 'we have not given a specific and detailed budget because it is not our role to,' Cummings shrugged.[59] They were not the government.

But the Leave campaign did contain a lot of familiar faces from the government, and that was enough to convince some – perhaps many – people. 'I would go mad if this money doesn't go into the NHS, I will go mad,' fretted a Sunderland voter called Shirley Bain to the *Guardian* a few weeks after the referendum vote. 'I want to be assured that this money – because that's why I voted to come out.'[60] When in March 2017 pro-Remain Labour MP Chuka Umunna generously presented the government with an opportunity to write the £350 million a year guarantee for the NHS into the legislation for their Brexit negotiations, Theresa May, who at least nominally supported Remain before transforming herself into the hardest of hard Brexiteers, declined to take him up on it.[61]

Even those who tried to keep on top of the details often found themselves in a muddle about exactly who was saying what. You could find plenty of otherwise clued-up Remain voters complaining post-referendum about Nigel Farage's disowning of the £350 million pledge. For once the UKIP leader was telling the truth – as the key frontman of rival campaign group Leave.EU, he had had nothing to do with the bus, preferring to focus his own publicity campaign on out-and-out racism instead. When Farage had chosen to throw around figures for the UK's 'membership fee' – as he did in his televised debate with Nick Clegg in April 2014 – he had made up a different figure, rounding up to '£55 million a day'.[62] Arron Banks, Farage's friend and funder, knew the score. 'It was taking an American-style media approach,' he told journalists as, on the other side of the Atlantic, Donald Trump closed in on the Republican nomination for US president. 'What they said early on was "facts don't work" and that's it. The Remain campaign featured fact, fact, fact, fact, fact. It just doesn't work. You have got to connect with people emotionally. It's the Trump success.'[63]

Three days after the referendum result, former Conservative leader Iain Duncan Smith, a man who has always taken a creative approach to both numbers and reality, was asked about his commitment to the £350 million pledge. 'I never said that during the course of the election,' he declared.[64] Most news reports of his denial were illustrated with photographs of him giving interviews during the campaign standing in front of a very familiar vehicle. The letters behind his head were nearly as big as he was: 'We send the EU £350 million a week. Let's fund our NHS instead.'

> ## 'Turkey (population 76 million) is joining the EU'

Vote Leave poster,
22 May 2016

Subtle it was not. The image was of a European passport forming an open door, through which a trail of footprints – not just immigrants, but dirty immigrants! – was marching.[65] There was nothing to explain why it would be so terrible for Turkey to become a member of the EU other than the fact its people were, well, Turkish. The only possible significance of the 'population 76 million' parenthetical was to imply that as soon as they were able, every single one of them would be on their way here, overwhelming the country – which seemed, to be honest, a bit unlikely. For good measure the Leave campaign suggested in an accompanying briefing note that they would all be bringing weapons with them: 'Crime is far higher in Turkey than the UK. Gun ownership is also more widespread.'[66]

The biggest problem with the poster, distributed for the most part online, was that it was nonsense. Turkey was not joining the EU, in any sense of the present tense. The country had applied to join when the EU was still the EC, way back in 1987. It had had to wait a full decade before even being declared 'eligible' for accession discussions. Those didn't start until 2005. And at the time of Britain's referendum, out of thirty-five policy areas where it was necessary for Turkey to meet EU membership conditions, it qualified in a single one. Negotiations in twenty other areas – including free movement of workers, financial services, social policy and employment, and foreign, security and defence policy – had not even opened. The country's military occupation of northern Cyprus, which it invaded in 1974, was a big issue. The European Commission, whose representatives were appointed by member governments, had noted in 2015 that Turkey was, if anything, moving backwards when it came to its application, with 'significant backsliding' in the past two years, notably 'in the areas of freedom of expression and freedom of assembly'.[67] A draconian crackdown by President Recep Tayyip Erdoğan after the attempted coup in July 2016 sent the country further towards the back of the queue.

What Turkey did have, however, was refugees. About 3 million people fleeing the Syrian civil war had ended up inside the country's borders, and the news was full of pictures of migrants attempting to cross the Mediterranean from Turkey (and too often dying in their attempt). The EU had opened talks about a resettlement scheme that might help to ease the pressure, but it would not involve the UK taking in anyone. While the European Commission made noises about speeding up the glacial pace of accession talks – or rather, about 'preparations… now underway to progress towards the opening' of talks, which was not quite the same thing – they had specifically ruled out anyone new joining within five years.[68] What's more, every single country that was already in the EU had a veto over new members, and more than one of them had indicated a willingness to use that veto in the case of Turkey. And this was a real veto, not a Cameronesque one: since each country had to approve new members as part of the council of heads of government, and also sign a treaty with every national member government, legal experts branded it a 'double veto'.

The Leave campaign dealt with this contradictory evidence by pretending it away. 'We're not going to be consulted or asked to vote: they are going to join, it's a matter of when,' declared government minister Penny Mordaunt on the BBC's *Andrew Marr Show*. Challenged twice about Britain having a right to veto, she said: 'It doesn't. The British people are not going to be able to have a say.'[69] Cameron was so infuriated that he called a special press conference to denounce this 'complete untruth'. 'It's irresponsible and it's wrong,' he declared, 'and it's time that the Leave campaign was called out on the nonsense that they're peddling.' It would, he said, be 'literally decades' before Turkey would even be in a position to become a member – 'at the current rate of progress they will probably get round to joining in about the year 3000.'[70]

Did it work? Nope. Just as they had done with the £350 million for the NHS, the Leave campaign doubled down. Although Boris Johnson, who has Turkish ancestry, apparently felt this particular claim was beyond the pale, his colleague Michael Gove was happy to lead the charge: 'With the terrorism threat that we face only growing, it is hard to see how it could possibly be in our security interests to open visa-free travel to 77 million Turkish citizens' – the population seemed to have exploded in no time at all – 'and to create a border-free zone from Iraq, Iran and Syria to the English Channel.'[71] Vote Leave released a map on which the ongoing war zones of Syria and Iraq, neither of which could apply for EU membership, were highlighted. 'You are telling lies and you are scaring people,' the mayor of London and Remain campaigner Sadiq Khan told Johnson at a televised debate as he brandished a copy of the map. 'This map shows in red, Turkey, but the only countries named in this map are Syria and Iraq. That's scaremongering, Boris, and you should be ashamed.'[72]

The lies about Turkey even managed the impressive feat of giving Nigel Farage the moral high ground in the very week he unveiled a poster depicting a line of Syrian refugees with the caption 'Breaking Point'; the image was quickly denounced as reminiscent of Nazi propaganda. Gove claimed he had taken one look at it and 'shuddered. I thought it was the wrong thing to do.'[73] Farage replied: 'Have you seen their posters? They have been doing very strong posters, not only about Turkey but the number of terrorists and criminals that have come into Britain under free movement rules.'[74]

None of it discouraged Dominic Cummings, Gove's former protégé who had made a name for himself as chief headbanger of the Vote Leave campaign. Insiders reported that, following the initial row, he delightedly told staff that 'Every week is Turkey week' and instructed them, whenever possible, to get to work 'Turkifying' stories before releasing them to the public.[75] Police figures would later show that racist attacks and other hate crimes rose as much as 58 per cent in the weeks immediately following the Brexit vote.[76]

7

WHERE POWER LIES

These are the big lies, the ones that were truly matters of life and death.

They are the lies uttered by those in charge, told because they felt it was their *duty* to lie: that by doing so, they were serving what is often called the 'greater good' and that the end justified the means. They are the lies told because the people in power convinced themselves that they knew best. That they had a superior ability to see 'the bigger picture' and discern the 'moral truth' of a situation (as opposed to the boring, black-and-white details bogging down the folks closer to ground level). The lies told because it was the 'right' thing to do.

In some cases, the lie was the result of disinterested decisions taken in the cold, blinding light of committee rooms – the ones connected by those infamous corridors of power. Officials charged with looking after the best interests of the country were unquestioningly allowed to calculate what those best interests must be: subsequently events beyond the scope of any bureaucratic war-gaming spun out of their control. In other cases, the lie came from the passionate intensity of a true believer, the elected official whose fervent self-belief had taken him or her all the way to the very top of the political hierarchy and, in the process, provided a sheaf of insulation from the doubts and questioning voices which beset the rest of us at every turn.

When truth is not spoken to power, the powerful do not always speak the truth.

* * * * *

'It was not sailing away from the Falklands. It was in an area which was a danger to our ships and to our people on them.'

Margaret Thatcher,
BBC Nationwide, 24 May 1983

It was exactly one month after the Argentine invasion of the Falkland Islands that Margaret Thatcher agreed to the sinking of the *Belgrano*. She took the decision on the morning of 2 May 1982 at Chequers, her weekend retreat, in the absence of the full war cabinet, who were due to gather later that afternoon. But she was careful to consult with the government's chief law officer, Attorney General Sir Michael Havers, because she knew full well that she was drifting into difficult legal waters.

Argentina had invaded the remote islands off the tip of South America – a Crown colony since 1841 – on 2 April. Britain had declared a 'total exclusion zone' around the Falklands – within which they declared any Argentine ships or aircraft would be attacked – on 26 April. It had taken that long for the ships of the British task force to get close enough to enforce the zone. When the head of the navy had informed Thatcher of the timeline for reaching the islands, she had burst out in shock: 'Three weeks? Surely you mean three days?'[1]

By May, however, she was fully up to speed, and had agreed to vary the official rules of engagement for what she insisted on calling a 'conflict' rather than a war so that the Argentine aircraft carrier *Veinticinco de Mayo* could be attacked *outside* the total exclusion zone. Capable of covering five hundred miles a day and stocked with fighter aircraft that could roam five hundred more, the aircraft carrier was too much of a threat to British troops; an attack could be justified under the self-defence rules of the UN Charter, since the ship was steaming towards them. The problem was that the British couldn't find it: it was out there somewhere in the South Atlantic, but no one knew precisely where.

They did, however, know the position of another Argentine boat, the cruiser *General Belgrano*. Intercepted messages had revealed that it was 'deploying to a position 54.00S 060.00W to attack targets'.[2] A British submarine, HMS *Conqueror*, was shadowing it through the ocean; naval commanders suspected it was part of a pincer movement, along with the *25 de Mayo*, which was closing in on the British task force in preparation for 'a major Argentine attack'.[3] But with the rules of engagement as they stood, and the *Belgrano* still outside the total exclusion zone, they could do nothing about it. Rear Admiral John Woodward, the task force commander, came up with a cunning plan to push the problem in front of the prime minister: he issued orders for the submarine to sink the *Belgrano* in the knowledge that these orders would be countermanded by military HQ back in Britain.[4] As a result of Woodward's feint, the chiefs of staff immediately went to Thatcher, seeking her permission to vary the rules of engagement in order to permit the attack.

It didn't take long – about twenty minutes – for her to agree. 'You don't wait for them to get to your ships,' she said later.[5] That night the *Conqueror* torpedoed the *Belgrano* twice; around two hundred men were killed in the explosions, and the ship began to sink immediately. Its captain gave the order to abandon ship after twenty minutes and 850 crew took to the life rafts. Confusion on board nearby ships, bad weather and damage to the *Belgrano*'s radio systems (making it unable to put out a distress signal) led to only 770 of the crew being rescued.[6] *The Sun*, then in its most frothily jingoistic phase, celebrated the attack with the headline

'GOTCHA!' They thought better of it when they realized the possible scale of losses, and changed the headline in later editions to 'DID 1200 ARGIES DROWN?'[7]

The scale of the losses was not the only problem. In between Woodward's countermanded orders and Thatcher's rubber-stamped ones, the *Belgrano* had changed course. At the time of the attack, it was heading west towards the South American mainland, not north towards the Falklands. But when Defence Secretary John Nott gave his account of the incident to the Commons the following day, he did not mention this, telling MPs that the ship had been 'close to the total exclusion zone and was closing on elements of our task force, which was only hours away'. He concluded: 'It must be a matter of deep concern to the House at the loss of life from these engagements including the sinking of the *General Belgrano*. But our first duty must be the protection of our own ships and men. There may be further attacks on our forces – and they must be allowed to act in self-defence. We cannot deny them that right.'[8]

On 29 November, five months after Britain had successfully retaken the Falklands, a junior defence minister, Peter Blaker, finally confirmed the *Belgrano*'s direction of travel: 'Throughout 2 May, the cruiser and her escorts had made many changes of course. At the moment she was torpedoed, about 8 p.m. London time, *General Belgrano* was on a course of 280 deg.'[9] That could have meant, as the government were subsequently at pains to stress, that the ship was travelling parallel to the perimeter of the total exclusion zone, ready to turn and head into it to launch an attack as soon as an order was given. But it could also mean, as observed by the MP who had managed to winkle the information out of the Ministry of Defence, that the ship was 'on course for the Straits of Magellan and her home port of Uschaia in the southern Argentine'.[10]

The questioner was Labour MP Tam Dalyell. He was a veteran conspiracy theorist, in many cases not without good cause, and in this particular case he and many others were convinced that the *Belgrano* had been sunk in order to scupper a peace plan which the US and Argentina's neighbour Peru had been attempting to broker, so that Mrs Thatcher could pursue a war she had decided she had to win at all costs. In a 1987 polemic against the prime minister, Dalyell thundered: 'I say she is guilty of gross deception. I say… she is guilty of calculated murder, not for the national interests of our country, not for the protection of our servicemen, but for her own political ends.'[11] The timings did indeed look suspicious – the statement directly before Nott's on the day after the attack had been an update from Foreign Secretary Francis Pym on the progress of his talks in America, and he said that 'we are working actively on various ideas, including those put forward by the President of Peru.'[12] But Pym had not made it back from Washington in time for the meeting at which the attack on the *Belgrano* was authorized; he only updated the war cabinet on the fresh proposals from the government in Lima on the Sunday afternoon.[13]

Whatever the precise sequence of diplomatic events, Dalyell managed to expose what looked like a serious cover-up of the circumstances of the *Belgrano*'s sinking. 'Again by parliamentary question I established that there were no elements of the Task Force west of where the *Belgrano* had been sunk, so use of the word "converging" was downright wrong,' he said.[14] But the government seemed determined to apply the old World War II motto 'Loose Lips Sink Ships' retrospectively. When on 14 December Dalyell asked a follow-up question about the precise details of the ship's course, Blaker bluntly told him: 'It would not be in the public interest to go into details.'[15] Two days later the prime minister herself snapped back at him: 'The precise courses being steered at any particular moment were incidental to the indications we possessed of the threat to the Task Force.'[16]

Thatcher did not appreciate queries about her tactics, as she had made very plain to the journalists who attempted to ask follow-up questions about the retaking of South Georgia early in the Falklands campaign. She had shot down their enquiries with 'just rejoice at that news and congratulate our forces and the marines'.[17] Her government had erupted into fury when, on BBC2's *Newsnight*, Peter Snow had introduced information from military briefings with the phrase 'if we believe the British'.[18] And a general attitude of 'keep quiet and trust in us' presided across government: it was still – rather unbelievably – official policy to not even admit the existence of the secret services, even as James Bond celebrated his twelfth cinematic outing, in *For Your Eyes Only*, with a congratulatory cameo from impressionists of Maggie and Denis.

A full year after the attack on the *Belgrano*, Mrs Thatcher appeared on the BBC's early evening current affairs show *Nationwide* as part of the 1983 General Election campaign. 'We'll be inviting viewers around the country to put Mrs. Thatcher "on the spot", as we call it,' announced a chirpy Sue Lawley.[19] If the prime minister was expecting friendly, soft-lobbed questions, she was in for a surprise. From the very first question – in which one Janet Blair from Exeter grilled her on why she talked about 'Victorian values' when those had involved 'child labour, unemancipated women, rigid class barriers, almost impossible poverty traps, and a variety of frigid morality which rejected fun and generally helped to maintain the status quo' – the tone was unremittingly hostile.[20] A university lecturer haranguing Thatcher about unemployment levels and a vicar complaining about tax breaks for the rich followed. Then Lawley threw to the BBC's Bristol studio, where a Mrs Diana Gould was waiting:

GOULD: Mrs Thatcher, why when the *Belgrano*, the Argentinian battleship, was outside the exclusion zone and actually sailing away from the Falklands, why did you give the orders to sink it?

THATCHER: But it was not sailing away from the Falklands.

This was simply an outright lie, and the prime minister knew it. Her interrogator was not the sort of woman who was going to let Thatcher get away with it. Gould had a double first in physical geography from Cambridge, specializing in the region around the Falklands, and she had served in the Women's Royal Naval Service – the Wrens. What's more, she had made sure to swot up very carefully on all the facts ahead of her TV appearance.

GOULD: Mrs Thatcher, you started your answer by saying it was not sailing away from the Falklands. It was on a bearing of 280 and it was already west of the Falklands, so I'm sorry but I cannot see how you can say it was not sailing away from the Falklands when it was sunk.

THATCHER: When it was sunk it was a danger to our ships.

GOULD: No, but you have just said at the beginning of your answer that it was not sailing away from the Falklands, and I'm asking you to correct that statement.

THATCHER: Yes, but it was in an area outside the exclusion zone, which I think is what you are saying is 'sailing away.'

LAWLEY: We're arguing about which way it was facing at the time.

THATCHER: It was a danger to our ships.

GOULD: Mrs Thatcher, I am saying that it was on a bearing 280, which is a bearing just north of west. It was already west of the Falklands and therefore nobody with any imagination can put it sailing other than away from the Falklands.

THATCHER: Mrs – I'm sorry, I've forgotten your name.

LAWLEY: Mrs Gould.

THATCHER: Mrs Gould, when orders were given to sink it and
  when it was sunk it was a danger to our ships. Now, you
  accept that, do you?
GOULD: No, I don't.
THATCHER: Well I'm sorry, it was.[21]

The next question was about nuclear holocaust. It probably came
as light relief.

'Q: Can it be transmitted to humans?

A: There is no evidence that it is transmissible to humans.'

Briefing for press officers on BSE in cattle,
Ministry of Agriculture, Fisheries and Food, 15 October 1987

The first case of BSE, bovine spongiform encephalopathy, was identified by the Central Veterinary Laboratory in a cow from a herd in West Sussex in November 1986. The official inquiry into the disease concluded that officials at the Ministry of Agriculture, Fisheries and Food (MAFF) had 'appreciated from the outset the possibility that BSE might have implications for human health'.[22] But it would be a full decade before Health Secretary Stephen Dorrell admitted to the House of Commons that 'the most likely explanation' for a spate of young people suffering from the horrific brain disease Creutzfeldt–Jakob was 'that those cases are linked to exposure to BSE' from eating beef as children.[23] For much of the intervening decade, officials and ministers did their damnedest to reassure the public that there was no danger to humans from doing just that.

Very early on government scientists identified the problem: the farming industry had turned herbivores into carnivores, cannibals even, by grinding down dead animals and adding their remains, in the form of 'meat and bone meal', to the feed mix given to living ones. It wasn't only cattle that were fed cattle; their remains were put into pig and poultry feed too. Thus, even after the meal officially went off the menu for cows thanks to a ban in July 1988, they continued to scoff the stuff due to cross-contamination of feed. In addition, farmers and feed traders continued to use up stocks of infected feed for months after the ban. Lab tests confirmed that BSE could be passed on by a speck of infected tissue 'as small as a peppercorn', and British cattle continued to catch the disease at a rate of thousands per week. In the end about 170,000 cows either died of the disease or had to be destroyed once they started showing symptoms, which included tremors, frenzied and aggressive behaviour, and the loss of control over their own hind legs.[24] Many more were slaughtered as a precaution.

Vets warned about a possible risk to humans right from the outset. The head of pathology at the Central Veterinary Laboratory reported to colleagues in December 1986 that it could 'have severe repercussions to the export trade and possibly also for humans, if for example it was discovered that humans with spongiform encephalopathies had close associations with the cattle'. In the same paperwork he also set the tone for the way that officialdom would deal with the threat – in reassuring whispers: 'It is for these reasons that I have classified this document confidential. At present I would recommend playing it low key.'[25] Many years later the government inquiry into the crisis found: 'Gathering of data about the extent of the spread of BSE was impeded in the first half of 1987 by an embargo… on making information about the new disease public.'[26] Just in case that wasn't clear enough, the inquiry's chair, Lord Phillips of Worth Matravers, spelt it out at the launch of his report: 'We do think, and have found, that there was what you might call a cover-up in the first six months.'[27]

The same caution was evident in the vets' official notification to their bosses at the MAFF after the disease was identified in seven separate herds in June 1987. 'There is no evidence that the bovine disorder is transmissible to humans,' they wrote. 'Irresponsible or ill-informed publicity is likely to be unhelpful since it might lead to hysterical demands for immediate, draconian government measures'.[28] The news was passed on to the minister in charge, John

MacGregor, the following month, with the warning that it 'would give rise to concern about any human health risks, although there is no reason at all to believe that such risks exist'.[29]

Unfortunately they were all working on a false assumption: that the new disease was related to scrapie, a similar illness that attacks the nervous system of sheep which had never been passed on to humans since it had first been identified in the early eighteenth century. Because everyone was working on this hypothesis, the disease remained the purlieu of vets, not doctors, for far too long. It was not until March 1988 that anyone even got round to notifying the Department of Health about it. Until then most of the discussions within government were focused on who would pay the bill if a mass slaughter programme had to be introduced. Indeed, MacGregor, who had only just agreed the MAFF's budget with the Treasury, wrote that he was 'concerned at the thought of a Government scheme, it runs the risk of reopening the compensation question',[30] while one of his top officials cunningly suggested that 'we can argue that the Animal Health Act does not say how much compensation should be paid, and in the circumstances, given that BSE-affected animals will have little market value anyway, we would be justified in paying only a small amount.'[31]

BSE was not like scrapie. Amazingly, the first person to suggest that the government might just want to consider the dangers of infected carcasses entering the food chain seems not to have been within the government at all. Instead it was the aristocratic car collector and gay icon Lord Montagu of Beaulieu, who wrote to the MAFF in December 1987 after a conversation with one of his tenant farmers. 'I understand little or no research has been done on whether the disease can be transmitted to humans through the consumption of beef from infected animals, and until this is known, it seems quite wrong to me that... there is a substantial financial incentive on farmers to sell a carcass for human consumption, as I understand it is worth approximately £300, as against a price of £50 if sold for pet food.'[32]

It was the government's chief medical officer, Sir Donald Acheson, who determined that 'there was insufficient evidence for him to be able to rule out the risk to human health posed by BSE.' For this reason he asked that an 'expert group' be set up to look into the matter.[33] This group, chaired by biologist Sir Richard Southwood, advised in June 1988 that cattle showing signs of BSE should be slaughtered and their carcasses destroyed (despite 'concerns with respect to public expenditure').[34] But when they released their final report a full year later the only recommendation they made about food was that 'manufacturers of baby foods should avoid the use of ruminant offal and thymus' – the latter a gland in the neck which they pointed out 'can currently be described on food labels as meat'.[35]

It was far from the only quease-inducing ingredient that would have to be revisited as the BSE crisis escalated. Concerns were raised about 'mechanically recovered meat', unappetizing scraps that were pressure-blasted off cows' skeletons and added to processed products such as pies, sausages and burgers, often along with fragments of spinal cord. Lord Phillips' inquiry found the 'MAFF discounted these concerns without subjecting them to rigorous consideration', and that a 'breakdown in communications' meant that no action was taken on mechanically recovered meat until 1995.[36] Neither the MAFF nor the Department of Health alerted the DTI to the risk of animal products in cosmetics, where the biggest danger came from 'premium products such as anti-ageing creams applied to the skin, eyes or mucous membranes, which might contain lightly-processed brain extracts, placental material, spleen and thymus'.[37] In every area, there was 'an absence of a sense of urgency' and 'a slow tempo of action' – it took a full three years to issue guidance to workers in hospitals, laboratories and mortuaries about the danger of handling 'risk tissues', with a supposedly 'fast-track' warning letter taking fourteen months to be drafted and sent out.[38] Despite a specific request in 1990 that schools be alerted to the risk of science lessons that involved pupils dissecting cow eyeballs, no advice went out for two and a half years.[39] And when the right thing was done – such as the banning in June 1989 of the bits of cow offal most likely to carry disease, which went above and beyond the recommendations of the Southwood report – it was 'presented to the public in terms that underplayed its importance as a public health measure', which meant that people failed to appreciate it when they discovered, much later, that such meaty treats as brains, spleens and spinal cords had been dangerous after all.[40]

Throughout, the public were being reassured that it was perfectly safe to carry on eating beef. MacGregor's successor as minister at the MAFF, John Gummer, famously summoned photographers in May 1990 to witness him sharing a beef burger with his four-year-old daughter.[41] On the same day Acheson reiterated official advice that 'beef can be eaten safely by everyone, both adults and children, including patients in hospital'.[42] Ironically, he was probably right, but only because the actions taken the previous year had done much to stamp out the risks. As the Phillips inquiry observed a decade later, 'the possibility of risk to humans was not communicated to the public or those whose job it was to implement and enforce the precautionary measures.'[43] Lord Phillips' panel also noted that there had been 'a belief in the Health and Safety Executive that action was being taken simply as a response to political and media pressures'.[44] When the Health and Safety Executive are dismissing things as health and safety gone mad, you know something has gone seriously wrong.

'The government did not lie to the public about BSE,' the Phillips inquiry concluded in 2000, when over eighty patients, some already dead, some still in the process of dying horribly, had been identified as contracting Creutzfeldt–Jakob disease as a result of eating infected meat many years before. 'It believed that the risks posed by BSE to humans were remote. The government was preoccupied with preventing an alarmist over-reaction to BSE because it believed the risk was remote. It is now clear that this campaign of reassurance was a mistake.'[45]

The mishandling of BSE fostered public mistrust of not just politicians, but of officials of all kinds, and of scientists too. Worse, it turned us into ripe targets for overreaction in future health scares. It was just a few short years later that Andrew Wakefield popped up with his bogus theory of a link between the MMR vaccine and autism.[46] Stopping your children from eating beef burgers because you are worried about the health risk is one thing; stopping them from being vaccinated against measles, mumps and rubella has considerably more serious – and potentially more widespread – consequences.

'I spoke to many policemen in the makeshift mortuary afterwards. They told me they were hampered, harassed, punched, kicked and urinated on by Liverpool fans. I kept quiet about this because I did not want to inflame a delicate situation. But it is a fact that these are the stories they told me and they had no reason to lie.'

Irvine Patnick MP, interview,
White's News Agency, 18 April 1989

It is sometimes said that journalism is the first draft of history. But journalism is essentially the act of recording what your sources tell you, and if those sources are lying through their teeth, you have a problem even before you start typing. There are ways of safeguarding against this danger. The most obvious one is to speak to as many people as possible and check their stories against each other, 'double-sourcing', or preferably triple- or quadruple-sourcing, every claim. But you'd be surprised how often multiple, and apparently trustworthy, witnesses turn out to all be passing on the same, unreliable evidence from a single dodgy outlet.

That is what happened to White's News, a respected local press agency in Sheffield, on the day after ninety-six Liverpool fans were crushed to death. The tragedy had occurred after the gates to Sheffield Wednesday's football ground at Hillsborough had been opened to allow gathering crowds into the penned-in stands, which were already full. White's News filed to their newspaper clients a story carrying quotes from a number of police officers who had been at the scene, as well as a local spokesman for the

Police Federation, which represents rank and file officers, and local MP Irvine Patnick. What one of those papers chose to do next – pumping up the story beyond all recognition and splashing it on the front page under the headline 'THE TRUTH', when it was anything but – is well known. But there was a fundamental problem with the story before it got anywhere near *The Sun*'s editors, because the police force that was in charge on the day was engaged in a determined cover-up.[47]

The Police Federation was a wholehearted participant – its representative, PC Paul Middup, said that 'putting our side of the story over to the press and media' was his priority following the tragedy.[48] And Patnick – he was quite open about this – was only passing on what he had been told by the police themselves. 'I saw the bruising on their bodies and the state they were in and there is no doubt in my mind it is true,' he ranted to White's. 'All this happened to them and yet they carried on doing their job trying to save lives and now they are being blamed.'[49]

It was a deliberate effort to deflect the blame from where it truly belonged. In the words of the independent panel set up to study the tragedy twenty years later, 'from the outset SYP [South Yorkshire Police] sought to establish a case emphasising exceptional levels of drunkenness and aggression among Liverpool fans, alleging that many arrived at the stadium late, without tickets and determined to force entry.'[50] The truth – that officers in charge had simply made a series of terrible decisions about crowd control, which led directly to the carnage – was to be hidden at all costs.

Patnick was not the only politician to be drawn into the web of lies. The day after the disaster, Prime Minister Margaret Thatcher and Home Secretary Douglas Hurd visited the stadium and were briefed by SYP Chief Constable Peter Wright and several of his senior officers. There is no record of exactly what they were told, but the

PM's chief press secretary, Bernard Ingham, came away from the subsequent briefing firmly convinced that 'tanked-up yobs... had turned up in very large numbers to try to force their way into the ground'. In a letter he wrote many years later he said: 'I have no intention of apologising for my views which are sincerely held on the basis of what I heard first hand at Hillsborough.'[51] In another, he argued that 'To blame the police, even though they may have made mistakes, is contemptible.'[52]

Certainly Mrs Thatcher, who was predisposed both by her nature and by her gratitude for their loyal service during the miners' strike of 1984–5 to take the police side in any dispute, was unwilling to condone any criticism of the SYP in the first official report on Hillsborough, which was published by Lord Justice Taylor in August 1989. The evidence offered by police to his inquiry, it would later infamously be established, had been subject to 'review and alteration' by colleagues and lawyers on a massive scale, in order to 'remove or amend comments unfavourable to South Yorkshire Police'.[53] Yet the judge still managed to state categorically that fans' behaviour had played no part in the tragedy. He noted that 'not a single witness' had been found to support the allegations of stealing from and urinating on victims which had been made to the media, and suggested that 'those who made them, and those who disseminated them, would have done better to hold their peace.'[54] Taylor laid the blame for the tragedy squarely on 'the failure of police control' – and he condemned the quality of evidence offered by senior officers who were 'defensive and evasive witnesses'.[55] 'It is a matter of regret that at the hearing, and in their submissions, the South Yorkshire Police were not prepared to concede they were in any respect at fault in what occurred.... the police case was to blame the fans for being late and drunk.... It would have been more seemly and encouraging for the future if responsibility had been faced.'[56]

The prime minister was having none of this. It would, as a senior civil servant pointed out, be likely to 'sap confidence in the police force'. On a copy of Hurd's proposed official response to Taylor's report, Thatcher scribbled: 'What do we mean by "welcoming the broad thrust of the report"? The broad thrust is devastating criticism of the police. Is that for us to welcome?' Her office sent a note to the home secretary requesting a change of wording: 'She considers that the statement should welcome the thoroughness of the report and its recommendations rather than "the broad thrust of the report", given the criticisms it makes of the police.'[57] Most of Taylor's recommendations were concerned with changes to the design of football grounds, rather than what he had revealed about the police. Such a lukewarm response to the rest of his findings – complimenting a report's 'thoroughness' is but a small step up from complimenting the nice font it's written in – can only have encouraged South Yorkshire Police in their determination to carry on lying for the next two decades.

'The Thatcher government, because they needed the police to be a partisan force, particularly for the miners' strike and other industrial troubles, created a culture of impunity in the police service and they really were immune from outside influences,' mused former Labour home secretary Jack Straw when the report of the Hillsborough Independent Panel was released in 2012. 'They thought they could rule the roost. And that is what we actually saw in South Yorkshire.'[58]

Many people, including Hurd, expected the chief constable to resign after Taylor's interim report came out. In the end South Yorkshire Police Authority felt confident enough to reject his offer to go, and the force declined to bring any disciplinary charges against any of its officers. When the Police Complaints Authority intervened to say they ought to, the chief superintendent who had taken the fatal decision to open the gates was allowed to retire rather than face them.

Patnick was also unconvinced by Taylor's findings. In 1990, after West Midlands Police had been appointed to investigate the behaviour of their sister force, he continued to lobby on behalf of his local bobbies. 'I do think that the South Yorkshire police's evidence was not fully taken into account at the Inquiry,' he wrote in a covering note for a lengthy package of material supplied by the South Yorkshire Police Federation.[59] The material was intended to demonstrate how 'the police did behave magnificently on this occasion in very difficult circumstances', and alleged – entirely falsely – that lawyers had prevented the judge from seeing evidence that the whole thing really was the fault of drunken fans.[60]

In April 2016, the jury at a second inquest into the Hillsborough tragedy determined that all ninety-six victims had been unlawfully killed, and that there had been a series of failings by South Yorkshire Police both before and during the disaster. They also concluded that there had not been 'any behaviour on the part of the football supporters which caused or contributed to the dangerous situation'.[61] In the spring of 2017, the Crown Prosecution Service were considering criminal charges against twenty-three suspects, both individuals and organizations, in relation to the disaster, including manslaughter by gross negligence, perverting the course of justice and misconduct in public office.

For his part, Sir Irvine Patnick recanted shortly before his death in 2012:

> I would like to put on the record how appalled and
> shocked I was to discover the extent of the deceit and
> cover-up surrounding these events. It is now clear that
> the information I received from some police officers at

the time was wholly inaccurate, misleading and plain wrong.

However, I totally accept responsibility for passing such information on without asking further questions. So, many years after this tragic event, I am deeply and sincerely sorry for the part I played in adding to the pain and suffering of the victims' families.[62]

'A licence is required for the export to Iraq of goods which are subject to control.... Applications for such licences are examined in particular against the guidelines on the export of defence equipment to Iran and Iraq announced to the House by my right hon. and learned Friend the Foreign and Commonwealth Secretary on 29 October 1985.'

Alan Clark,
House of Commons, 20 April 1989

When three directors of Midlands company Matrix Churchill were arrested in February 1991, just days after the end of the first Gulf War, and charged with exporting machine tools used to make weapons to Iraq, it looked like an open-and-shut case. Certainly that was the opinion of Geoffrey Robertson QC, the lawyer hired to represent the company's managing director, Paul Henderson. The MD appeared to be

> a businessman clever enough to deceive ministers and DTI officials while flying back and forth to Baghdad to superintend the installation of his machine tools in the arms factories. There was extremely prejudicial evidence that bombs made by Matrix Churchill had been found on battlefields where British soldiers had fallen: once the jury heard that it would be the end of any chance of acquittal.[63]

But Matrix Churchill had not been acting alone. The government had been in on the whole thing. Henderson and his colleagues had faked their export applications, which claimed the tools were for non-military purposes, with the connivance of those DTI officials, and with the explicit encouragement of one of the department's ministers. In January 1988 Henderson had visited trade minister Alan Clark as part of a deputation from the Machine Tool Technologies Association, to discuss the difficulties in getting export licences to sell their goods – which could be used for all sorts of innocent manufacturing purposes as well as crafting guns and bombs – to Iraq, as a result of the stringent restrictions imposed a few years earlier when the country had been at war with its neighbour Iran. Clark had been explicitly charged by his boss and heroine Mrs Thatcher with promoting British exports, and his own unique morality – shag-happy Hitler fan, obsessed with animal rights, not in the slightest bit bothered about human beings – meant he was unable to see why that shouldn't include warmongers like Saddam Hussein. He regarded the restrictions agreed between his department and the Foreign Office as 'irksome, tiresome and intrusive', and was quite happy to advise the manufacturers that 'the intended use of the machines should be couched in such a manner as to emphasize the peaceful aspect to which they will be put. Applications should stress the record of "general engineering" usage of machine tools.'[64] Clark would later describe this as being 'economical… with the actualité. There was nothing misleading to make a formal or introductory comment that the Iraqis would be using the current orders for "general engineering purposes"…. All I didn't say was "and for making munitions".'[65]

The minister was not the only representative of the British state to have encouraged Henderson either. That same year the businessman had been recruited as an informant by MI6, who had requested he pass on information he picked up on his trips to Baghdad. Since Saddam did not look kindly on people he suspected of spying – in 1990 he hanged an *Observer* journalist, Farzad Bazoft, after torturing a false confession out of him – this was a very risky sideline indeed. Henderson's secret-service handler testified in disguise at his abortive trial in 1992 that he was 'a very, very brave man…. There are very few people who would take such risks and take them so much in their stride'.[66]

The government approved the first batch of Matrix Churchill's machine tools going to Iraq one month after Henderson's meeting with Clark. Given that the end address for the consignment was the Nassr munitions factory, this would qualify as the most blatant blind-eye-turning in history, were it not trumped for the title by the fact, revealed at the trial, that they had also approved a consignment of rifles and shotguns to the same address under the pretence they were for 'sporting purposes'.[67] But between the Matrix Churchill delivery in February 1988 and the arrests of the company directors three years later, something very awkward had happened: Saddam Hussein had invaded Kuwait, and British soldiers had been killed in the resulting war – very possibly using weapons produced using equipment the British government had approved the sale of. As a subsequently disclosed Whitehall memo put it, any trial carried the risk of having 'the DTI's dirty washing aired in court'.[68] The Foreign Office wrote to Number 10 to warn Prime Minister John Major that 'the trial may be embarrassing for the Government…. The press may use disclosures in an unhelpful sense to suggest that ministers knowingly broke their own guidelines.'[69]

A massive cover-up was launched. No fewer than six government ministers from four different departments signed public-interest immunity certificates claiming that it was 'necessary for the proper functioning of the public service' to withhold the paperwork which Henderson and his colleagues needed to defend themselves at their trial.[70] Officials even prepared one certificate for Home Secretary Kenneth Clarke to sign which played the ultimate card,[71] suggesting that to release official documents would be 'likely to prejudice national security by revealing matters, knowledge of which would assist those whose purpose is to injure the security of the UK and whose actions in the past have shown that they are willing to kill innocent civilians'.[72] The British government was prepared to let three British businessmen, one having spied for his country, go to prison in order to hide its own role in the crimes those men had allegedly committed.

The plot failed, partly thanks to the judge taking a dim view of such draconian secrecy measures, but mostly thanks to Alan Clark. Even before the trial started he had changed his story twice: first, when allegations about his meeting with Matrix Churchill emerged, he had dismissed them as 'rubbish, trash and sensational';[73] then, he had admitted giving the exporters a nod and a wink because 'it was clear to me that the interests of the West were well served by Iran and Iraq fighting each other, the longer the better'.[74] His witness statement ahead of the trial reverted to the official line, but in the box he was only too happy to admit that the phrasing of the export licences had been 'a matter for Whitehall cosmetics to keep the record ambiguous' – something he had personally encouraged.[75] Robertson, who cross-examined Clark, reckoned he was the only figure from Whitehall and Westminster involved in the trial who 'genuinely cared about the possibility of Paul Henderson's innocence'.[76] Clark's testimony blew the prosecution out of the water. The trial was abandoned the next day, 9 November 1992.

Clark admitted something else in the witness box too: that the arms export guidelines everyone thought the government was working from, which banned any 'lethal equipment' from going to either Iraq or Iran, had been secretly changed, several years back, to 'tilt to Iraq', which at that pre-Gulf War point was Britain's preferred party in the region.[77] This caused panic in Whitehall, because minister after minister was on record over the years telling the Commons that the guidelines – known as the Howe guidelines for Foreign Secretary Sir Geoffrey Howe – were the same as they had ever been. The prime minister himself, John Major, had stated just a few months earlier that the policy had not changed between 1985 and the invasion of Iraq in 1990.[78] Now a memo from his private secretary brought him awkward news: 'It emerges that the Howe guidelines of 1985 were amended by ministers in December 1988, but the amendment was never announced to Parliament.'[79]

The change had followed a ceasefire in the war between Iran and Iraq. It was agreed between the three departments that had to agree export licences for arms and related equipment: the Ministry of Defence, the Department of Trade and Industry and the Foreign Office. William Waldegrave, the minister responsible at the last department, claimed he had been bullied by his counterparts at the other two ministries into both agreeing to relax the restrictions and not announcing them, even though he thought it was 'a serious mistake; both regimes were still dangerous, not only to their immediate neighbours but further afield.... Both had appalling human rights records'.[80] There is little sign of such hand-wringing in the note he scribbled in the margin of an internal memo from 1989 warning that Iraq could be using imported machine tools to develop nuclear weapons: 'screwdrivers can be required to make atom bombs!'[81] Fancying himself as one of the few intellectuals in government, Waldegrave personally drafted a response to potential questions:

> The form of words we agreed to use if we are now pressed in Parliament over the guidelines was the following: 'The guidelines on the export of defence equipment to Iran and Iraq are kept under constant review, and are applied in the light of the prevailing circumstances'....[82]

You would look at that sentence for a long time before you read the words 'have changed'.

At the Scott inquiry, the lengthy judicial investigation into the whole business which the prime minister was forced to call after the collapse of the Matrix Churchill trial, Waldegrave tried to argue that – despite everyone concerned working from different guidelines from the end of 1988 onwards – the fact they had not been announced made it 'perfectly clear they were never changed'.[83] At his own appearance, Alan Clark cut through the crap once again to point out that this was a 'slightly Alice-in-Wonderland suggestion'.[84]

It was far from the only tortuous logic on display at the inquiry. Mrs Thatcher, confronted with a Downing Street minute requesting that she be 'kept very closely in touch and at every stage consulted on all relevant decisions' about the arms guidelines, said that the change wouldn't have been brought to her attention because it was 'not a change of policy but a change of circumstance'.[85] Former minister Tristan Garel-Jones tried to argue that when he had claimed the release of official documents to the trial could have caused 'unquantifiable damage to the functions of security and intelligence', he wasn't exaggerating, because 'the word "unquantifiable" can mean unquantifiably large or unquantifiably small'.[86] Robin Butler, the head of the Home Civil Service, said it was perfectly possible when drafting responses to parliamentary questions to give 'an accurate but incomplete answer… an answer which in itself is true, [although] it did not give a full picture'.[87] Ian McDonald, an official at the MoD, was reduced to spluttering that 'truth is a very difficult concept'.[88]

One of the few straightforward answers came from Mark Higson, a former civil servant who said he had left his job on the Foreign Office's Iraq desk partly because of the 'sham' of dishonest ministerial statements about the exports policy. Asked why he thought the relaxation of rules had not been announced, he said: 'we were getting, you know, tens and tens of letters about gassing of the Kurds and political prisoners or hostages or whatever. It would have been unacceptable.... There would have been trouble from the public and members of Parliament if we had announced publicly that there was a relaxation in favour of Iraq.'[89]

As Lord Scott established in the 1,800-word report he delivered in 1996, the fact was that the British government had secretly adopted 'a more liberal policy on defence sales to Iraq'.[90] They had agreed to sell Saddam Hussein the tools he needed to make weapons, despite being warned that he was working on what would later come to be known as weapons of mass destruction. And they had lied to the British people about it.

Who could possibly have guessed that this sort of thing might eventually come back to bite them?

'The document discloses that his military planning allows for some of the WMD to be ready within 45 minutes of an order to use them.'

Tony Blair, Iraq's Weapons of Mass Destruction: The Assessment of the British Government, *24 September 2002*

I do not believe Tony Blair lied about his reasons for taking the country to war against Saddam Hussein. I think he genuinely believed that the Iraqi leader possessed WMDs, and was preparing to use them.

Thing is, I do not think he held that belief on any kind of sound evidential basis.

Most prime ministers go mad eventually. Harold Wilson got there by his second stint in Downing Street, when he started seeing plots and paranoia everywhere he looked. It took Margaret Thatcher until her third term, when she stopped trying to keep any of her colleagues on side and decided she was the only woman who could save the world. Gordon Brown, amazingly, managed to lose his grip on reality even before he made it to Number 10, so utterly consumed did he become with a determination to oust his predecessor. Blair began to slip the surly bonds of earth when he returned to Downing Street in 2001.

It was then that he became infused with the messianic fervour that has stuck with him ever since – a conviction that he had somehow moved so far beyond the conventional political wisdoms of left and right that he alone was afforded a vision of what was best not just for Britain but for everyone. Emotional truth counted for far more than historical truth. In the days after the 9/11 attacks he had attended a memorial service in Manhattan, talked about the London Blitz and told his hosts: 'As you stood by us those days, we stand side by side with you now.'[91] This solemn pronouncement ignored the inconvenient detail that the two years when the greatest number of German bombs were raining down on London, America was maintaining a position of studied neutrality.

There was no evidence of any connection between Saddam Hussein and the attacks on America, but nevertheless Blair was carried along with President George W. Bush's belief that there must be. In his 2010 memoir *A Journey* he writes: 'I thought I could see something deeper, that at a certain level down beneath the surface there was an alliance taking shape between rogue states and terrorist groups.'[92]

His American partner in the misadventure was open about his belief that God gave him his orders directly. Blair, who hid his own fervent religiosity while he was in Downing Street, seemed to take his inspiration from somewhere within. In his party conference speech from 2004, he fessed up, in his usual staccato fashion, to having been mistaken about those WMDs:

> The evidence about Saddam having actual biological and chemical weapons, as opposed to the capability to develop them, has turned out to be wrong.

> I acknowledge that and accept it.

> …the problem is, I can apologise for the information that turned out to be wrong, but I can't, sincerely at least, apologise for removing Saddam.

> The world is a better place with Saddam in prison not in power.…

Do I know I'm right?

Judgements aren't the same as facts.

Instinct is not science.

I'm like any other human being, as fallible and as capable of being wrong.

I only know what I believe.[93]

That was Blair's starting point: what he believed. Then all he had to do was find the evidence to fit around it.

This was exactly how the infamous dossier that he commissioned in the autumn of 2002 was compiled. The most damning bits of intelligence were cherry-picked, then wrapped up to look as damning as they possibly could. Yes, of course, as Downing Street communications boss Alastair Campbell has always furiously insisted, the security services had 'ownership' of the document. But they knew exactly what their job was, because the prime minister had announced on 3 September that the dossier would demonstrate how Saddam 'is without any question still trying to develop that chemical, biological, potentially nuclear capability'.[94]

Besides, while the metaphorical pen might have been held by Joint Intelligence Committee (JIC) chief John Scarlett, it was Campbell who chaired meetings at which the dossier's contents were discussed 'from the presentational point of view'. Writing in his diary, he was explicit as to the point of the exercise: 'Today was about beginning to turn the tide of public opinion and it was going to be very tough indeed…. It had to be revelatory and we needed to show that it was new and informative and part of a bigger case.'[95] The extent of the influence he and other Number 10 spin doctors had over the way the dossier was written is evident from the welter of documents that have been released to the no fewer than three official inquiries that have studied its compilation. 'Re dossier, substantial rewrite... as per TB's discussion' runs one email, sent from Campbell to Blair's chief of staff Jonathan Powell on 5 September 2002.[96] Another spinner, Godric Smith, emailed Campbell six days later to say, 'I think there is material here we can work with but it is in a bit of a muddle and needs a lot more clarity in the guts of it'.[97] Eight days after that, his colleague Tom Kelly pointed out: 'The weakness, obviously, is our inability to say that he could pull the nuclear trigger any time soon.'[98] And Desmond Bowen from the Cabinet Office defence secretariat emailed Scarlett directly on 11 September with the following advice:

> In looking at the WMD sections, you will clearly want to be as firm and authoritative as you can be. You will clearly need to judge the extent to which you need to hedge your judgements with, for example, 'it is almost certain' and similar caveats.
>
> I appreciate that this can increase the authenticity of the document in terms of it being a proper assessment, but that needs to be weighed against the use that will be made by the opponents of action who will add up the judgements on which we do not have absolute clarity.[99]

The effect was to strip out every qualification, nuance and doubt from material that the JIC – and every other intelligence body – warned was 'sporadic and patchy' at best.[100] Nothing was added, but plenty was taken away. Emails between intelligence officials who were shown what had been done with their information complain about 'iffy drafting' and claims that were 'likely to mislead'.[101] Some of the changes seemed to go even further. In one case, a sentence detailing how Iraq 'would not be able to produce a nuclear weapon' if sanctions remained in place, and would need 'at least five years' to do so if they were lifted, was changed in a subsequent draft to 'Iraq could produce a nuclear weapon in between one and two years.'[102]

This beefing-up went on right to the end of the process. On 19 September – after the deadline that JIC members had been given for making any changes to the dossier – Number 10 was continuing to tinker. 'I think the statement on p19 that "Saddam is able to use chemical and biological weapons if he believes his regime is under threat" is a bit of a problem,' Jonathan Powell wrote to Scarlett. 'It backs up the… argument that there is no CBW [chemical and biological warfare] threat and we will only create one if we attack him. I think you should redraft the para.'[103] Scarlett promptly did so, though none of his intelligence colleagues had objected to the phrasing over three previous drafts. 'We concluded that it was not right, the way that this was phrased, and therefore we took that out,' he would tell the inquiry, chaired by Lord Hutton, looking into the death of Ministry of Defence expert and former UN weapons inspector Dr David Kelly and the whole dossier debacle. The following summer, Blair continued to insist to that old troublemaker Tam Dalyell that 'At no time during the process did anyone attempt to override the intelligence judgements of the Chairman of the JIC and his Committee.'[104]

Thirteen years later the Chilcot inquiry – the third exhaustive official investigation of the claims and counterclaims that swirled around Saddam's WMDs ahead of the invasion – drew a subtly different conclusion:

> The urgency and certainty with which the Government stated that Iraq was a threat that had to be dealt with fuelled the demand for publication of the dossier.…
> The dossier was designed to 'make the case' and secure Parliamentary and public support for the Government's

position that action was urgently required to secure
Iraq's disarmament.... The assessed intelligence had *not*
established beyond doubt either that Saddam Hussein
had continued to produce chemical and biological
weapons or that efforts to develop nuclear weapons
continued. The JIC should have made that clear to Mr
Blair.[105]

Let us follow just one claim through the process of drafting and
publishing the dossier – the one flagged up to BBC reporter Andrew
Gilligan by David Kelly. It is perhaps the most notorious claim. And
it was particularly problematic, bringing the full vengeance of the
government, dragged by a near-demented Alastair Campbell, down
upon both journalist and source.

On 5 September the Joint Intelligence Committee received some
information from MI6 to consider for the dossier. It came from an
Iraqi military source, but only at third hand. They phrased it as
such: 'Iraq has probably dispersed its special weapons, including
its CBW weapons. Intelligence also indicates that from forward-
deployed storage sites, chemical and biological munitions could
be with military units and ready for firing within 45 minutes.'[106]

By the time the information made it into the dossier, on 10
September, it had been stripped of the opening qualification, about
the material being hidden and not immediately to hand. Instead
of a delay, the forty-five minutes had become an issue of rapidity.
Iraq 'Envisages the use of WMD in its current military planning and
could deploy such weapons within 45 minutes of the order being
given. Within the last month intelligence has suggested that the
Iraqi military would be able to use their chemical and biological
weapons within 45 minutes of being ordered to do so.'[107] By 16
September the claim had been weakened slightly – 'The Iraqi

military *may* be able to deploy…' – but it had also been bumped up into the dossier's executive summary.

On 17 September doubts were raised about that wording from both ends of the spectrum. A member of the MoD's Defence Intelligence staff complained that it was 'rather strong since it is based on a single source'. Instead, the person proposed, it 'Could say intelligence suggests…'.[108] Campbell, meanwhile, emailed Scarlett to object to the word 'may', and got a reply that it would be 'tightened'.[109] It morphed into the definitive 'Iraqi military are able to deploy these weapons within 45 minutes of a decision to do so.'[110]

This led members of the Defence Intelligence staff to raise some serious concerns about the claim on 19 September. There were, they told their bosses, 'a number of questions in our minds relating to the intelligence on the military plans for the use of chemical and biological weapons, particularly about the times mentioned and the failure to differentiate between the two types of weapons', either long-range missiles which posed a threat to other countries, or short-range munitions that could only be used on a battlefield.[111] On 20 September another pointed out: 'it is not clear what is meant by "weapons are deployable within 45 minutes". The judgement is too strong considering the intelligence on which it is based.'[112] They were thanked for their input.

The dossier was finally published on 24 September. The forty-five-minute claim was highlighted in a signed foreword by the prime minister himself: Saddam's 'military planning allows for some of the WMD to be ready within 45 minutes of an order to use them.'[113] Blair flagged this up in the Commons too:

> I am aware, of course, that people will have to take
> elements of this on the good faith of our intelligence
> services, but this is what they are telling me, the
> British Prime Minister, and my senior colleagues. The

intelligence picture that they paint is one accumulated over the last four years. It is extensive, detailed and authoritative. It concludes that Iraq has chemical and biological weapons, that Saddam has continued to produce them, that he has existing and active military plans for the use of chemical and biological weapons, which could be activated within 45 minutes, including against his own Shia population, and that he is actively trying to acquire nuclear weapons capability.[114]

During the drafting of the dossier, Powell had emailed Campbell – copying Scarlett in – to ask a rhetorical question: 'Alastair – what will be the headline in the *Standard* on day of publication? What do we want it to be?'[115] On 24 September he got his answer. London's evening newspaper went with '45 Minutes from Attack'. The following morning's *Sun* was even more apocalyptic: '45 Minutes from Doom'. Years later, in his memoirs, Blair would admit that the claim was 'highlighted by some papers the next day in a form we should, in retrospect, have corrected', but at the time it can only have felt like a case of 'job done'.[116]

Two years later former cabinet secretary Sir Robin Butler and a committee of privy counsellors delivered a cool and measured assessment of the intelligence and its use in the dossier before the war. They pointed out that when it came to the forty-five-minute claim, 'The intelligence report itself was vague and ambiguous. The time period given was the sort of period which a military expert would expect; in fact it is somewhat longer than a well-organised military unit might aspire to.'[117] They discovered that no one had really known what sort of munitions were being referred to, what their range might be. Not making this clear in the dossier 'was unhelpful to an understanding of the issue…. [A] more accurate representation… of the report would have highlighted the uncertainties in the intelligence by saying: "A source has claimed some weapons may be deployable within 45 minutes of an order to use them, but the exact nature of the weapons, the agents involved and the context of their use is not clear.'"[118] Not quite as sexy, is it?

But then, as it turned out, the information might well have been nonsense anyway. 'We have been informed by SIS' – officials always insist on calling MI6 by its proper name rather than the one everyone else uses – 'that the validity of the intelligence report on which the 45-minute claim was based has come into question,' noted Butler. 'Post-war source validation by SIS… has thrown doubt on the reliability of one of the links in the reporting chain affecting [the] intelligence report.'[119] By then, of course, Saddam Hussein had demonstrated that he didn't have chemical or biological weapons of either the long-range or battlefield variety, by the simple method of failing to use them when coalition forces had invaded.

In many ways, none of it mattered: George W. Bush was determined to oust Saddam Hussein from Iraq, and Tony Blair was determined to go along with America come what may. As Sir John Chilcot put it in his 2016 comprehensive report on the Iraq War, the prime minister had no choice but to make WMDs his excuse: 'based on consistent legal advice, the UK could not share the US objective of regime change. The UK government therefore set as its objective the disarmament of Iraq in accordance with the obligations imposed in a series of [UN] Security Council resolutions.'[120] Blair hoped to haul a war that was already inevitable onto some kind of legal and internationally justifiable footing, but everyone, on every side, was starting with a desired endpoint and working backwards. In July 2002 the head of MI6, Sir Richard Dearlove, told a Downing Street meeting that in Washington 'the intelligence and facts were being fixed around the policy'.[121] Rather than taking it as a warning, the prime minister seemed to have taken it as advice.

Of course both Blair and Bush received generous help from Saddam himself, who had been quite happy to fulfil the role of international bogeyman previously undertaken by Colonel Gaddafi (as we saw in chapter 5). He had spent the years since 1998, when he kicked out UN weapons inspectors, taunting the world with the possibility that he might be redeveloping chemical, biological and even nuclear weapons; he was hardly in a position to complain when they chose to believe him.

The world almost certainly is a better place for not having Saddam Hussein in it any more. Trouble is, almost everyone who has rolled into the gap he left behind has been just as, if not more, appalling.

One final note: don't get muddled and think the document we have been discussing here was the one that became known as the 'dodgy dossier'. That one, 'Iraq: Its Infrastructure of Concealment Deception and Intimidation', was totally different. It was published by Downing Street in February 2003 as everyone geared up for an invasion the White House had pencilled in for the following month. When it was published, Blair was at pains to stress just how hush-hush its sources were: 'It is obviously difficult when we publish intelligence reports, but I hope that people have some sense of the integrity of our security services. They are not publishing this, or giving us this information, and making it up. It is the intelligence that they are receiving, and we are passing it on to people.'[122] Three days later much of its contents turned out to have been cut-and-pasted, typos and all, from an academic article by a postgraduate student in California.[123]

8

BREAKING THEIR WORD

In the early years of the twenty-first century it sometimes seemed as though we could only watch as things spun out of control. Wars without end or aim; financial failures and meltdowns beyond the scope of comprehension. Again and again villainy was exposed on a massive scale – bankers who gambled with all our futures, media titans presiding over criminal enterprises, even paedophiles like Cyril Smith and Jimmy Savile whose political patronage helped them get away with unimaginable crimes for decades. In every case the perpetrators seemed to slip away without punishment. The public could rage all they wanted – an unprecedented number of them took to the streets to try to tell their leaders that war with Iraq would be an unmitigated disaster – but it made no difference.

Politicians seemed to be able to offer little more than false assurances, and with each broken promise and disingenuous rationale, the public's trust ebbed away. When all else failed, the politicians tried to dress themselves up in new clothes: George W.

Bush, a man whose own military career was chequered, to say the least, donning a flight suit to swagger through a premature victory rally; Gordon Brown, one of the central pillars of government for a decade, presenting himself as a new broom sweeping through Downing Street; David Cameron, the Old-Etonian epitome of a Tory toff, dressed down as a green-minded, hoodie-hugging man of the people. As Brown's much-repeated pledge of an 'end to boom and bust' exploded spectacularly, those who would soon oust him and form the country's first coalition government in sixty-five years made solemn promises of their own – which they felt not the slightest compunction to keep.

When even the politicians appeared impotent – and not overly bothered by that fact – was it any wonder that the public began to throw their support behind anyone, or anything, that promised to shake up a system that seemed broken beyond repair?

* * * * *

'Mission Accomplished'

Banner, televised presidential address,
USS Abraham Lincoln, 1 May 2003

It was a hell of a spectacle. The plane made a complicated 'tailhook' landing on the deck of the aircraft carrier, docking onto the arresting gear at a speed of 150 miles an hour and then decelerating to a halt within just a few hundred feet. As it taxied around, its wings folding gracefully in upon themselves, the markings on its fuselage came into view of the assembled TV cameras: 'Navy – 1' on the tail, and on the left side of the cockpit, 'George W. Bush – Commander in Chief'. Through the smoked windscreen a figure in a white helmet and flight suit could be seen, apparently making his post-flight checks. It couldn't be, could it?

It was. As the crew assembled on the flight deck, out climbed the forty-third President of the United States, George W. Bush, helmet now beneath his arm as he saluted them. So much for those jokes about him being a man who couldn't even eat a pretzel without choking and falling over; so much for all that gossip about how he had gone AWOL from the Air National Guard during the Vietnam War and lost his authorization as a pilot. For a good twenty seconds he strutted about, giving the impression he had been flying solo. Then he gave a thumbs up and two copilots sheepishly ambled behind him to pose for the photographers. The president had to make his way towards the cameras through a storm of backslapping and handshaking. 'Yes, I flew it,' he confirmed to the waiting journalists, skipping over the question of who exactly had been at the controls during the impressive landing. 'Yeah, of course, I liked it.'[1]

Soon afterwards, out of his flight suit and in jacket and tie, he made his way to a podium that had been set up on deck in front of a vast banner hung across the ship's tower. 'Mission Accomplished', it read, across a stars and stripes background. 'Admiral Kelly, Captain Card, officers and sailors of the USS *Abraham Lincoln*, my fellow Americans,' he began. 'Major combat operations in Iraq have ended. In the battle of Iraq, the United States and our allies have prevailed.'[2]

It is hard to say which part of the operation was more nonsensical. For all the laddish briefings – Vice President Dick Cheney had chortled, 'he's going to fly onto the carrier and do a trap – that is, they'll catch him with cable arresting gear. No president's ever done that before. And I'm not sure he told [his wife] Laura what he is going to do either!'[3] – the plane's regular pilot, Commander John 'Skip' Lussier, was firmly in charge, handing over the controls to the president only for a brief period when they were high in the sky. (Lussier obligingly told the press that the pair 'were just rapping, like flight school buds' during the flight.[4]) The ship, which had been deployed to the Persian Gulf, was now sitting not far off the coast from San Diego, which, despite explicit press briefings to the contrary, put it well within the range of the helicopter the president typically used to get around. He just fancied some *Top Gun* antics and the chance to play dress-up alongside people who had genuinely been risking their lives over the previous months. Condoleezza Rice, his secretary of state, and the 120 journalists who were brought in to witness the stunt arrived by significantly less glamorous transport.

As for the speech, Bush could not have been more wrong. The fighting in Iraq had barely begun. As 2003 wore on the country settled into a grim cycle of guerrilla warfare and suicide bombings. Despite the capture of Saddam Hussein on 13 December 2003, the violence was escalating. US troops were still in the country when Bush left office five years later, vainly protesting that 'I believe we can win.'[5] At the time of Bush's speech, just over a hundred US servicemen and women had lost their lives in Iraq; by the time his successor Barack Obama pulled the last troops out in 2011, the total stood at nearly 4,500.[6] Combat operations had gone on for seven years, longer than either World War I or World War II.

As the fighting drew on, White House spin doctors took pains to draw attention to the bits towards the end of his 'Mission Accomplished' speech where the president said: 'We have difficult work to do in Iraq' and 'The transition from dictatorship to democracy will take time', rather than the opening statement.[7] But there was no mistaking the central message, even had it not been emblazoned across the ship's tower in letters several feet high. Bush's people even tried to disown the banner too. It had, they insisted, been the crew's idea, and had been intended to celebrate that the USS *Abraham Lincoln*'s own record 290-day deployment was at an end and its five-thousand-strong crew were on their way home. The US Navy pointed out that while they might have hung it up, it was the White House who had got it made.[8] The president's visit, incidentally, had delayed the crew's return to their loved ones – they had originally been due home in January – by a day, so that he could spend a night on board before they sailed into dock. If he had the chance to play at sailors, he was going to get his money's worth.[9]

What did 'major combat operations' mean, anyway? It was a very carefully chosen turn of phrase. As the highly partisan Fox News reported at the time: 'He will not declare victory in the war, hoping to avoid triggering Geneva Convention rules that require the release of prisoners of war, the end of the pursuit of enemy leaders, and the designation of the United States as an occupying power once victory is declared.'[10] The first reports of American troops torturing and degrading Iraqi prisoners at Abu Ghraib began to emerge before the year was out.

'It is not going to happen. The Prime Minister has said it is not acceptable and therefore it won't be accepted.'

Harriet Harman, BBC Andrew Marr Show, 1 March 2009

In October 2008 the British government, along with many others around the world, were faced with an unprecedented crisis in the banking system. Financial institutions, overexposed to 'toxic' sub-prime loans made largely in the US but bundled up and sold on as securities around the world, had been forced to write down the value of their own assets, while simultaneously finding themselves unable to borrow money from one another. Gordon Brown and his chancellor, Alistair Darling, had already had to nationalize one bank, Northern Rock, earlier in the year; now, over the space of one desperate weekend, they were forced to commit enormous amounts of public money to buy shares in several other, much bigger ones as they teetered on the brink of collapse.

The government had very little choice, because if they didn't act, customers were going to find cashpoints closed, cards useless and their money effectively evaporated – all within a matter of hours. £37 billion of taxpayers' money was poured into Lloyds (whose takeover of the even more exposed HBOS had been personally brokered by Gordon Brown a month earlier[11]) and the Royal Bank of Scotland, whose rapacious overexpansion in recent years had left it living far, far beyond its means, in return for substantial shares in both institutions.[12] It would not be the end of the story. Lloyds–HBOS would eventually soak up £20.5 billion, with the government taking a 43 per cent share in return (it has since paid all of it back).[13] RBS needed even more – £45 billion – with taxpayers taking over a huge 79 per cent shareholding.[14] Nine years on, despite George Osborne insisting on selling off some of the shares at a loss, we still retain 73 per cent of the bank. RBS has staggered from disaster to disaster ever since, recording cumulative losses of over £58 billion.[15]

It was a take-it-or-leave-it deal, with Darling calling the bankers' bluff by telling them he was going to bed at midnight on Sunday and it was up to them to decide if they still wanted to have a business when the financial markets opened the next morning. RBS boss Sir Fred Goodwin, who had continuously insisted that the problems were not as severe as everyone was saying, and even tried to talk down the amount of cash his bank needed, apparently complained: 'This is not a negotiation; it is a drive-by shooting.'[16] Despite the fact that his own departure, and that of his HBOS counterpart Andy Hornby, were a precondition of the eventual deal, Goodwin did very well for himself in the negotiations.

With Darling departing to the land of Nod, it was left to his financial services secretary to look after the small print. Paul Myners had got through the fraught negotiations of the previous days on barely any sleep at all. He had only become a government minister a few days previously when Brown gave him a peerage and hoicked him into the Treasury as part of the 'government of all the talents' he was determined to recruit from outside the usual channels. He had spent decades in financial services himself, so big pay packets did not shock him in the same way they do mere mortals, but he vehemently insisted that he had made it very clear during the three-way negotiations with Goodwin and the RBS board that there could be 'no reward for failure'.[17]

The failure of RBS could be laid squarely at the feet of its overweening CEO, who had pushed through the takeovers of no fewer than twenty-six other institutions during his seven years at the helm, culminating in the aggressive acquisition of Dutch bank ABN Ambro, which had finally scuppered the company. Under his leadership the bank had spent £350 million on a new HQ outside Edinburgh; Goodwin's own office suite was decked out in top-of-the-range materials and so large that it was used to house no fewer than eighty people after his departure.[18] His pay packet in 2007 had been £4.2 million.[19]

The board had always been in awe of Goodwin – the Financial Services Authority would later criticize them for their inability to rein him in – and when Myners pointed out that some sort of 'gesture' was needed, Bob Scott, the chair of the RBS remuneration committee, told Myners quite frankly: 'Sir Fred Goodwin was not the sort of person to give things up'.[20] They did manage to get him to surrender his entitlement to a year's salary in lieu of notice – something Darling subsequently praised as 'doing the right thing' – but in an agreement signed in the early hours of Monday morning, the board also agreed to allow him to 'retire' rather than be sacked.[21] Under the terms of his contract this meant his pension pot automatically shot up from an already stonking £8 million to a flabbergasting £16 million. He would be entitled to £703,000 every year for the rest of his life. And he was only fifty years old.

None of this came out publicly for months. It was not until February 2009 that the Treasury select committee, conducting its own postmortem into the bailouts the previous autumn, started to ask some awkward questions. 'One of the many frustrating things about the pension is the manner in which its startlingly generous terms have been made public,' their report on the matter noted. 'Only gradually has one surprising fact after another emerged, and we have had the feeling that we have been obliged to prise away until eventually the information was forthcoming.'[22]

UK Financial Investments, the limited company the government had set up to manage the public stakes in the nationalized banks, blushingly admitted they had only just discovered that what they had thought was 'an unavoidable legal commitment' to give Goodwin his pension in full had actually been 'partly discretionary'.[23] But that discretion had long since been exercised. When he was asked about it, Myners stropped that he had had quite a lot of other things on his mind that weekend and 'it is not the job of the government minister to negotiate or settle the details of individual transactions.'[24]

Some of his colleagues begged to differ. Gordon Brown – who had taken very little interest in the rules governing financial services during his time as chancellor, only dipping in occasionally to publicly boast about his 'light touch regulation' – now stormed: 'This is unjustifiable, unacceptable and we are going to clean up the banks so that this doesn't happen again.'[25] His deputy leader, Harriet Harman, was even clearer. 'It's not going to happen. The Prime Minister has said it is not acceptable and therefore it won't be accepted.' The problem was that it already had been accepted, months before. But Harman, surprisingly for a former lawyer, seemed unable to grasp this problem. 'It might be enforceable in a court of law, but it's not enforceable in the court of public opinion, and that's where the Government steps in.'[26]

Trouble is, all they could step in with was a polite request. Myners interrupted Goodwin's peaceful retirement by phoning him at home in Edinbugh and, in Goodwin's words, requesting that he 'consider voluntarily taking a material reduction in my pension entitlement as a "gesture"'.[27] The former bank boss made his reply public:

> I am told that the topic of my pension was specifically raised with you by both the Chairman of the Group

remuneration committee, and the Group Chairman, and
you indicated that you were aware of my entitlement,
and that no further 'gestures' would be required.... Whilst
I suspect that you will not now agree with it, I hope you
can understand my rationale for declining your request to
voluntarily reduce my pension entitlement.[28]

He remained deaf to all similar entreaties. At the bank's shareholder
meeting that April, one angry attendee denounced Goodwin as a
'benefit scrounger', but it didn't matter; he had left the building for
good.[29] Unions pointed out that more junior RBS staff – let alone
the nine thousand sacked by the bank in a fruitless attempt to
balance the books after its near-collapse – did not get quite such
a generous deal.[30] The *Telegraph* denounced it as 'a giant bonus
for foes of capitalism'.[31]

Several months later Goodwin did finally agree to surrender some
of his pension pot – but only as a result of legal threats from his
former employer, not action from the government. He was still
left with an income of £342,000 a year, and he got to keep the
£2.7 million he had already taken out as a lump sum. The reduction
– £4 million – was equivalent to slightly less than half of the
increase he had received for not being sacked.[32]

In January 2012, as controversy raged over whether his successor,
Stephen Hester, should receive a bonus of nearly £1 million
despite RBS still being deep in the red with no prospect of profits,
Goodwin was stripped of the knighthood he had received eight
years earlier for 'services to banking'. The BBC called it 'a very
British humiliation'.[33] But it was a symbolic one, and that was all
that the state could manage. Though the post-Goodwin RBS has
been hit by fine after fine for crimes as varied as mis-selling of
payment protection insurance (PPI), interest-rate rigging, fixing
foreign exchange markets, failures to correctly report transactions

and mortgage mis-selling in the run-up to the crash, the Crown Office in Scotland announced in 2016 that there was 'insufficient evidence in law of criminal conduct either in relation to RBS as an institution or any directors or other senior management' over the events which directly preceded the bailout.[34] Maybe it hurt as much as everyone would like it to have done – the threat of being stripped of his knighthood seemed to be enough to force former BHS boss Sir Philip Green to stump up £363 million of his own cash for the pensions of his own staff in 2017.[35]

At least Goodwin's de-Sir-ification was less of an empty gesture than another that was contemplated the same year. After Jimmy Savile was exposed as a lifelong sexual predator who had preyed on children and adults alike, there was a campaign to take away his knighthood too. It was both pointless and impossible: he was already dead.

'I did not condone phone hacking, nor do I have any recollection of incidences where phone hacking took place…. As far as I am aware there is no evidence linking the non-royal phone hacking by Glenn Mulcaire with any member of the *News of the World* staff.'

Andy Coulson, testimony,
House of Commons Culture Select Committee, 21 July 2009

Despite departing his full-time employment in Downing Street at the height of the Hutton inquiry in 2003 – he'd shattered the spin doctors' first rule of never becoming the story – Alastair Campbell cast a very long shadow indeed. Four years later opposition leader David Cameron was still convinced that to fulfil his avowed intention to become 'the heir to Blair' he too needed a former tabloid journalist by his side as communications director. Even then his choice of Andy Coulson was an eccentric one. Campbell had been political editor of both the *Daily Mirror* and *Today*; Coulson had edited the 'Bizarre' showbiz column in *The Sun*, where he specialized in having his photo taken with his arm round pop stars. The worst Campbell had done during his newspaper career was punch another journalist who was celebrating the death of the crook Robert Maxwell; Coulson, by contrast, had been forced to step down as editor of the *News of the World* after his royal editor, Clive Goodman, and a private detective on a £2,000-per-week retainer were jailed for hacking messages on mobile phones, many of them belonging to members of the royal household.

Coulson maintained he knew nothing about it, and that the practice was limited to just those two underlings, but there were plenty of reasons to suspect he was lying. He was notorious as a hands-on editor who wanted to know every detail of the stories that made it into his paper. The handful of test cases on which the two men were tried included an MP, two prominent figures from the football world, the publicist Max Clifford (who had publicly fallen out with the *News of the World* and was refusing to deal with its editor) and a supermodel, none of whom would appear to have been of interest to the royal editor. The judge at the trial had even noted that in those cases the detective 'had not dealt with Goodman but with others' at the paper.[36]

The editors of both the *Guardian* and *Daily Mail* warned the Conservative leader that hiring Coulson was a bad idea.[37] They were ignored. Cameron got a strong recommendation from a newspaper boss whose advice counted for more with him: Rebekah Brooks from *The Sun*. She had preceded Coulson as editor of the *News of the World* during the period when the paper hacked the phone of murdered schoolgirl Milly Dowler, and the pair of them had also been cheating on their spouses with each other for several years.[38] But very few people knew about either of those things at the time.

Cameron and Brooks were great friends. They were frequently in and out of each other's Cotswolds homes and went riding together, and he used to sign off his regular texts to her 'LOL', supposedly under the impression it meant 'lots of love' rather than 'laugh out loud'.[39] In 2009 she told him: 'I am so rooting for you… not just as a proud friend but because professionally we are definitely in this together.'[40] But he was far from the only politician she and her senior colleagues at News International were pally with. Prime Minister Gordon Brown's wife, Sarah, had hosted a 'slumber party' at Chequers for Brooks, Rupert Murdoch's daughter Elisabeth and his then wife Wendi Deng. Tony Blair had gone one better by serving as godfather to one of Murdoch and Deng's daughters when she was baptized in the river Jordan. (Blair fell out with the media tycoon when it later came out that Wendi had taken a shine to his 'such good body and... really really good legs Butt', and started trying to arrange encounters when her husband wasn't around.[41])

On top of maintaining good relations with these various rival politicians, Brooks was able to keep Coulson up to date on the cover-up she was overseeing at News International. She and other executives were busy negotiating bigger and bigger legal settlements with victims of phone hacking to disguise the fact that the practice of phone hacking had been rampant across both the news and features departments of the *News of the World*.[42] When word leaked in 2009 that police evidence suggested between two thousand and three thousand phones had been illegally hacked by Coulson's staff – actually an underestimate – the company issued a flat denial, and Cameron announced he was 'very relaxed about the story'.[43]

Coulson did have to go in front of a parliamentary select committee, where he once again denied all knowledge of lawbreaking and insisted it was all the fault of Goodman, a single 'rogue reporter'.[44] He scoffed at suggestions his staff had hacked the phones of Labour cabinet ministers, despite the fact that he had personally listened to the messages of former home secretary David Blunkett before fronting him up about his relationship with a married woman. Blunkett was one of many figures to receive a hush-hush payoff from News International.[45] To keep things really cosy, they gave him a job too.[46]

Brooks was called in front of the same group of MPs – she claimed to have been tipped off this was going to happen by another buddy in Downing Street, Gordon Brown – but she felt confident enough to decline their invitation with an officious put-down: 'my attendance... would be pointless and a waste of the Committee's time.'[47] It's not that surprising she wasn't keen to chat. When she had gone in front of a similar committee in 2003 (while she was editor of *The Sun*), she had accidentally blurted out, 'we have paid the police for information in the past,' a straightforward admission of a crime.[48] But she didn't need to worry; nothing had happened as a result.

And nothing happened to Coulson, who moved with Cameron to Number 10 after the 2010 General Election. One of their first visitors was Rupert Murdoch, a regular caller on every prime minister all the way back to Harold Wilson. 'They… don't want me to be photographed going out the front door or I don't want to be,' he would later tell the Leveson inquiry into the British press when asked why he used the back entrance to Downing Street, 'but it also happens to be a shortcut to my apartment, so it's quite okay.'[49]

In 2011, however, things began to spin out of News International's control. As the storm broke Brooks requested a 'discreet' meeting with Coulson to advise him he should probably leave his job at Number 10 because some 'pretty incriminating evidence' had emerged.[50] 'I am very sorry that Andy Coulson has decided to resign as my director of communications,' the prime minister announced. With a blithe disregard for the chronology of the affair, Cameron complained that his right-hand man had 'resigned from *News of the World* when he found out what was happening, I feel that he has been punished twice for the same offence. I choose to judge him by the work he's done for me, for the government and for the country'.[51]

Most of the country chose instead to judge Coulson on the facts that became incontrovertible not long afterwards. He and his colleagues on the *News of the World* had hacked the mobile phone of a murdered schoolgirl, as well as hundreds of others, including families of those injured or killed in terrorist bombings and relatives of servicemen and -women killed in Iraq and Afghanistan. At the end of an epic eight-month trial he was found guilty of conspiracy to unlawfully intercept voicemails. Four of his senior editorial staff pleaded guilty to the same charges.[52]

The fact that Brooks was found not guilty at the same trial tended to overshadow just what a big deal this was: the prime minister had hired a criminal after his crimes had begun to be uncovered and ignored the warnings, installing him right at the heart of Downing Street. 'I am extremely sorry that I employed him,' Cameron blustered directly after Coulson was found guilty. 'It was the wrong decision.'[53] It was the wrong decision to speak out then too – in a magnificent example of the independence of the British judiciary, Mr Justice Saunders slapped down the prime minister for speaking out before the jury had returned their verdicts on all the charges in the trial.[54]

During the Leveson inquiry, as revelations arrived thick and fast about the favours and freebies that were being exchanged not just between the press and politicians but senior police officers too (the evidence required to convict Coulson and his colleagues had been sitting in Scotland Yard since 2006), it looked – for a few glorious months – as if things might change. No such luck. By 2017 Rebekah Brooks was back in her old job. Coulson had a new job at the *Telegraph*. Murdoch *père* continued to enjoy access to Downing Street – he met Theresa May within weeks of her taking over from Cameron. Five years on from Lord Justice Leveson's inquiry into the 'culture, practice and ethics of the press', its most notable result had been that fewer national newspapers than before are signed up to any kind of press regulator.

> 'I pledge to vote against any increase in fees in the next parliament and to pressure the government to introduce a fairer alternative.'

Nick Clegg,
signed pledge to National Union of Students, 26 April 2010

Sometimes, very odd things happen in politics. Unfamiliar faces come into public view. Voices which sound different say things that don't sound like the sort of things politicians say. It happened in the autumn of 2015, when a new generation decided that Jeremy Corbyn was an exciting new force in politics, because they hadn't noticed he had been a career politician since before they were born and the only reason he had failed to make any impact before was that he had always been useless. And it happened in the run-up to the 2010 General Election, when the nation fell head-over-heels for Nick Clegg.

Seems impossible, doesn't it? Many of us have successfully wiped it out of our minds. But it really did happen. 'NICK CLEGG IS NEARLY AS POPULAR AS WINSTON CHURCHILL' thundered a headline in the *Sunday Times* days after the Lib Dem leader went head-to-head on television with Gordon Brown and David Cameron.[55] The following day's *Guardian* asked 'NICK CLEGG – THE BRITISH OBAMA?' – and managed to keep a straight face.[56] One opinion poll in the run-up to the election put the Lib Dems ahead of both the Conservatives and Labour, which really would have broken the political mould.[57]

A lot of it was down to Clegg's performance in that TV debate, where familiarity had bred contempt for his two rivals. 'You're going to be told tonight by these two that the only choice you can make is between two old parties who've been running things for years,' Clegg pouted charismatically into the camera. 'I'm here to persuade you that there is an alternative.'[58] Viewers practically rolled over to have their tummies tickled: a poll on the night gave him 43 per cent of audience support, against 26 per cent for Cameron and 20 per cent for the sitting prime minister.[59] Gordon Brown's government *was* as tired as he looked: not-so-New Labour had been in power for thirteen years, and had taken over the position of clapped-out incumbents previously occupied by John Major's Conservatives ahead of the 1997 election. No one had really taken to David Cameron. (I'm not sure they ever did, even when they voted him into Number 10 twice.) Clegg seemed like a breath of fresh air, rather than a long-serving member of both European and Westminster parliaments who had hauled his party back in a decidedly right-wing direction following the defenestration of his popular but pissed predecessor Charles Kennedy.

There was another reason for 'Cleggmania': the fact that he pitched himself directly to students, with a promise ahead of Lord Browne's review of university funding, due later that year, that he would absolutely, unequivocally vote against any rise in tuition fees. His party stood behind him: four hundred Lib Dem parliamentary candidates added their names to a pledge organized by the National Union of Students (NUS) alongside fifty-six of the party's other sitting MPs.[60]

Not only that, but Clegg told the students' representatives that he would go further than they were asking. 'You've got people leaving university with this dead weight of debt, around £24,000, round their neck,' he told the NUS conference in a specially recorded video message on 13 April. 'We used to want to be able to scrap tuition fees overnight. Because money is tight it is going to take a little longer. We have a plan to do that over six years. But it is a plan that works.'[61] They believed it so strongly they even put it in the party manifesto: fees to be phased out totally in six years, but scrapped for final-year students immediately.

The promise was something those of us with longer memories had reason to be wary about. The Labour MP I voted for as a third-year student in 1997 distributed leaflets which assured us of her implacable opposition to tuition fees being introduced; just over a year later she voted with the government to bring them in. In their 2001 manifesto Labour promised not to introduce top-up fees, which could triple the amount students had to pay; they duly brought them in two years after being re-elected. The flip-flop did at least cause one of the biggest backbench rebellions of Tony Blair's time in Downing Street. In his memoirs he said it was 'the closest I came to losing my job'.[62] But he was also candid about how much a manifesto commitment counts for: 'frankly it would have been absurd to postpone the decisions necessary for the country because of it.'[63]

The country went to the polls on 6 May, and another rather odd thing happened. The country returned a hung parliament, as everyone had predicted, but all the vocal support for the Lib Dems, all that Cleggmania, translated into... a minimal increase in their vote and the *loss* of five Commons seats. Nevertheless, with his fifty-seven MPs, Clegg had all the power. He instantly began horse-trading with both the Conservatives and (with considerably less enthusiasm) Labour to see what his party could get in return for their support. He was surprised to discover quite how much the Tories were willing to offer. A member of the negotiating team told journalist Andrew Rawnsley: 'We'd say what about a, b and c, and they'd say we're surprised you haven't asked for d and e as well.'[64] There was, however, one big sticking point, a principle on which Clegg was not willing to compromise under any circumstances... a referendum on whether proportional representation should be introduced to the voting system. Tuition fees barely even featured.

It would later turn out that the head of the Lib Dems' negotiating team, Danny Alexander, had advised two months ahead of the election that in the event of a hung parliament, the party should 'seek agreement on part time students and leave the rest.'[65]

On 12 May Clegg stood in the Downing Street garden alongside Cameron as they announced the terms by which they would govern Britain in coalition for the next five years. Tuition fees were way down in the small print. The Lib Dems hadn't actually agreed to vote for a rise in fees if that was what the Browne review recommended when the report was published in the autumn. Instead they were allowed to abstain from the vote – but they didn't even all manage to do that. When the issue of raising the cap on fees from £3,375 to £9,000 came before the Commons in December 2010, twenty-one Lib Dems voted against it, and twenty-seven – including Clegg – came out in support.

They were the sort of numbers the Lib Dems could only dream of following the next general election. In 2015 all but eight of them were swept out of parliament, including three of the five cabinet ministers they had wangled places for in the coalition agreement, although a chastened Clegg hung on to his own seat.

His former partner, meanwhile, was returned to government with a majority of his very own. But Cameron's perfidy had been no lesser than Clegg's. Prior to the 2010 General Election he repeatedly promised that under his rule there would be 'no more of the tiresome, meddlesome, top-down re-structures that have dominated the last decade of the NHS'.[66] Within two months of being elected, his government announced a massive re-structure which independent think tank The King's Fund called 'perhaps the most significant and far-reaching in the history of the NHS'.[67] Pushed through against the vocal opposition of medical experts, and at a cost of nearly £3 billion, it created what the think tank called 'an unwieldy structure… with leadership fractured between several national bodies, a bewilderingly complex regulatory system and a strategic vacuum in place of system leadership.'[68] Cameron, never a man to bother himself with the finer details of government when there was chillaxing to be done and box sets to be watched, sailed on regardless.

254 ■ THE LIES OF THE LAND

> 'The coalition Government have inherited from their predecessors the largest budget deficit of any economy in Europe, with the single exception of Ireland. One pound in every four we spend is being borrowed....The formal mandate we set is that the structural current deficit should be in balance in the final year of the five-year forecast period, which is 2015–16.'
>
> *George Osborne, budget speech,*
> *House of Commons, 22 June 2010*

The Conservatives won the 2010 election – well, nearly won; they needed the Lib Dems to help them take power – because they hammered home a message to the British people that Labour could not be trusted with the economy. All right, it might be true that the emergency measures Gordon Brown and Alistair Darling had taken to rescue the banks had set the global agenda in how to tackle the 2008 crisis, and the country was already pulling out of the resulting recession. But the message that David Cameron and his sidekick George Osborne repeated – until it achieved such resonance that Labour even seemed to believe it themselves by the time the next election rolled round – was that Labour had drastically overspent, recklessly overborrowed and generally behaved like fiscal Viv Nicholsons for the past thirteen years.

When Osborne stood at the dispatch box to deliver his first budget as chancellor in the summer of 2010, he vowed that things were (finally) going to be different. He called it his 'emergency budget', a title he liked so much that he would pull it out again, to rather less effect, during the Brexit campaign. 'This Budget is needed to deal with our country's debts. This Budget is needed to give confidence to our economy. This is the unavoidable Budget,' he intoned. 'I am not going to hide hard choices from the British people or bury them in the small print.... The British people are going to hear them straight from me, here at this Dispatch Box.'[69]

One message that the British people heard, loud and clear, was that Osborne was going to get the deficit down. They might not all have known exactly what the deficit was – the amount that the government has to borrow to cover the difference between what it receives in tax and what it spends – but they understood that it was a bad thing, and it needed to be eliminated. No one disputed that it was running at an unprecedentedly high level – 10.2 per of gross domestic product (GDP), the measure of what the UK's economy was actually worth.[70] Even Darling, Osborne's predecessor as chancellor, had been talking about the need to get it down, though he had had great difficulty convincing Brown, who had grown so addicted to announcing giveaways (genuine or not) that he was terrified to even utter the word 'cut'. In the pre-budget report the previous year, Darling said he aimed to slice the deficit in half by 2014.[71]

But Osborne committed himself to going further than that. He would, he said, within the same time scale, cut the deficit right back down to zero – and then beyond. 'Thanks to my action today,' he told the Commons, '[t]hat deficit will... be eliminated to plus 0.3% in 2014–15 and plus 0.8% in 2015–16. In other words, it will be in surplus.'[72]

It was the rationale behind the coalition government's programme of savage cuts to public services, what Cameron had already christened the 'age of austerity'.[73] Osborne was clear that 'the bulk of the reduction must come from lower spending rather than higher taxes. This country has overspent, it has not been under-taxed.'[74] He brought in swingeing cuts to investment in infrastructure, and his cabinet colleagues set about cutting waste with a vengeance, including such fripperies as public libraries, spare rooms, jobs for disabled people, welfare payments for children, lawyers for victims of domestic violence, prison officers, firefighters, police and soldiers. Trouble was, pulling money out of the economy and banging on endlessly about the need for us all to tighten our belts meant that *everyone*, consumers and businesses alike, spent less and hung on to their money. As a result, tax receipts went down too. Osborne had no choice but to carry on borrowing to cover the spending that had survived the budget, and by the time of the next general election, the country was £600 billion more in debt than it had been when the coalition took over.[75]

Osborne was forced to admit that getting rid of the deficit was 'clearly taking longer than one would have hoped' by the end of 2012.[76] By December the following year he had officially pushed back the target date for running a surplus to 2017–18.[77] By 2014–15 – the year he originally claimed we would be back in the black – he had moved the goalposts for achieving an overall budget surplus, not just the 'structural deficit' (the version with temporary economic effects stripped out which he had been talking about before) by 2020. He felt so confident about his promise that he put it in a new 'fiscal charter' to ensure that whoever was in government, 'This country has to live within its means.'[78] Independent experts at the Institute for Fiscal Studies were warning by March 2016 that there was 'only just the right side of 50–50' he would manage it,[79] and Osborne abandoned the target after the Brexit vote in the summer of 2016, shortly before he was kicked out of his job by Theresa May. As the financial year 2016–17 drew to a close, the Office for Budget Responsibility, which Osborne had set up to keep tabs on his figures, were predicting a deficit of £51.7 billion, or 2.6 per cent of national income. They expected it to get bigger the following year, before beginning to shrink, and the prospect for a surplus was distant: 'We do not expect to see a surplus in the next five years.'[80]

It's not Osborne's problem. He has decided to have a go at being a newspaper editor instead. Just in case that doesn't work out, he's taken on one or two other positions too. Together, they will push his income up to a decidedly non-austere £700,000 plus a year.[81]

'I'm not going to be calling a snap election. I've been very clear that I think we need that period of time, that stability to be able to deal with the issues that the country is facing and have that election in 2020.'

Theresa May,
BBC Andrew Marr Show, 4 September 2016

One of the very first announcements of the coalition government led by David Cameron was a fundamental change to the way politics worked in Britain. Starting in May 2010 no prime minister would be able to call an election at the time of their own choosing in order to capitalize on their own political advantage. Instead, as in many other democracies, elections would be held at strict intervals on set dates, and all sides would just have to take their chances. There would be no more shenanigans as in 1992 or the recent poll, when respective incumbents John Major and Gordon Brown had clung on to power until the very last possible minute in the hope that something, anything, might turn up to save their administrations from the knacker's yard. No more, either, the machinations of 1983 and 2001, when Thatcher and Blair chose to go to the country before they were obliged to, cashing in on a peak in popularity or hedging against the expectation of bad economic news.

'I'm the first prime minister in British history to give up the right unilaterally to ask the Queen for a dissolution of Parliament,' Cameron boasted. 'This is a huge change in our system, it's a big giving up of power.' He insisted – in words that would come to seem rather ironic seven years later – that it was 'a good arrangement to give us strong and stable government'.[82]

The date for the next election – the first Thursday in May 2015 – was set in stone as part of the coalition deal Cameron signed with the Lib Dems. The process was then formalized in the following year's Fixed-term Parliaments Act.[83] Against everyone's expectations, that pre-planned election resulted in a slim Conservative majority – and a prime minister who was stuck holding himself to the promise of a referendum on the question of Britain's continued membership in the EU. When that gamble didn't pay off quite as Cameron had hoped, the woman who succeeded him into Number 10 pronounced herself content to stick by its strictures.

'I think what's important, particularly having had the referendum vote, is that we have a period of stability,' May told the nation, brushing aside concerns that the only people to give her a mandate lived in her Maidenhead constituency. 'We'll be continuing the manifesto on which the Conservative government was elected in 2015, so I don't think there's a need for an election.... I'm not going to be calling a snap election. I've been very clear that we need that period of time, that stability to be able to deal with the issues that the country is facing and have that election in 2020'.[84]

Her tight-knit team kept reiterating this message over the coming months, even as the fortunes – and poll ratings – of opposition leader Jeremy Corbyn dwindled. 'It's not going to happen,' a spokesman told the *Telegraph* in March 2017. 'It's not something she plans to do or wishes to do.'[85] The *Financial Times* were similarly slapped down a few weeks later: 'There isn't going to be one. It's not going to happen. There is not going to be a general election.'[86] The last possible date when a national vote could be called to coincide with the local elections that May – which, along with just about everything else, the Conservatives were predicted to storm – came and went. It seemed we were definitely in for the long haul.

Then, on 18 April 2017, mere weeks after revealing a budget that made plain the new regime was not in the least bound by the manifesto commitments of its predecessors,[87] May performed a screeching U-turn. Standing at a hastily erected lectern in the middle of Downing Street, she announced that the country should go to the polls three years early, on 8 June 2017. 'I have concluded that the only way to guarantee certainty and stability for the years ahead is to hold this election and seek your support for the decisions I must take.'[88]

The opportunism was naked. The prime minister made it evident that she was not simply looking to improve on her party's tiddly seventeen-seat working majority, but to annihilate all opposition; her preferred option was a one-party state in which her actions could not be questioned. 'At this moment of enormous national significance, there should be unity here in Westminster, but instead, there is division,' she announced, blithely sweeping aside the three-hundred-year tradition of parliamentary opposition.[89] She insisted that 'every single vote for me and Conservative candidates will be a vote that strengthens my hand in the negotiations for Brexit', despite the fact that the only stage of the negotiations where a crushing majority could possibly help would be in the single vote she had grudgingly been forced to offer Parliament, on the final terms of the deal with the EU two years down the line.[90] A gargantuan band of backbench loyalists would be insurance against the increasing likelihood that she would not be presenting them with anything like a good deal, but it would not, as she was implying, make the slightest jot of difference with the EU negotiating team she was going to have to face down first.[91]

The Conservatives were jubilant. More shockingly, the opposition also agreed. The Labour leadership ordered its troops to vote in favour of a motion to activate one of the get-out clauses sneakily built into the 2011 Act, just as they had gone along with the government a few months earlier in the vote in favour of triggering Article 50 and committing the UK to leaving the EU. The Lib Dems, who with just nine seats must have figured they had little to lose, did the same. The Scottish Nationalists abstained. Only thirteen MPs voted against. And thus was the strangest, most dishonest and most downright unnecessary general election campaign in the history of the country kicked off.

And, against absolutely everyone's initial expectations, it ended in disaster for May, destroying her majority, her authority and her credibility. To paraphrase Wilde, to lose one prime minister to a reckless gamble on a completely unnecessary vote may be regarded as misfortune; to lose two really does look like carelessness.

9

WHOSE TRUTH IS IT ANYWAY?

As G. K. Chesterton definitely never said, once people stop believing in politicians, the problem is not that they believe nothing – but that they believe anything. And that is what seems to be happening today.

More and more young voters are searching for new, outsider voices in which to place their faith, and failing to spot that they are turning to the same old career politicians who will only let them down. But they are not alone. Even seasoned voters are grasping for straws and strawmen, throwing themselves behind various fringe figures who have somehow ended up dictating the show from the sidelines. Political certainties that had coalesced around the centre are crumbling away as new movements emerge from the far left and right – although these new movements, on close inspection, look very like the old movements, rebranded and with better online operations. Strange coalitions of the two extremes are spawning in the fertile ground of the Internet: left-wing groups that have always championed human rights are marching alongside Islam's most conservative campaigners; 'campus fascists' of the left are shouting down feminists and in turn being denounced by Marxist Milošević fans writing in the Murdoch press; the most right-wing flank of the US Republican Party appears to have formed an election-winning alliance with the Russians.

This is the age of both the nonsensical conspiracy theory and the covered-up reality that is too awful to be true. Blatant fictions are meme-ified and circulated without question, while inconvenient truths are denounced as 'smears' or 'fake news'. Intellectualism, investigation and even knowledge itself have all somehow come to be mistrusted. As Michael Gove put it at the height of the nakedly dishonest Brexit campaign, 'people in this country have had enough of experts.'[1]

In the absence of such authoritative voices, we are left to construct our own realities. And within our individual bubbles, we are increasingly choosing to believe some very odd things indeed.

* * * * *

'David Cameron made a secret visit to Shetland to see this important field. But the visit was hushed up along with the latest results of test drilling, which are rumoured to reveal even more oil…. It has even been suggested that workers on the field stand down till after the referendum.'

Joan McAlpine,
Daily Record, 25 August 2014

As the referendum on Scottish independence loomed in the summer of 2014, an extraordinary conspiracy theory started doing the rounds among campaigners for a 'yes' vote: oil giant BP had discovered new reserves worth £1 trillion in the Clair Ridge oilfield fifty miles off the Shetland Islands, but had been ordered to keep it a secret. Several bloggers and online activists claimed that workers had been ordered home on full pay until after the referendum. They had apparently been instructed to keep quiet, because the find would ensure Scotland had sufficient oil reserves not just to support itself after an independence vote, but for every man, woman and child to live in the lap of luxury. And the dastardly regime in London – government, BBC and press, they were all in it together – were not prepared to let them know anything about it.

How had the news leaked out? Well, as one graphic shared on social media summed it up, no less a figure than David Cameron 'sneaks into Shetland, the First PM in 34 years to visit…. The Prime Minister's plane was photographed when it landed'. Blurred shots of a small plane touching down, and a figure that was undeniably the prime minister strolling across a runway, accompanied the text.[2] You could actually get a much clearer photo of Cameron visiting Shetland from the prime minister's own Twitter account. The snapshot showed him stroking a tiny horse and was captioned: 'I enjoyed seeing some Shetland ponies with two children who are on holiday here.'[3] So 'sneaky' had his July visit been that he had made a speech in Lerwick Town Hall, laid a wreath at a war memorial and posed for press photographers on the deck of a fishing boat, outside a lighthouse and with the helicopter crew of the local search and rescue service. It had been widely reported throughout the Scottish media.

These inconvenient facts did not deter the conspiracy theorists. 'Questions over why a recent visit to the Shetland Islands by Prime Minister David Cameron was kept secret from the Scottish public and media, have been met with silence from Number 10 Downing Street,' roared the reputable-looking 'independent politics and current affairs site' Newsnet.scot on 7 August. It did, however, manage to wangle a response out of a bemused spokesperson at BP about the supposed trillion-dollar discovery. 'None of those statements are based on any fact.... The Cameron visit to Shetland had no connection to BP at all.... No crew... have been sent home on full pay....'[4]

Despite such reassurances, the rumours made their way into the mainstream a few weeks later when Joan McAlpine – an SNP member of the Scottish Parliament and a former journalist who really ought to have known better – used her weekly column in Scottish paper the *Daily Record* to air them.[5] The party's then-deputy leader Nicola Sturgeon told BuzzFeed: 'I have no evidence that there is any ongoing attempt to cover up discovered oil, but Westminster governments have, almost since North Sea oil was discovered, attempted to downplay it to the people of Scotland.'[6]

A Number 10 official who had been on the trip offered a slightly different take, saying the story was 'bollocks... the closest we got to an oil well was a trip around the harbour.'[7] A BP spokesperson pointed out that if the prime minister wanted to meet oil company executives, he would probably do it in London. No one even tried to explain why, even if the company had found extra oil in the area, Cameron would want to personally travel eight hundred miles just to look at the sea on top of it.

The government had given BP the go-ahead to exploit Clair Ridge in 2011. Platforms were due to be installed in 2015 and production scheduled to begin the following year. The company had long since announced that even with a proposed extraction rate of 120,000 barrels per day it would take them forty years to get out all the oil in the Clair Ridge area, which was itself an extension of the Clair field discovered way back in 1977. In the three years after the independence vote of 2014, the company did not announce any extra oil in the field (although they did manage to spill quite a bit of it in October 2016[8]). By that point the price of oil per barrel had dropped to forty-eight US dollars – less than half the level it had been at when Sturgeon made her own visit to Shetland the month before the referendum and predicted a looming 'oil boom' for a soon-to-be independent Scotland.

> 'Nick has been spoken to by experienced officers from the child abuse team and from the murder investigation team and they and I believe what Nick is saying is credible and true.'

Detective Superintendent Kenny McDonald,
appeal for information, 18 December 2014

A hysterical atmosphere gripped Britain following the revelations about royal intimate and friend of Mrs Thatcher, Jimmy Savile. Police, politicians and the press were all seized with guilt that they had looked the other way for so long; suddenly the pendulum swung and everyone saw paedophiles everywhere. Celebrity after celebrity had their reputations dragged through the mud over allegations dating back decades, only for police to drop all action, or for trials to end in acquittal. Some – Rolf Harris, Stuart Hall, Fred Talbot, Max Clifford – had their depravity exposed in court and went to prison.[9] The decades-long cover-up of the late Cyril Smith's sexual and physical abuse of boys and young men at Cambridge House hostel and Knowl View school, both in his constituency of Rochdale, came spilling out into the open.[10] Eventually, a joint report by police and the National Society for the Prevention of Cruelty to Children revealed that Savile's abuse had been on a scale that was scarcely imaginable.[11]

There was still more collateral damage. The BBC, which had failed to identify the predator hiding in their midst for several decades and then missed the chance to expose him even after his death, rushed to suggest that former Tory treasurer Lord McAlpine had been involved in a notorious abuse scandal centred on care homes in North Wales. In their reports the BBC had relied on a deeply damaged victim whose unreliability as a witness had been exposed in an earlier libel trial, and they hadn't bothered with the most rudimentary checks on his claims, which he almost instantly withdrew. The mistake cost the broadcaster, and others who had promulgated the accusations, dearly.

Into the middle of this arrived Nick. Or rather 'Nick' – as someone who claims to have been the victim of sexual abuse he is entitled to anonymity for life. Nick was a middle-aged man who said that, as a child, he had been abused by a paedophile ring which included his stepfather. He decided to get in touch with Exaro, a website-cum-news agency which had filled a gap in the market no one knew existed by making itself a one-stop shop for stories about high-profile child abusers. An Exaro staffer accompanied Nick when he made the first of five complaints to police between October 2014 and April 2015. By the end of the process his story had escalated: he now claimed to be able to positively identify several of the men who had abused him. 'Some of them were quite open about who they were. They had no fear at all of being caught, it didn't cross their mind,' he told the BBC in one of the media interviews he was conducting alongside those with the police.[12] One, he alleged, was a former prime minister, Ted Heath. Another was a past home secretary, Leon Brittan. A third, he said, was their fellow MP Harvey Proctor, outed as gay by the tabloids in 1987. Others included in Nick's allegations were the chief of the defence staff, other senior military figures and the then heads of both MI5 and MI6. VIP paedophiles did not come more VI than this.

It sounded too extreme to be true – especially when it came to the details of what Nick claimed had happened to him. On one of many occasions when he claimed he had been raped in the Dolphin Square apartment block, close to Westminster and home to many political figures, Nick said that Proctor had taken out a penknife and been about to cut off his genitals before Heath intervened; the more junior politician had changed his mind and decided to give the boy the penknife as a souvenir instead.[13] Nick apparently also accused Proctor of murdering two other child victims who he stabbed, beat and strangled.[14] Nick also said that he had witnessed another boy being deliberately run down in the street in Kingston upon Thames by members of the paedophile ring.[15] 'They amount to just about the worst allegations anyone can make against another person,' Proctor said when he bravely went public to deny all the claims about him in the summer of 2015. 'It is unbelievable because it is not true. My situation has transformed from Kafkaesque bewilderment to black farce incredulity.'[16]

But Scotland Yard were taking it very seriously indeed. An entire police investigation, Operation Midland, was set up based on Nick's allegations. Twenty-seven detectives and six civilian staff were seconded to work on it; it ran for sixteen months and cost £2.5 million.[17] Just one month in, the man in charge, Detective Superintendent Kenny McDonald, announced publicly that what Nick had told his officers about the three murders was not only 'credible' but – in unequivocal, black-and-white terms – 'true'.[18]

It may have been credible to some, but it was not true. No one ever came up with any corroborating evidence for Nick's claims. Police searches of the homes of Nick's alleged abusers turned up nothing. The most basic of checks into the story about the hit-and-run killing established there was no evidence of any such incident ever occurring. Proctor 'is an innocent man, as indeed are all the men named by "Nick",' concluded Sir Richard Henriques, the retired judge who was brought in to review the whole sorry affair and identify the 'significant failings' in the police's conduct of the investigation.[19] 'It is difficult, if not impossible, to articulate the emotional turmoil and distress that those persons and their families have had to endure.'[20]

Nick is, at the time of this writing in May 2017, under investigation by a different police force to see if he should be charged with perverting the course of justice. Henriques noted that there exists 'an important category of complainant, distinct from the deliberately untruthful, namely, "troubled people often have something that happened in life, even if it is not what they've reported".'[21] One of the tragedies of child abuse is that it can screw you up so much it makes you an unreliable witness as to what has actually happened to you. Publicity over high-profile cases prompts false memories as well as long-buried true ones.

In the meanwhile Exaro – which published reams of dubious claims about celebrity sex abusers and used to boast that Operation Midland 'only happened as a consequence of evidence that we found' – has gone out of business.[22] Newspapers which queued up to buy Exaro's exclusives, or which breathlessly chased claims made under the cover of parliamentary privilege by MPs such as Tom Watson, Zac Goldsmith and Simon Danczuk, now pour scorn on the police for their credulity.

Many of the rumours they'd fallen for had been doing the rounds for years. Brittan was in the headlines by 2014 for supposedly losing a 'dossier' on child abusers given to his department by an MP in the early eighties.[23] (The nudge-nudge coverage harked back to old allegations about Brittan's sex life that had been thoroughly debunked by journalists and blamed on what *Private Eye* called 'MI5 spooks and loonies who object to having a Jewish Home Secretary'.[24]) Tales of depravity at Dolphin Square had been aired in the early nineties, along with allegations about Lord McAlpine, in the notoriously unreliable *Scallywag* (which you may recall spreading inaccurate rumours about John Major in chapter 4). They had been circulating around dark, conspiracy-minded corners of the Internet for much of the intervening two decades.

The difference was that, by this time, people were ready to believe them.

> 'A distinguished Oxford contemporary claims Cameron once took part in an outrageous initiation ceremony involving a dead pig. His extraordinary suggestion is that the future PM inserted a private part of his anatomy into the animal's mouth.'

Daily Mail, *20 September 2015*

One of the first things journalists should do when somebody tells them something is consider why. Why are they telling me this? What's in it for them? How might they benefit from the story emerging? Do they have a grudge against the subject? Neither payoff nor payback is necessarily a reason to distrust the information, but any half-decent hack will keep a source's motivations in mind. Of course the very top priority, it should go without saying, is to establish whether what they are telling you is true or not.

When the *Daily Mail* blared the juiciest bit of former Conservative treasurer Lord Ashcroft's 'unauthorized biography' of the prime minister from its front page in September 2015, it was pretty upfront about the first possibility: the headline was 'REVENGE!' 'Today we lift the lid on the extraordinary feud between David Cameron and a billionaire Tory donor that has triggered the most explosive political biography of the decade,' the paper chortled. Ashcroft, who to refresh your memory from chapter 3, had never stood for office and had massively embarrassed the party by finally fessing up to his dubious tax status just ahead of the 2010 General Election, had been deeply offended when the new PM only offered him a relatively junior post in his government right after it. 'I regarded this as a declinable offer,' he whinged in his book. 'It would have been better had Cameron offered me nothing at all.'[25] So, in a vengeance plot straight out of the school playground, he decided to spread a rumour that the prime minister shagged pigs. Or rather, that when Cameron was at Oxford University, he had 'inserted a private part of his anatomy' – the book didn't specify which one, but it was pretty obvious – into the mouth of a dead one at a drinking society party.[26]

Ashcroft's source was another MP who was at Oxford at the same time. (David and Samantha Cameron apparently had a pretty good idea which one, and also blamed him for spreading hurtful rumours about their disabled son Ivan, who died at the age of six.) But even this person didn't claim to have witnessed the incident personally. As Ashcroft put it in his breathlessly bad prose: 'Lowering his voice, he claimed to have seen photographic evidence of this disgusting ritual.... The MP also gave us the dimensions of the alleged photograph, and provided the name of the individual who he claims has it in his keeping. The owner, however, has failed to respond to our approaches.' Ashcroft didn't even seem to believe it himself. 'Perhaps it is a case of mistaken identity. Yet it is an elaborate story for an otherwise credible figure to invent.'[27]

It was the sort of story that would be slapped down in seconds by the least experienced editor on a local free sheet. But because *Daily Mail* editor Paul Dacre hated Cameron almost as much as Ashcroft did, he was quite happy to run it on his front page. It probably didn't hurt that as a billionaire, Ashcroft had deep enough pockets to defend the paper from any ensuing libel claim. He had been quick to rush to the courts when baseless stories about his own behaviour were published, and nor was this the first occasion when he had taken his revenge by literary means. After suing *The Times* a decade previously he had not only written and published a book about the affair but sent free copies of it to MPs and libraries throughout the country. He is – and to be clear, this is just vulgar abuse and therefore unactionable – a very weird little man.

He was also struck down by illness on the eve of the serialization, so it was left to his co-author, Isabel Oakeshott, to do the publicity interviews. She had already been involved in one of the greatest possible sins against journalism, when her source for a story about the criminal activities of Lib Dem cabinet minister Chris Huhne (his ex-wife, Vicky Pryce), was unveiled and later imprisoned, despite Oakeshott initially promising her that the chances of prosecution 'were minor'.[28] Now Oakeshott compounded her offences by offering the most pathetic possible justification – or rather *lack* of justification – for the pig story, which had taken off like a rocket and was dominating the news. 'We didn't get to the bottom of that source's allegations, so we merely reported the account that the source gave us,' she shrugged on *Channel 4 News*. 'We didn't say whether we believe it to be true. It's up to other people to decide whether they give it any credibility or not.'[29] Asked about proof at the Cheltenham Literature Festival a few weeks later, she was even more insouciant. 'I think it rests on a really false premise, which is that things that are written in books need to have the same standard – if you like to use that word – as things that are written in newspapers,' she told the crowd. 'You might just as well say, "Well, you couldn't have put that in *Barbie Princess* magazine."'[30] By Oakeshott's logic, this being a book, I could justifiably write anything I wanted to about Oakeshott's own sexual behaviour. But I won't. I will merely note that Dacre was so impressed with her attitude to journalism that he gave her a job on the *Mail*, much to the disgust of the rest of the political team. She lasted a year.

For Cameron's part, he issued 'a very specific denial... for the specific issue raised' by Ashcroft and added that 'I can see why the book was written and I think everyone can see straight through it.'[31] And for all the appalling things David Cameron has done – only some of them as a student, when he admits belonging to the deliberately obnoxious, snobbish and restaurant-wrecking Bullingdon Club – there remains no evidence that he has ever inserted any part of himself into any part of a pig, however much people would like it to be true.

> 'I watched when the World Trade Center came tumbling down. And I watched in Jersey City, New Jersey, where thousands and thousands of people were cheering as that building was coming down. Thousands of people were cheering.'

Donald Trump,
campaign rally, Alabama, 21 November 2015

Donald Trump, property developer, bully, blowhard and reality TV star, stood in front of a rally of supporters in Birmingham, Alabama, and basked in their approval. Record crowds were turning up for him everywhere he went on the campaign trail. More than four thousand people had turned up to his first big event in July 2015, filling the venue in Phoenix, Arizona, to capacity. Trump claimed there were fifteen thousand at the event but officials 'don't want to admit' to it.[32] He knew exactly how to play his fans, and, as former Republican presidential candidate John McCain had put it, 'fired up the crazies'.[33] Racism generally did it: a rant about Mexicans always hit the spot.[34] Sometimes, like tonight, he got the chance to let them put some of it into practice; when black activist Mercutio Southall Jr started chanting 'Black lives matter!' in the middle of Trump's speech, the audience turned on him and started kicking and punching him as Trump shouted his approval from the podium: 'Get him out of here. Throw him out!'[35] 'Maybe he should have been roughed up, because it was absolutely disgusting what he was doing,' shrugged the future president on Fox News the following Sunday morning. 'I have a lot of fans, and they were not happy about it. And this was a very obnoxious guy who was a trouble-maker who was looking to make trouble.'[36]

Now it was the turn of the Muslims. The previous week he had linked recent terrorist attacks in Paris with President Barack Obama's plan to accept refugees from the Syrian civil war, telling a crowd in Texas, 'You'd have to be insane.'[37] Now he was telling them the bad guys were already in the US. The native New Yorker informed his Southern audience that he had personally witnessed 'thousands and thousands' of people in neighbouring New Jersey – a state with one of the biggest Muslim populations in the country – 'cheering' as they watched the World Trade Center towers collapse on 9/11.[38]

It was a baseless fiction that had been circulating online ever since that devastating day. George Stephanopoulos, who interviewed Trump on ABC News's Sunday morning programme *This Week*, told him so. 'You know, the police say that didn't happen and all those rumors have been on the Internet for some time. So did you misspeak yesterday?'

'It did happen. I saw it,' was Trump's blunt reply.

STEPHANOPOULOS: You saw that –
TRUMP: It was on television. I saw it. It did happen.
STEPHANOPOULOS: – with your own eyes?
TRUMP: George, it did happen.
STEPHANOPOULOS: Police say it didn't happen.
TRUMP: There were people that were cheering on the other side of New Jersey, where you have large Arab populations. They were cheering as the World Trade Center came down. I know it might not be politically correct for you to talk about it, but there were people cheering.... It was well covered at the time, George. Now I know they don't like to talk about it, but it was well covered at the time.[39]

Refuting Trump's lies is like nailing down jelly, but the *Washington Post*, whose 'Fact Checker' feature had been working overtime since Trump put himself forward as a Republican candidate, had a go. 'Extensive examination of news clips from that period turns up nothing,' said the paper, which has been one of the most respected investigative outlets in the world since it broke open the Watergate story in 1972, and one of the best resourced since Amazon billionaire Jeff Bezos bought it in 2013. They found that a local paper, the Newark *Star-Ledger*, had shot down the story as early as 18 September 2001, when it reported that 'rumours of rooftop celebrations of the attacks by Muslims here proved unfounded.'[40] Now the New Jersey Police Commissioner confirmed to the *Post*, who recorded his words in their own inimitable house style: 'That is totally false. That is patently false. That never happened. There were no flags burning, no one was dancing. That is [barnyard epithet].'[41] The New Jersey attorney general at the time of the attacks recalled investigating the 'disturbing' report. 'We followed up on that report instantly because of the implications if true. The word came back quickly from Jersey City, later from Paterson. False report. Never happened.'[42]

All that existed to support Trump's contention was a line from in the *Washington Post* itself, from an article written by Serge F. Kovaleski and Fredrick Kunkle: 'In Jersey City, within hours of two jetliners' plowing into the World Trade Center, law enforcement authorities detained and questioned a number of people who were allegedly seen celebrating the attacks and holding tailgate-style parties on rooftops while they watched the devastation on the other side of the river.'[43] Their story appeared seven days after the attacks, on the same day the *Star-Ledger* reported the allegations were unfounded. Now Kunkle explained their reporting: 'I specifically visited the Jersey City building and neighbourhood where the celebrations were purported to have happened. But I could never verify that report.'[44] Kovaleski told the *Post*'s Fact Checker: 'I certainly do not remember anyone saying that thousands or even hundreds of people were celebrating. That was not the case, as best as I can remember.'[45] Let alone the 'thousands and thousands' witnessed by Trump.[46]

A few weeks later defenders of the presidential candidate gleefully uncovered a local TV news report from 16 September 2001 that suggested people in a Jersey City neighbourhood had witnessed 'eight men celebrating' on a rooftop. Breitbart, the batshit-crazy rightwing website from which Trump would later recruit his chief strategist, Steve Bannon, ran the fourteen-year-old video clip under the headline 'TRUMP 100% VINDICATED'.[47] Eight men versus 'thousands and thousands': you do the math. The journalist who originally presented the story, Pablo Guzmán, felt moved to point out: 'The report never said thousands cheering on roofs.'[48]

But by then Trump himself had gone on the attack against those who dared to dispute his self-dictated version of reality. At a rally in South Carolina on 24 November, he told the crowd that he had had 'phone calls in my office by the hundreds' from people who also watched those New Jersey celebrations.[49] (Given the way he counts, it might just have been one, possibly the same 'extremely credible source' he claimed in August 2012 'called my office and told me that Barack Obama's birth certificate is a fraud'.[50]) Then, waving a copy of Kunkle and Kovaleski's fourteen-year-old report, he announced that it had been 'written by a nice reporter, now the poor guy, you've got to see this guy, "Uuh, I don't know what I said. Uuh, I don't remember." He's going like "I don't remember, uuh, maybe that's what I said."'[51] As he reeled off these made-up quotes, the man asking to be elected the so-called leader of the free world performed an impression every primary-school child would recognize: he stuck out his chin, opened his mouth wide and flapped his forearms around with the elbows tightly tucked in to his body. It was a universal, and universally offensive, signifier of a disabled person. And Serge Kovaleski has arthrogryposis, which causes congenital joint contractures that limit the movement of his arms and force him to hold the right one in a position very reminiscent of the one Trump had mimicked on stage.[52] It didn't appear to be a coincidence. Kovaleski later said: 'Donald and I were on a first-name basis for years. I've interviewed him in his office, I've talked to him at press conferences.'[53]

Even if we give Trump the benefit of the doubt he doesn't deserve and suppose that he really did 'have no idea who this reporter is… what he looks like', would you not be so devastated that you would immediately issue a grovelling apology and try to organize one of those contrite visits Gordon Brown was always having to do when he inadvertently offended people? Not the Donald. As ever, he doubled down. He added insult to injury in his denial – 'I have no idea who… Serge Kovalski [sic] is, what he looks like or his level of intelligence.' He used the opportunity to boast about himself: 'Despite having one of the all-time great memories, I certainly do not remember him.'[54] And when the furore refused to die down within the space of a day, he issued a second statement: 'Serge Kovaleski must think a lot of himself if he thinks I remember him from decades ago – if I ever met him at all, which I doubt I did. He should stop using his disability to grandstand'.[55]

Did his supporters believe his explanation that he 'merely mimicked what I thought would be a flustered reporter trying to get out of a statement he made long ago'?[56] Did they believe anything he said? Did it matter, when he could just call anyone who posed awkward queries about the fantasy world he was creating around himself 'fake news' and refuse to even listen to their questions, let alone answer?

Five months after he was elected as US president – in what he claimed was 'the biggest electoral college win since Ronald Reagan',[57] but was actually a smaller margin than those of George H. W. Bush in 1988, Bill Clinton in 1992 and 1996, and Barack Obama in 2008 and 2012 – Donald Trump gave an interview to *Time* magazine which was specifically focused on his relationship with truth. Like Humpty Dumpty's words, it appeared to mean 'just what I choose it to mean – neither more nor less'. The president refused to concede that he had ever said, could ever say, anything that turned out to be wrong, because 'I'm an instinctual person. I tend to be right.' One example that the interviewer threw back at him, seventeen months after the fact, was the tale of the celebrating Muslims on 9/11. 'Look at the reporter,' Trump shrugged. 'Well if you look at the reporter, he wrote the story in the *Washington Post*.'[58]

'Some things you won't hear on the BBC and MSM'

@JeremyCorbyn4PM, Twitter, 7 May 2016

Two days after Labour had become the first opposition party since 1985 to lose seats in local elections and fall behind the Conservatives in the Scottish Parliament, a Twitter account called JeremyCorbyn4PM – not an official one, but one of the most fervid fan accounts that had sprouted around the veteran leftie ahead of his surprise victory in the leadership election the year before – posted something rather striking. 'Some things you won't hear on the BBC and MSM,' ran the Tweet, using the derisive acronym for the 'mainstream' media. 'Labour is the most popular party and @jeremycorbyn has a huge mandate'.[59] The accompanying graphic – a Photoshop job that must have taken someone a bit of time to put together – offered evidence for both these claims: Labour leading the projected national share of the vote on election night with 31 per cent, and a list of the results in the leadership contest which showed him trouncing his rivals, Andy Burnham, Yvette Cooper and Liz Kendall.

There was just one problem, which was swiftly highlighted by other Twitter users, including Huw Edwards, presenter of the *BBC News at Ten*. Both images, as was obvious from the branding and the presence (in one of them) of swingometer-botherer Jeremy Vine, were taken from coverage on the BBC.

It was far from the only example. A few months later – before realizing it was a pointless task – I found myself taking issue with a much-shared Facebook post on the day of a protest against

Britain taking part in military action on Syria. It showed a sea of protesters streaming past Big Ben, with the accompanying text '2 million on anti-war March today in London. And not mentioned by the BBC.'[60] Even the organizers of the protest, Stop the War, only claimed five thousand people had turned up. The accompanying photo, an aerial shot taken by that most mainstream of media organizations, the photo agency Getty Images, had been taken thirteen years earlier: it showed the crowd at the 2003 march against the Iraq War which may or may not have numbered 2 million. The BBC had posted reporters to the more recent protest throughout the afternoon, delivering frequent pieces to camera for their twenty-four-hour news channel. It had been the lead story – albeit bundled up with details of the divisions in Labour ahead of the parliamentary vote on military action – on that night's *News at Ten*.

Articles on self-appointed 'alternative news' sites regularly cite reports in the *Daily Mail* or Sky News as evidence that the MSM is deliberately neglecting stories. Challenge any of these online truth tellers and you will get the same catch-22 response: they wouldn't know, because they don't look at the mainstream media, because they can't trust it, because it doesn't show these things. Often the exercise reaches its most self-satisfied peaks in the wake of terror attacks on Western countries, when Internet users vocally blame media racism for the fact they couldn't be bothered to read reports about similar incidents in other parts of the world. From here it is a short hop to the right-wing insistence that non-existent issues – sharia law being imposed on Britain, terror attacks in Sweden and American suburbs – are being deliberately hushed up. Of course it might be because the mainstream media have looked into them and found no evidence of anything – but then, they would say that, wouldn't they?

This way, madness lies.

'In the emails, you will read this Comet Ping Pong seems to be a hot-spot, serving as a fundraiser location for both Obama and Hillary Clinton. Why would they choose a pizza joint supposedly kid-friendly with the main attraction being PING PONG TABLES??... at very best, these are very odd, probably Satanic people. At worst, they are part of a massive pedophile and human trafficking ring that involves some of the world's most powerful people.'

Anonymous, blog devoted to 'Pizzagate', 7 November 2016

Delusions are catching. When the man who would be president lives in a fantasy world of his own creation, why should his followers do anything else?

In November 2016, just days before the US election, a very peculiar story seeded itself in a fertile corner of the Internet and began to spread. It stated that Democratic presidential candidate Hillary Clinton was somehow involved in a child-trafficking paedophile ring that centred on an impractically public venue: a pizza restaurant in Washington DC.

The story was ingeniously crafted. There were elements of reality in the recipe – dubious info-dumpers WikiLeaks, almost certainly with the help of Russian forces determined to disrupt the election, *had* recently posted a number of Clinton campaign chief John

Podesta's personal emails online, including ones to a man called James Alefantis discussing having a fundraising event for Clinton at the restaurant he owned, Comet Ping Pong. Alefantis had once been romantically involved with another prominent Clinton campaigner, David Brock. From there, it leapfrogged off into the craziest corners of conspiracy theory. The 'evidence' included the restaurant's menu and signs for many neighbouring businesses, which, they said, contained 'pedophilic symbols' reminiscent of those generally – and barmily – credited to the so-called Illuminati. Characters who regularly featured in such paranoid fantasies, ranging from the Rothschild family to Lady Gaga, Beyoncé and Jay Z, were present and correct around the edges of this one too. 'I am honestly horribly frightened at what we've uncovered,' one of the posters wrote, 'and I fear for the life of those who try to expose it, including my own.'[61]

'Theory' would be a generous title for what it all amounted to: random emails and images torn out of context and generously doused with supposition and some warped mischief. It all swirled around web communities 4chan and Reddit, specifically a Reddit subforum of Trump supporters called 'r/The_Donald'. Chants of 'Lock her up!' had become a staple of Trump rallies, and those with the loudest voices were quite happy to believe Hillary was guilty of any crime you could come up with. Those who had detested the Clintons ever since the Ken Starr days had long been convinced the couple were capable of any and every debauchery. Even the charitable work of the Clinton Foundation in countries such as Haiti had been recast as something considerably more sinister. 'Is it a coincidence Clinton Foundation only works in countries that do not issue birth certificates?' demanded one foaming propagator of the Pizzagate meme.[62]

And so the story bloomed and sent out shoots through a gamut of online forums, Facebook pages and fake news sites. Alefantis's social media pages and those of anyone associated with him – even if they had simply 'liked' his business's Facebook page – were mined for suspicious material. Any photograph featuring a child was held up as evidence of nefariousness; customers who posted innocent family snaps found those photos reproduced across the Internet with their own children identified as the victims of the supposed paedophile ring. One photo circulated on Twitter of what was supposedly an 'Enormous refrigerated room under Comet Ping Pong' with the hashtag #Killroom. In vain did Alefantis protest that his restaurant didn't even have a basement.

'Everyone associated with the business is making semi-overt, semi-tongue-in-cheek, and semi-sarcastic inferences towards sex with minors,' claimed one fervent believer. Before long, in a perfect example of people searching for deeper meanings where the most obvious ones would do, it was determined that whenever anyone connected to the pizza restaurant used the word 'pizza', they were actually using a code word for children trafficked for sex – as opposed to, you know, pizza.[63] By the end of November, Alefantis and his staff were receiving so much abuse online and in phone calls and text messages that he hired security to protect his business. The police in DC were detailed to keep an eye on his restaurant.[64]

Enter Alex Jones, the bloviating broadcaster behind the Infowars website, which transformed conspiracy theorizing into a quite lucrative business. Jones, who sometimes stripped down to his XXL waist to deliver his wide-eyed right-wing rants to camera, had previously claimed that both the 9/11 attacks and the mass murder of elementary-school students in Sandy Hook, Connecticut, in 2012 were faked, inspiring his online supporters to shower hate mail down on the grieving relatives of their victims.[65] But he is not some fringe character: his website gets around 3.9 million monthly views and his five-days-a-week radio programme is syndicated to more than one hundred stations across the US.[66] In 2015 he had been given a huge credibility boost when Donald Trump himself appeared on his programme and told him: 'Your reputation is amazing. I will not let you down.'[67] And Jones did not let Trump down either. Just ahead of polling day he informed his followers that 'Hillary Clinton's ties to satanic rituals and the occult have been well-documented for decades', that she had been a regular attendee at a 'witch's church' during her husband's presidency and that 'many FBI agents consider Clinton to be "the Antichrist personified."'[68]

On 27 November Jones waded into the restaurant business. 'Pizzagate is real,' he barked on his show. 'The question is: How real is it? What is it? Something's going on. Something's being covered up. It needs to be investigated…. You have to investigate it for yourself.'[69]

One self-confessed listener did exactly as he was told. On 4 December Edgar Welch, a twenty-eight-year-old father of two, drove 350 miles from his home in North Carolina to take a 'closer look' at the place he had read and heard so much about, in the hope that he would be able to 'shine some light on it'.[70] According to court documents, he decided somewhere along the way that he had a duty to rescue the children he was convinced were being held captive in the restaurant. In texts he sent to a friend, Welch said he was 'raiding a pedo ring, possibly sacraficing [sic] the lives of a few for the lives of many. Standing up against a corrupt system that kidnaps, tortures and rapes babies and children in our own back yard.'[71]

He walked into Comet Ping Pong carrying an assault rifle and a handgun. Terrified customers – including a number of families with children – fled the building. Welch fired three shots, but surrendered to police when, in his own words, he had convinced himself that there was no evidence 'children were being harbored in the restaurant'. He would later plead guilty to assault with a dangerous weapon and interstate transport of a firearm. The police report on his arrest made it clear that he had been following up nothing more than a 'fictitious online conspiracy theory'.[72]

Alex Jones finally admitted the same in March 2017, issuing an apology to the beleaguered restaurant owner and admitting: 'To my knowledge today, neither Mr. Alefantis, nor his restaurant Comet Ping Pong, were involved in any human trafficking…. I want our viewers and listeners to know that we regret any negative impact our commentaries may have had… we hope that anyone else involved in commenting on Pizzagate will do the same thing.'[73] The following month, as part of a custody battle with his wife Kelly, Jones's lawyers told a court in Texas he hadn't really believed any of the ideas he had been aggressively pushing on his audience over the previous twenty years: 'He's playing a character. He is a performance artist.'[74]

But the story will not die. At its height in November 2016, bewildered staff at Comet Ping Pong counted five Twitter posts per minute with the hashtag '#pizzagate'.[75] In May 2017, they were still running at twelve per hour – and that is just counting the ones from people pushing the conspiracy, not the few pointing out it has long since been thoroughly debunked.[76]

When no one believes anything any more, this is where we end up.

CONCLUSION

So what do we do? How can we stop politicians from lying? And how can we convince ourselves to start believing them again when they actually are telling the truth?

A few simple measures would at a stroke remove at least some of the motivations for dishonesty. Encouraging more independent candidates into politics at all levels would do away with the deadening disciplinary pressure to stick to a party line you might not believe in; it would also reward the public with more candidates with experience of the real world, as opposed to the current uninspiring crop of PPE-degree-and-four-years-as-a-special-adviser fodder who dominate both sides of the House. Not only might independent MPs have something useful to say, but with less to lose career-wise, they would feel more free to say it. Fat chance, though. The party system is horribly, deeply entrenched. As one example, in 2012 a new layer of bureaucracy was created in the form of police and crime commissioners to oversee forces throughout England and Wales. No one really wanted them, but the coalition government claimed we did, and there is no reason on earth for such posts to be party-political. But of the forty candidates elected to the posts in 2016, all but three were representatives of Labour, the Conservatives or (in Wales) Plaid Cymru.

Okay, then, there must be other practical measures we could take. Doing away with the system of political donations would remove all possibility of wealthy individuals purchasing either policy or peerages – say, instead, every party was allotted a pound of public money per vote, according to their share of the ballot at the most recent general election. Relative to other public spending commitments, the bill would be tiny, and it would ensure that everyone would compete on, if not quite a level playing field, at least a terrain that was determined by the voters. It would also ensure that those of us voting un-tactically in constituencies where our chosen party stands no chance of winning still get to award them some tangible benefit. While we're at it, can we flush out the House of Lords every five years and fill its benches with party peers elected according to the share of the vote, as opposed to the first-past-the-post system of the Commons? This would at least partially redress patently unfair situations like UKIP bagging 12.6 per cent of the vote in 2015 and getting just one elected representative in return. There wouldn't even be any need for the current crop of peers to give up their jobs: they could put themselves forward again on an 'additional member' system like those in the Scottish Parliament and Welsh and London assemblies.

Naturally, these sort of measures are so straightforward and fair no government would ever dare try to push them through, for fear of disadvantaging themselves. Although obviously, they would lie and say that wasn't the reason.

None of these measures would directly address the non-party financial motivations for lying, however. Here, sunlight is the best disinfectant, as the hygienically inaccurate saying goes.

The new rules for registering MPs' financial interests brought in by the parliamentary authorities in 2009, which did away with such meaningless declaration brackets as 'up to £5,000', were a big step in the right direction, but they should be extended yet further. Why should we be allowed to know that Boris Johnson earned £22,916.66 for ten hours' work writing his columns for the *Daily Telegraph* in May 2015, but only that Baron (John) Prescott of Kingston upon Hull receives an unspecified 'fee' for his ones in the *Sunday Mirror*?[1] Why, too, should openness not be extended to the people who really run the country, the senior civil servants, who are regularly flattered with freebies and smooched with sinecures – or at least the possibility of future ones – by the very firms to whom they award vast and remunerative public sector contracts? Journalists, and indeed proper human beings, are currently expected to jump through the multiple hoops erected by (and, more pertinently, despite of) the Freedom of Information Act in order to find out such things. Extending and strengthening its strictures would, if nothing else, serve the purpose of really annoying Tony Blair, who declared that this particular legislation was 'utterly undermining of sensible government' and called himself a 'naïve, foolish, irresponsible nincompoop' for introducing it.[2]

Oh dear, we're not doing very well, are we? You will further note that the most recently elected President of the United States, where they have traditionally tended to be rather better at this openness thing than we are, is the first inhabitant of the White House since Richard Nixon not to release his tax returns or tax data.[3]

Well, let's look on one bright side. We probably can't solve the psychological problems of either the compulsive risk-takers or the wannabe Messiahs, representatives of whom we have met in these pages, but at least they may no longer feel forced to lie about who they choose to lie down with any more. The prudery that compelled politicians to disguise their sex lives seems to have all but faded away. Public morals have shifted so far that between 1997 and 2017 we went from a general election campaign where an official Conservative candidate felt free to describe his gay opponent as 'Bent Ben' (and claim that he followed a 'sterile, disease-ridden, God-forsaken occupation') to one where both major party leaders, who were openly Christian, felt duty-bound to declare they didn't consider gay sex a sin before even getting properly on the stump.[4]

If we hope to change anything perhaps we have to start with ourselves. An awful lot of the fault for the current state of affairs lies with the voters, and our determination to assume the worst of those who put themselves forward for office, and as the last chapter showed, too many of us are willingly putting our critical faculties into cold storage. The much-vaunted democratization the Internet was supposed to create has in practice created a level playing field on which the BBC and *Washington Post* compete with professional lobbying groups, political parties both mainstream and extreme, the propaganda wing of the Russian government and whatever your racist cousin got cross about most recently. Each source assumes an equal authority as you scroll infinitely past them on your Facebook feed. It is not so much that everything has been elevated to paper-of-record status, as that everything has been lowered to the twenty-first-century equivalent of you'll-never-guess-what-a-bloke-in-the-pub-just-told-me.

What we choose to take in appeals to our natural desire to believe the worst, and by doing so proclaim ourselves the best. In 2005 the American satirist Stephen Colbert coined the word 'truthiness' for the sort of things that *feel* right on a gut level – the sort of things that people *want* to believe. He was using the term to describe the way Bush and Blair approached the Iraq War, but it applies equally to nearly every 'fact' that was swallowed during the EU referendum campaign. And it applies to nearly every click and swipe of approval on whatever anonymous meme is doing the rounds today. Since the beginning of 2017, there has been growing consternation about the activities of a company called Cambridge Analytica and its role exploiting data on behalf of both the Brexit and Trump electoral campaigns. Those fretting the loudest about the topic push up its prominence by sharing articles about it online.[5] We can't really campaign about the nefarious actions of Russian hackers or sinister firms disseminating disinformation on the Internet when we ourselves are providing the means for their activities.

Look, I know I'm as guilty as anyone. In my darker moments I describe my job as 'professional cynic', and what have I been doing for the past three-hundred pages but been hammering home the message that many, though not all, politicians are appalling charlatans? But then again, you've been reading it, and at least I was willing to show my workings.

Asking a question is always more worthwhile than just emitting a snort of disbelief. (It probably exercises more facial muscles too, and it's definitely better for the brain.) When the leader of the free world behaves like a spoilt toddler, the best thing we might do is follow the same path, and keep on incessantly asking our elders: 'But why? But why? But why?'

ACKNOWLEDGEMENTS

Thank you to Mike Harpley at Atlantic Books who, four days after the EU referendum, invited me to his office to listen patiently as I rambled about politics, the media and the general state of the world for longer than was really necessary, then quietly suggested a much better idea for a book. Thanks to my agent, David Smith, for helping me tease that idea out into a real plan. And thanks, too, to the friends and colleagues who have helped nurture that plan into the book you're holding: Richard Brooks, Adam Curtis, Tristan Davies, Veneta Hooper, Jane Mackenzie, Patrick Maguire, Heather Mills, Sarah Shannon, Emily Travis, Imogen Wall, Francis Wheen and Camilla Wright. Michael Tierney kept me going, sane and fed throughout the writing process.

Robin Dennis, my editor, helped reshape and refine the material into a much better form. She helped me see the woods at a point where I was scraping my nose right up against the bark of the trees. Nearly everyone I talked to during the writing process made the same joke, that a book about political liars would be the longest one ever written; less amusingly, the version that went to Robin nearly was, and she showed great expertise and patience in whittling it down to more manageable proportions. Man, you should see the ones that got away.

Thanks too to Theresa May for finding out when my deadline for handing in the finished manuscript was and then choosing *the very next morning* to call a general election. Very funny. You got me. Although not, it turns out, as badly as you got yourself.

I have drawn on the hard work of many other journalists and authors for this book. The endnotes make that obvious, but there are several particular giants on whose shoulders I am not so much standing but crowd-surfing: Michael Bloch, Tom Bower, Michael Crick, Nick Jones, David Leigh, Ben Macintyre, Kevin Maguire, Charles Moore, Peter Oborne, Matthew Parris, Sonia Purnell, Andrew Rawnsley and Tim Shipman.

The errors, omissions and errant opinions I added all by myself.

NOTES

Introduction

1. Foges, Clare, 'Foxhunting Carries a Toxic Scent for the Tories', *The Times*, 15 May 2017, https://www.thetimes.co.uk/article/foxhunting-carries-a-toxic-scent-for-the-tories-3hgqwqq7l
2. UN Security Council Resolution 1441, http://www.un.org/Depts/unmovic/documents/1441.pdf
3. Blair, Tony, *A Journey: My Political Life*, London, Penguin, 2011, p607
4. Ipsos MORI, 'Veracity Index 2016', 4 December 2016, https://www.ipsos.com/ipsos-mori/en-uk/enough-experts-ipsos-mori-veracity-index-2016
5. 'Labour Calls to Curb John Whittingdale's Powers After Escort Relationship', BBC News, 13 April 2016, http://www.bbc.co.uk/news/uk-politics-36031743
6. Taher, Abul, and Nick Craven, 'MPs' Porn Star Lover "Shown Cabinet Papers": John Whittingdale in New Sex Scandal as Second Lover Reveals Affair', *Mail on Sunday*, 16 April 2016, http://www.dailymail.co.uk/news/article-3543701/MP-s-porn-star-lover-shown-Cabinet-papers-John-Whittingdale-new-sex-scandal-SECOND-lover-reveals-affair.html

1. Out of Deference

1. Conservative Party Television Election Broadcast, BBC, 16 October 1951, video available at http://blogs.bl.uk/thenewsroom/2014/07/why-is-this-lying-bastard-lying-to-me.html
2. Colville, John, diary entry, 23 May 1952, quoted in Martin Gilbert, *Winston S. Churchill: Never Despair: 1945–1965*, London, William Heinemann, 1988, p731
3. Gilbert, p846
4. Ibid., p846
5. Lord Moran, *Winston Churchill: The Struggle for Survival 1940–1965*, London, Constable, 1966, p408
6. Ibid., p406
7. Gilbert, p847
8. Moran, p409
9. Gilbert, p850
10. Ibid.
11. Ibid., p851
12. Moran, p410

13. Quoted in Kynaston, David, *Family Britain: 1951–57*, London, Bloomsbury, 2009, p314

14. Colville, John, *The Fringes of Power: Downing Street Diaries, 1939–55*, London, Hodder, 1985, p669

15. Gilbert, p854

16. Ibid.

17. Ibid., p858

18. Jenkins, Roy, *Churchill*, London, Pan, 2002, p866

19. Quoted in Kynaston, p315

20. Gilbert, p857

21. Philby, Kim, *My Silent War*, London, Panther, 1969, p171

22. Macintyre, Ben, *A Spy Among Friends: Kim Philby and the Great Betrayal*, London, Bloomsbury, 2014, p150

23. Quoted in ibid., p154

24. Philby, p176

25. Macintyre, p161

26. Ibid., p158

27. Ibid., p20

28. Quoted in ibid., p100

29. Quoted in ibid., p138

30. Ibid., p164

31. Quoted in ibid., p183

32. Hansard, HC (series 5) vol 545, col 29, 25 October 1955, http://hansard. millbanksystems.com/volumes/5C/545

33. Hennessy, Peter, *Having It So Good: Britain in the Fifties*, London, Allen Lane, 2006, p315

34. Quoted in Macintyre, p188

35. Hansard, HC (series 5) vol 545, col 1497, 7 November 1955

36. Hansard, HC (series 5) vol 545, col 1549, 7 November 1955

37. 'Colonel Lipton Withdraws', *The Times*, 11 November 1955, quoted in Macintyre, p192

38. Macintyre, p191

39. Lownie, Andrew, *Stalin's Englishman: The Lives of Guy Burgess*, London, Hodder & Stoughton, 2016, p274

40. Macintyre, p255

41. Page, Bruce, David Leitch and Phillip Knightley, *The Philby Conspiracy*, London, Doubleday, 1968, p49

42. Eden, Anthony, Broadcast to the Nation, BBC, 8 August 1956; Gorst, Anthony, and Lewis Johnman, *The Suez Crisis*, Abingdon, Routledge, 2013, p69

43. Hennessy, p426

44. Hall, Simon, *1956: The World in Revolt*, New York, Pegasus, 2016, p263

45. *Voice of the Arabs*, Cairo Radio, 16 May 1967, quoted in Laqueur, Walter, *The Road to War*, London, Pelican, 1969, p82

46. Text as reproduced in Avi Shlaim, 'The Protocol of Sèvres, 1956: Anatomy of a War Plot', *International Affairs*, vol 73 no 3, July 1997, pp509–30

47. Hansard, HC (series 5) vol 558, col 1631, 1 November 1956, http://hansard. millbanksystems.com/volumes/5C/558

48. Hansard, HC (series 5) vol 558, col 1648, 1 November 1956

49. Beckett, Francis, and Tony Russell, *1956: The Year That Changed Britain*, London, Biteback, 2015, e3242

50. Boyle, Peter G., (ed), *The Eden–Eisenhower Correspondence, 1955–1957*, Chapel Hill, University of North Carolina Press, 2006, p157

51. Beckett and Russell, e22676

52. Kyle, Keith, *Suez: Britain's End of Empire in the Middle East*, London, I. B. Tauris, 2011, p457

53. Thorpe, D. R., *Supermac: The Life of Harold Macmillan*, London, Pimlico, 2011, p364

54. The quote at the start of the chapter in Hansard, HC (series 5) vol 562, col 1518, 20 December 1956, http:// hansard.millbanksystems.com/volumes /5C/562

2. Sex Lies

1. '"It's Such a Shock… But Men Think They Can Get Away with It These Days" – Mother-in-Law Georgina', *Mirror*, 26 October 2006, http://www.mirror.co.uk/news/uk-news/its-such-a-shock-but-men-think-they-can-703908

2. Thurlbeck, Neville, 'Lib-Dem Oaten's 3-in-Bed Rent Boy Shame', *News of the World*, 22 January 2006

3. Hansard, HC (series 5), vol 674, col 809–10, 22 March 1963, http://hansard.millbanksystems.com/volumes/5C/674

4. Keeler, Christine, with Sandy Fawkes, *Nothing But…*, London, New English Library, 1983, p15

5. Ibid., pp62–4

6. Ibid., pp65–6

7. Ibid., p68

8. Ibid.

9. Ibid., p71

10. Ibid., pp73–4

11. Davenport-Hines, Richard, *An English Affair: Sex, Class and Power in the Age of Profumo*, London, HarperPress, 2013, p275

12. Ibid., p277

13. Parris, Matthew, and Kevin Maguire, *Great Parliamentary Scandals: Five Centuries of Calumny, Smear and Innuendo*, London, Chrysalis, 2004, p152

14. Davenport-Hines, p291

15. Leader, 'It *Is* a Moral Issue', *The Times*, 11 June 1963, quoted in ibid., p296

16. Muggeridge, Malcolm, 'The Slow, Sure Death of the Upper Classes', *Sunday Mirror*, 23 June 1963, quoted in ibid., p308

17. Hansard, HC (series 5) vol 679, col 35, 17 June 1963, http://hansard.millbanksystems.com/volumes/5C/679

18. Macqueen, Adam, *The Prime Minister's Ironing Board and Other State Secrets: True Stories from the Government Archives*, London, Little, Brown, 2013, p172

19. Keeler and Fawkes, p153

20. Keays, Sara, *A Question of Judgement*, London, Quintessential Press, 1985, p33

21. 'Lord Parkinson: Obituary', *Telegraph*, 25 January 2016, http://www.telegraph.co.uk/news/obituaries/12120308/Lord-Parkinson-obituary.html

22. Keays, p14

23. Ibid., p17

24. Ibid., p20

25. Ibid., p19

26. Ibid., p22

27. Ibid., p41

28. Ibid., p43

29. Ibid.

30. Ibid., p44

31. Ibid., p47

32. Moore, Charles, *Margaret Thatcher: The Authorized Biography, Volume 2: Everything She Wants*, London, Penguin, 2016, p62

33. Quoted in Parris and Maguire, p252

34. Keays, p55

35. Ibid., p51

36. Ibid., p57

37. Ibid., p70

38. 'Parkinson Admits Love Affair', *The Times*, 6 October 1983

39. Ibid.

40. Keays, p156

41. Moore, p89

42. Craig, Olga, 'The Only Promise Cecil Parkinson Ever Kept – Never to See His Daughter', *Telegraph*, 6 January 2002, http://www.telegraph.co.uk/news/politics/conservative/12120477/The-only-promise-Cecil-Parkinson-ever-kept-never-to-see-his-daughter.html

43. 'Lord Parkinson: Obituary', *Telegraph*

44. Sanderson, Daniel, '"Shut up! You Stupid, Smelly Little Git!": Listen to Tory Bigwig David Mellor's F-Word Rant at Black Cab Driver', *The Sun*, 25 November 2014, https://www.thesun.co.uk/archives/news/546071/shut-up-you-stupid-sweaty-little-git

45. Durham, Michael, 'Mellor's Wife Pleads for Truce in Public Row', *Independent*, 22 July 1992, http://www.independent.co.uk/news/uk/mellors-wife-pleads-for-truce-in-public-row-1534910.html

46. Merrin, Tom, 'Well We All Get Our Just Deserts', *Daily Mirror*, 25 September 1992

47. Vallely, Paul, 'Politics Is Not for Children', *Independent*, 7 February 1999, http://www.independent.co.uk/life-style/focus-politics-is-not-for-children-1069382.html

48. Timmins, Nicholas, 'Mellor Visits Wife's Parents as Major Repeats Support', *Independent*, 24 July 1992, http://www.independent.co.uk/news/uk/mellor-visits-wifes-parents-as-major-repeats-support-1535235.html

49. Boggan, Steve, 'Mellor Rides Out Storm as Press Bickers', *Independent*, 26 July 1992, http://www.independent.co.uk/news/mellor-rides-out-storm-as-press-bickers-1535874.html

50. Reid, Sue, 'Absolutely Nothing Attracted Me to Him Physically, but I Did Love Him: Antonia de Sancha Insists She Has No Regrets About the Affair That Ruined David Mellor's Marriage and Career', *Mail on Sunday*, 1 February 2013, http://www.dailymail.co.uk/news/article-2272170/Antonia-Sancha-Has-regrets-affair-David-Mellor.html

51. Clifford, Max, and Angela Levin, *Max Clifford: Read All About It*, London, Virgin Books, 2005, p117

52. Langdon, Julia, 'Antonia Goes Back to Basics', *Guardian*, 19 February 1994

53. Reid, 'Absolutely Nothing Attracted Me to Him Physically'

54. Langdon, 'Antonia Goes Back to Basics'

55. Chittenden, Maurice, 'Revealed: Chinks in Stories that Pillory Mellor', *Sunday Times*, 13 September 1992

56. Evans, Richard, 'Mellor Lambasts Popular Press for Morbid Intrusion', *The Times*, 22 December 1989; Greenslade, Roy, 'A Decade of Diplomacy', *Guardian*, 5 February 2001, https://www.theguardian.com/media/2001/feb/05/mondaymediasection.pressandpublishing

57. Fallon, Ivan, 'Scandal: The Mellor Affair', *Sunday Times*, 26 July 1992

58. Evans, Richard, 'Watchdog Gives Tacit Support to Press Coverage of Mellor', *Financial Times*, 23 July 1992

59. Fallon, 'Scandal: The Mellor Affair'

60. Dawnay, Ivo, 'Mellor Weathers Deluge of Media Criticism', *Financial Times*, 24 July 1992

61. Mellor, David, interview, *Newsnight*, BBC 2, 23 September 1992

62. Dawnay, 'Mellor Weathers Deluge'

63. Clinton, Bill, Address to the Nation on Monica Lewinsky, 17 August 1998, transcript available at http://www.ucl.ac.uk/USHistory/Making/address.htm

64. Noah, Timothy, 'Bill Clinton and the Meaning of "Is"', Slate, 13 September 1998, http://www.slate.com/articles/news_and_politics/chatterbox/1998/09/bill_clinton_and_the_meaning_of_is.html

65. Starr, Kenneth, *Referral from Independent Counsel Kenneth W. Starr in Conformity with the Requirements of Title 28, United States Code, Section 595(c)*, Washington, Government Printing Office, 1998, p16

66. Kuntz, Phil (ed), *The Evidence: The Starr Report*, New York, Simon & Schuster, 2010, p390

67. 'Hillary Clinton Defends Her Husband', BBC News, 27 January 1998, http://news.bbc.co.uk/1/hi/51010.stm

68. 'Clinton Confesses', BBC News, 18 August 1998, http://news.bbc.co.uk/1/hi/world/americas/153099.stm

69. Berlusconi, Silvio, interview with *La Stampa* quoted in Hooper, John, 'Silvio Berlusconi's Office Intervened on Behalf of Teenage Girl Suspected of Theft', *Guardian*, 29 October 2010, https://www.theguardian.com/world/2010/oct/29/silvio-berlusconi-office

70. Hooper, John, 'Silvio Berlusconi Denounces Furore over Links with 17-Year-Old Girl', *Guardian*, 28 October 2010, https://www.theguardian.com/world/2010/oct/28/silvio-berlusconi-denounces-furore

71. Hooper, 'Silvio Berlusconi's Office Intervened'

72. Squires, Nick, 'Silvio Berlusconi Convinced That Ruby the Heart Stealer Was Mubarak's Granddaughter', *Telegraph*, 6 October 2012, http://www.telegraph.co.uk/news/worldnews/silvio-berlusconi/9591504/Silvio-Berlusconi-convinced-that-Ruby-the-Heart-Stealer-was-Mubaraks-granddaughter.html

73. Squires, Nick, 'Silvio Berlusconi in Prostitution Investigation', *Telegraph*, 14 January 2011, http://www.telegraph.co.uk/news/worldnews/europe/italy/8260230/Silvio-Berlusconi-in-prostitution-investigation.html

74. Squires, Nick, 'Nicole Minetti: I Was in Love with Silvio Berlusconi', *Telegraph*, 7 June 2013, http://www.telegraph.co.uk/news/worldnews/silvio-berlusconi/10105702/Nicole-Minetti-I-was-in-love-with-Silvio-Berlusconi.html

75. Dinmore, Guy, 'Berlusconi Resists Calls to Quit over Sex Scandal', *Financial Times*, 2 November 2010, https://www.ft.com/content/c8a4ad18-e6d2-11df-8894-00144feab49a

76. Ibid.

77. 'Berlusconi "Most Persecuted Man"', BBC News, 9 October 2009, http://news.bbc.co.uk/1/hi/world/europe/8300184.stm

78. 'A Step Too Far', *The Economist*, 4 November 2010, http://www.economist.com/node/17417722

79. Mackenzie, James, 'Berlusconi Says Liking Girls "Better than Being Gay"', Reuters, 3 November 2010, http://in.reuters.com/article/idINIndia-52620420101102

80. 'Berlusconi's Wife to Divorce Him', BBC News, 3 May 2009, http://news.bbc.co.uk/1/hi/world/europe/8031520.stm

81. 'Profile: Karima El Mahroug', BBC News, 24 June 2013, http://www.bbc.co.uk/news/mobile/world-europe-12473645

3. Financial Fibbing

1. Madonnell, Hamish, and Michael Savage, 'I'm Not Wealthy Says Corbyn, Despite £138,000 Salary', *The Times*, 27 August 2016, https://www.thetimes.co.uk/article/i-m-not-wealthy-says-corbyn-despite-138-000-salary-t8f8qzxt0

2. 'Pay and Expenses for MPs', UK Parliament, http://www.parliament.

uk/about/mps-and-lords/members/pay-mps; 'Earnings and Working Hours', Office for National Statistics, https://www.ons.gov.uk/employmentandlabourmarket/peopleinwork/earningsandworkinghours

3. 'Mayor's £250,000 Chicken Feed', BBC News, 14 July 2009, http://news.bbc.co.uk/1/hi/england/london/8148899.stm

4. Gillard, Michael, *A Little Pot of Money: The Story of Reginald Maudling and the Real Estate Fund of America*, London, Private Eye, 1974, p31

5. Cameron, Sue, 'Sorry, Old Cock', *Financial Times*, 9 June 2010, http://www.ft.com/cms/s/0/28215d56-735e-11df-ae73-00144feabdc0.html

6. 'Members' Pay and Allowances: A Brief History', UK Parliament, http://researchbriefings.parliament.uk/ResearchBriefing/Summary/SN05075

7. Parris, Matthew, and Kevin Maguire, *Great Parliamentary Scandals: Five Centuries of Calumny, Smear and Innuendo*, London, Chrysalis, 2004, p183

8. Parris and Maguire, p184

9. Ibid.

10. Sandbrook, Dominic, *State of Emergency: The Way We Were: Britain 1970–74*, London, Penguin, 2011, e9833

11. 'Mortgages, Offshore Funds, the Yankees and Prison', *Connersville News Examiner*, 13 January 2016, http://www.newsexaminer.com/news/local/mortgages-offshore-funds-the-yankees-and-prison/article_a077a814-cc4a-5583-94a5-f079bc2277fb.html

12. Parris and Maguire, p185

13. Ibid., p181

14. 'The Tragedy of Maudling', *The Sun*, 19 July 1972, reproduced in Parris and Maguire, p182

15. Sandbrook, e9818

16. Ibid.

17. 'Resolutions of the House Relating to the Conduct of Members', UK Parliament, https://www.publications.parliament.uk/pa/cm201012/cmcode/1885/188508.htm

18. Parris and Maguire, p186

19. Wood, Nicholas, and Andrew Pierce, 'Suspension for Two MPs in Cash Row', *The Times*, 11 July 1994

20. Bower, Tom, *Fayed: The Unauthorized Biography*, London, Macmillan, 1998, p40

21. 'In the Courts: Fayed v. Sanity', *Private Eye*, 16 March 2007

22. Leigh, David, and Ed Vulliamy, *Sleaze: The Corruption of Parliament*, London, Fourth Estate, 1998, p102

23. Ibid., p64

24. 'Al Fayed: A Unique Story of Rags to Riches', BBC News, 12 February 1998, http://news.bbc.co.uk/1/hi/uk/55867.stm

25. Bower, p120

26. Leigh and Vulliamy, p18

27. Ibid., p31

28. 'Ian Greer, Lobbyist: Obituary', *Telegraph*, 17 November 2015, http://www.telegraph.co.uk/news/obituaries/12001034/Ian-Greer-lobbyist-obituary.html

29. Leigh and Vulliamy, p64

30. Ibid., p47

31. Ibid., p136

32. Ibid., p82

33. Ibid., p83

34. Al-Fayed, Mohamed, witness statement, 23 June 1995, as reproduced in House of Commons, *First Report of Committee on Standards and Privileges*, appendix 3, UK Parliament, https://www.publications.parliament.uk/pa/cm199798/cmselect/cmstnprv/030ii/sp0105.htm

35. Parris and Maguire, p359

36. Leigh and Vulliamy, p87

37. Ibid., p89

38. Ibid., p88

39. Cusick, James, 'Mystery Origins of Brothers' Paper Fortunes', *Independent*, 26 October 1994

40. Hansard, HC (series 6), vol 207, col 144W, 13 May 1992, http://hansard. millbanksystems.com/volumes/6C/207

41. Leigh and Vulliamy, p154

42. Ibid., p155–6

43. Hencke, David, 'Tory MPs Were Paid to Plant Questions Says Harrods Chief', *Guardian*, 20 October 1994, https:// www.theguardian.com/politics/1994/ oct/20/conservatives.uk

44. Heseltine, Michael, letter to the Parliamentary Commissioner for Standards, 27 February 1997, reproduced in House of Commons, *First Report of Select Committee on Standards and Privileges*, appendix 92, https://www.publications.parliament. uk/pa/cm199798/cmselect/cmstnprv/ 030ii/sp01132.htm

45. 'Hamilton Loses Libel Case', BBC News, 21 December 1999, http://news.bbc. co.uk/1/hi/uk/573630.stm

46. *Guardian*, letter from the Editor to the Parliamentary Commissioner for Standards, 8 October 1996, reproduced as in *First Report of Select Committee on Standards and Privileges*, appendix 15, https://www.publications.parliament. uk/pa/cm199798/cmselect/cmstnprv/ 030ii/sp0124.htm

47. 'Committee on Standards in Public Life: Terms of Reference', UK Government, https://www.gov.uk/government/ organisations/the-committee-on- standards-in-public-life/about/terms-of- reference

48. Leigh and Vulliamy, p44

49. Ibid., p188

50. Ibid., p248

51. Ibid., p215

52. Ibid., p231

53. Hencke, David, David Leigh and David Pallister, 'A Liar and a Cheat', *Guardian*, 1 October 1996, https:// www.theguardian.com/politics/1996/ oct/01/conservatives.uk

54. Leigh, David, and David Pallister, 'Hamilton Admits: I Took Money', *Guardian*, 2 October 1996, https:// www.theguardian.com/politics/1996/ oct/02/conservatives.uk

55. House of Commons, 'Minutes of Oral Hearings, 20 February 1997', *First Report of Select Committee on Standards and Privileges*, https:// www.publications.parliament.uk/pa/ cm199798/cmselect/cmstnprv/030iii/ sp0101.htmhttps://www.publications. parliament.uk/pa/cm199798/cmselect/ cmstnprv/030iii/sp0141.htm

56. 'Conclusions', *First Report of Select Committee on Standards and Privileges*, https://www.publications. parliament.uk/pa/cm199798/cmselect/ cmstnprv/030i/sp0139.htm

57. 'Judge's Warning over Fayed Evidence', BBC News, 17 December 1999, http:/ /news.bbc.co.uk/1/hi/uk/570618.stm; 'Hamilton Loses Libel Case', BBC News, 21 December 1999, http://news.bbc. co.uk/1/hi/uk/573630.stm

58. *Nine O'Clock News*, BBC 1, 8 April 1997

59. Glaze, Ben, 'Nigel Farage Launches Bid to Block UKIP Rival Neil Hamilton', *Mirror*, 8 February 2016, http://www.mirror.co.uk/news/ uk-news/nigel-farage-launches-bid- block-7334514

60. Hansard, HC (series 6) vol 278, col 95, 21 May 1996, http://hansard.mill banksystems.com/volumes/6C/278

61. Blair, Tony, Speech to Labour Party Conference, Brighton, 30 September

1997, transcript available at British Political Speech Archive, http://www.britishpoliticalspeech.org/speech-archive.htm?speech=203

62. Rawnsley, Andrew, *Servants of the People: The Inside Story of New Labour*, London, Hamish Hamilton, 2000, p94

63. Ibid.

64. Hooper, John, 'David Mills: A Career Punctuated by Several Lapses of Judgement', *Guardian*, 17 February 2009, https://www.theguardian.com/politics/2009/feb/17/david-mills-berlusconi-trial

65. Rentoul, John, *Tony Blair: Prime Minister*, London, Little, Brown, 2001, p366

66. Ibid., p364

67. Quoted in Rawnsley, p92

68. Rentoul, p364

69. Campbell, Alastair, *Power and the People: 1997–1999 – The Alastair Campbell Diaries Volume 2*, London, Hutchinson, 2011, p202

70. Rawnsley, p97

71. Ibid., p91

72. Ibid., p98

73. Ibid., p97

74. Ibid.

75. Campbell, p206

76. Ibid., p205

77. Rawnsley, p101

78. Ibid., p99

79. Ibid., p102

80. *On the Record*, BBC 1, 16 November 1997, transcript available at http://www.bbc.co.uk/otr/intext/Blair16.11.97.html

81. Rentoul, p368

82. Mandelson, Peter, *The Third Man: Life at the Heart of New Labour*, London, HarperCollins, 2011, p243

83. Blair, Tony, interview, *On the Record*, BBC 1, 16 November 1997, transcript available at http://www.bbc.co.uk/otr/intext/Blair16.11.97.html

84. Macintyre, Donald, *Mandelson and the Making of New Labour*, London, HarperCollins, 2000, p488

85. Civil Servants' and MPs' Salaries, House of Commons Library Research Briefing, July 2013, http://researchbriefings.files.parliament.uk/documents/SN06689/SN06689.pdf

86. Mandelson, p269

87. Mandelson, p271

88. Rawnsley, p220

89. Robinson, Geoffrey, *The Unconventional Minister: My Life Inside New Labour*, London, Michael Joseph, 2000, p6

90. Mandelson, p271

91. Rawnsley, p213

92. Mandelson, p273

93. Ibid.

94. 'Declaring an Interest', BBC News, 22 December 1998, http://news.bbc.co.uk/1/hi/uk_politics/240465.stm

95. Mandelson, p273

96. Rawnsley, p223

97. Mandelson, p275

98. Blair, Tony, *A Journey: My Political Life*, London, Penguin, 2011, p220

99. Ibid.

100. Robinson, p11

101. Leader of the Opposition (William Hague), letter to Prime Minister, 23 May 1999, reproduced in Written Evidence from Cabinet Office to Public Administration Committee, 17 March 2010, website of UK Parliament, https://www.publications.parliament.uk/pa/cm200910/cmselect/cmpubadm/470/470we02.htm

102. Savage, Michael, 'Pressure on Hague over His Role in Ashcroft's Peerage', *Independent*, 3 March 2010, http://www.independent.co.uk/news/uk/

politics/pressure-on-hague-over-his-role-in-ashcrofts-peerage-1914998.html

103. Political Honours Scrutiny Committee, letter to Prime Minister, 27 March 2000, reproduced in Written Evidence from Cabinet Office to Public Administration Committee, 17 March 2010

104. Lord Ashcroft, memo to Rt Hon William Hague MP, 23 March 2000, reproduced in Written Evidence from Cabinet Office to Public Administration Committee, 17 March 2010

105. Secretary of the Political Honours Committee (Gay Catto), letter to Sir Hayden Phillips, 9 May 2000, reproduced in Written Evidence from Cabinet Office to Public Administration Committee, 17 March 2010

106. Phillips, Sir Hayden, letter to Rt Hon James Arbuthnot, June 2000, reproduced in Written Evidence from Cabinet Office to Public Administration Committee, 17 March 2010

107. Catto, Gay, letter to Sir Hayden Phillips, 22 June 2000, reproduced in Written Evidence from Cabinet Office to Public Administration Committee, 17 March 2010

108. Phillips, Sir Hayden, letter to Gay Catto, 29 June 2000, reproduced in Written Evidence from Cabinet Office to Public Administration Committee, 17 March 2010

109. Cobain, Ian, 'Ashcroft: New Questions About His Peerage, His Tax and His Home', *Guardian*, 9 November 2007, https://www.theguardian.com/politics/2007/nov/09/uk.conservatives2

110. Ibid.

111. Lord Ashcroft, 'A Broken Promise and Why I Wrote This Book: Lord Ashcroft Reveals How He Went from Supporter to Critic of David Cameron', *Daily Mail*, 20 September 2015, http://www.dailymail.co.uk/news/article-3242581/A-broken-promise-wrote-book-LORD-ASHCROFT-reveals-went-supporter-critic-Cameron.html

112. Roberts, Bob, 'Lord Ashcroft Tax Scandal: The Unpaid £127million', *Mirror*, 2 March 2010, http://www.mirror.co.uk/news/uk-news/lord-ashcroft-tax-scandal-unpaid-204696

113. Stratton, Allegra, and Polly Curtis, 'Hague Only Found Out About Ashcroft Tax Deal a Few Months Ago', *Guardian*, 3 March 2010, https://www.theguardian.com/politics/2010/mar/03/william-hague-lord-ashcroft

114. Arbuthnot, James, letter to Sir Hayden Phillips, 12 July 2000, reproduced in Written Evidence from Cabinet Office to Public Administration Committee, 17 March 2010, https://www.publications.parliament.uk/pa/cm200910/cmselect/cmpubadm/470/470we02.htm

115. 'CPS Decision: "Cash For Honours" Case – Explanatory Document', Crown Prosecution Service, 20 July 2007, http://www.cps.gov.uk/news/latest_news/146_07_document

116. Moore, Charles, *Margaret Thatcher: The Authorized Biography, Volume 2: Everything She Wants*, London, Penguin, 2016, p78

117. Blair, p686

118. 'MPs' "John Lewis List"', BBC News, 13 March 2008, http://news.bbc.co.uk/1/hi/uk_politics/7295150.stm

119. Dawar, Anil, 'MPs Fight to Block Expenses Revelations', *Guardian*, 7 May 2008, https://www.theguardian.com/politics/2008/may/07/houseofcommons

120. Öpik, Lembit, interview, BBC Wales, 13 May 2009; Bell, Sir Stuart, interview, *Newsnight*, BBC 2, 30 March 2009

121. Winnett, Robert, and Gordon Rayner, *No Expenses Spared*, London, Corgi, 2010, e1619

122. Porter, Andrew, 'MPs' Expenses: Ten Worst Moments Caught on Film', *Telegraph*, 3 June 2009, http://www.telegraph.co.uk/news/newstopics/mps-expenses/5436939/Hazel-Blears-avoided-capital-gains-tax-on-two-properties-MPs-expenses.html

123. Winnett and Rayner, e4666

124. Ibid., e1634

125. Hope, Chrisopher, 'Michael Gove "Flipped" Homes', *Telegraph*, 11 May 2009, http://www.telegraph.co.uk/news/newstopics/mps-expenses/5305434/Michael-Gove-flipped-homes-MPs-expenses.html

126. Winnett and Rayner

127. Winnett, Robert, 'Oliver Letwin's Tennis Court Repairs', *Telegraph*, 11 May 2009, http://www.telegraph.co.uk/news/newstopics/mps-expenses/5305385/Oliver-Letwins-tennis-court-repairs-MPs-expenses.html

128. Watt, Holly, 'Alan Duncan Charged £598 for Lawnmower Repairs', *Telegraph*, 5 November 2009, http://www.telegraph.co.uk/news/newstopics/mps-expenses/6508903/MPs-expenses-Alan-Duncan-charged-598-for-lawnmower-repairs.html

129. Rayner, Gordon, 'Sir Gerald Kaufman's £1,800 Rug and an £8,865 Claim for a Television', *Telegraph*, 16 May 2009, http://www.telegraph.co.uk/news/newstopics/mps-expenses/5330816/Sir-Gerald-Kaufmans-1800-rug-and-an-8865-claim-for-a-television-MPs-expenses.html

130. Prince, Rosa, 'Taxpayer Charged for Michael Ancram's Pool', *Telegraph*, 12 May 2009, http://www.telegraph.co.uk/news/newstopics/mps-expenses/5309953/MPs-expenses-Taxpayer-charged-for-Michael-Ancrams-pool.html

131. Hope, Christopher, 'David Davis, the Council Estate Lad Who Claimed £5,700 for a Portico', *Telegraph*, 12 May 2009, http://www.telegraph.co.uk/news/newstopics/mps-expenses/5309646/MPs-expenses-David-Davies-the-council-estate-lad-who-claimed-5700-for-a-portico.html

132. Watt, Holly, 'Taxpayer Picks Up Bill for Sir Michael Spicer's Chandelier', *Telegraph*, 12 May 2009, http://www.telegraph.co.uk/news/newstopics/mps-expenses/5310404/MPs-expenses-Taxpayer-picks-up-bill-for-Sir-Michael-Spicers-chandelier.html

133. Pierce, Andrew, and Chris Irvine, 'Anthony Steen to Stand Down as MP at Next Election', *Telegraph*, 20 May 2009, http://www.telegraph.co.uk/news/newstopics/mps-expenses/5357365/MPs-expenses-Anthony-Steen-to-stand-down-as-MP-at-next-election.html

134. Prince, Rosa, 'Cleaning the Moat at Douglas Hogg's Manor', *Telegraph*, 12 May 2009, http://www.telegraph.co.uk/news/newstopics/mps-expenses/5310069/MPs-expenses-Clearing-the-moat-at-Douglas-Hoggs-manor.html

135. Ibid.

136. Allen, Nick, 'Sir Peter Viggers Claimed for £1,600 Floating Duck Island', *Telegraph*, 21 May 2009, http://www.telegraph.co.uk/news/newstopics/mps-expenses/5357568/MPs-expenses-Sir-Peter-Viggers-claimed-for-1600-floating-duck-island.html

137. Hope, Christopher, and Jon Swaine, 'Sir Nicholas and Ann Winterton to Stand Down from Parliament', *Telegraph*, 15 May 2009, http://www.telegraph.co.uk/news/newstopics/mps-expenses/5326205/Sir-Nicholas-and-Ann-Winterton-to-stand-down-from-parliament-MPs-expenses.html

138. Sparrow, Andrew, 'Derek Conway Apologises for Overpaying Son with Public Money', *Guardian*, 29 January 2009, https://www.theguardian.com/politics/2009/jan/29/derek-conway-fined

139. 'Ex-MP Elliot Morley Jailed for Expenses Fraud', BBC News, 20 May 2011, http://www.bbc.co.uk/news/uk-politics-13467137

140. 'David Chaytor Jailed over False Claims', BBC News, 7 January 2011, http://www.bbc.co.uk/news/uk-politics-12127327

141. 'Fraud MP Margaret Moran Given Supervision Order', BBC News, 14 December 2012, http://www.bbc.co.uk/news/uk-england-beds-bucks-herts-20725315

142. 'Denis MacShane Jailed for MPs' Expenses Fraud', BBC News, 23 December 2013, http://www.bbc.co.uk/news/uk-politics-25492017

143. 'Lord Hanningfield Jailed for Fiddling Expenses', BBC News, 1 July 2011, http://www.bbc.co.uk/news/uk-politics-13989329

144. Boden, Nicola, 'MPs' Expenses Farce: Scathing Report Orders Half of Them to Repay £1.3m but Judge Says "They've Done Nothing Wrong"', *Daily Mail*, 5 February 2010, http://www.dailymail.co.uk/news/article-1248422/Sir-Thomas-Legg-orders-MPs-repay-1-3million-overclaimed-expenses.html

145. Winnett and Rayner, e3826

146. Hinsliff, Gaby, Caroline Davies and Toby Helm, 'The Week Britain Turned Its Anger on Politicians', *Observer*, 17 May 2009, https://www.theguardian.com/politics/2009/may/17/mps-pay-expenses-poll-tax

147. Dorries, Nadine, 'Clarification', The Blog of Nadine Dorries, 21 May 2009, http://blog.dorries.org/id-1387-2009_5_Clarification.aspx

148. Mulholland, Hélène, 'Police Will Not Investigate Leaks to Media', *Guardian*, 19 May 2009, https://www.theguardian.com/global/2009/may/19/expenses-leak-police

149. 'MPs Expenses', Downing Street YouTube Channel, 21 April 2009, https://www.youtube.com/watch?v=sBX-j5l6ShpA

150. 'Brown Apology over MPs' Expenses', BBC News, 11 May 2009, http://news.bbc.co.uk/1/hi/uk_politics/8043447.stm

151. 'Expenses Focus Turns on Tory MPs', BBC News, 11 May 2009, http://news.bbc.co.uk/1/hi/uk_politics/8043057.stm

152. Rayner, Gordon, 'David Cameron Repays £680 Bill for Wisteria Removal', *Telegraph*, 13 May 2009, http://www.telegraph.co.uk/news/newstopics/mps-expenses/5315163/David-Cameron-repays-680-bill-for-wisteria-removal-MPs-expenses.html

4. Gamblers' Conceits

1. Shales, Tom, 'Nixon's Long Look Back', *Washington Post*, 6 April 1984, https://www.washingtonpost.com/archive/lifestyle/1984/04/06/nixons-long-look-back/7f45cc9a-d7d9-4af6-9a7d-923890e357d4

2. Wheen, Francis, *Strange Days Indeed: The Golden Age of Paranoia*, London, Fourth Estate, 2009, p97

3. 'Listen: "Blow the Safe and Get It"', transcript available at University of

Virginia, http://www.upress.virginia.edu
/2014/07/28/listen-blow-safe-and-get-it

4. Wheen, p114

5. Nixon, Richard, news conference,
San Clemente, California, 29 August
1972, transcript available at American
Presidency Project, University of
California Santa Barbara, http://www.
presidency.ucsb.edu/ws/?pid=3548

6. *The Nixon Interviews with David Frost*,
syndicated broadcast, 19 May 1977

7. Wheen, p37

8. 'Transcript of a Recording of a
Meeting Between the President and
H. R. Haldeman in the Oval Office
on June 23, 1972 from 10:04 to 11:39
a.m.', Richard Nixon Presidential
Library, https://www.nixonlibrary.gov
/forresearchers/find/tapes/watergate/
trial/exhibit_01.pdf

9. 'Transcript of a Recording of a Meeting
Among the President, John Dean and
H. R. Haldeman in the Oval Office,
on March 21, 1973, from 10:12 to
11:55 a.m.', Richard Nixon Presidential
Library, https://www.nixonlibrary.gov
/forresearchers/find/tapes/watergate/
trial/exhibit_12.pdf

10. Wheen, p117

11. Bernstein, Carl, and Bob Woodward,
All The President's Men, New York,
Simon and Schuster, 2012, p331

12. Macqueen, Adam, *The Prime Minister's
Ironing Board and Other State Secrets*,
London, Little, Brown, 2013, p149

13. 'Proclamation 4311: Granting Pardon
to Richard Nixon', 8 September 1974,
available at American Presidency
Project, University of California Santa
Barbara, http://www.presidency.ucsb.
edu/ws/?pid=4696

14. Bloch, Michael, *Jeremy Thorpe*, London,
Little, Brown, 2014, pxi

15. Ibid., p357

16. Ibid., p145

17. Ibid., p273

18. Ibid., p222

19. Preston, John, *A Very English Scandal:
Sex, Lies and a Murder Plot at the Heart
of the Establishment*, London, Penguin,
2016, p13

20. Bloch, p528

21. Ibid., p495

22. Ibid., p192

23. Preston, p29

24. Bloch, p142

25. Ibid., p230

26. Ibid., p305

27. Ibid., p422

28. Ibid., p382

29. Ibid., p383

30. Ibid., p402

31. Ibid., p428

32. Ibid., p463

33. Preston, p216

34. Ibid., p216

35. Bloch, p444

36. Ibid., p457

37. Ibid., p460

38. Preston, p240

39. Bloch, p474

40. Preston, p304

41. *Private Eye*, 23 July 2004

42. Crick, Michael, *Jeffrey Archer: Stranger
Than Fiction*, London, Fourth Estate,
2000, p270

43. Ibid., p275

44. Ibid., p264

45. Rawnsley, Andrew, 'Archer Wins
Record £500,000 Damages', *Guardian*,
25 July 1987, https://www.theguardian.
com/uk/1987/jul/25/archer.politics

46. Quoted in Crick, p291

47. Ibid., p296

48. Ibid., p299

49. Ibid., p300

50. Reid, Tim, 'Archer "Paid Aide To Miss
Libel Trial"', *Times*, 13 June 2001

51. 'Jeffrey Archer: A Life of Lies',
Panorama, BBC 1, 19 July 2001,

transcript at http://news.bbc.co.uk /hi/english/static/audio_video/ programmes/panorama/transcripts/ transcript_19_07_01.txt

52. Crick, p413
53. Ibid., p445
54. 'Jeffrey Archer Quits over False Alibi', *News of the World*, 21 November 1999; 'The Archer Tapes', BBC News, 19 July 2001, http://news.bbc.co.uk/1/hi/uk/ 1436200.stm
55. Crick, p449
56. 'Tories Punish Archer', BBC News, 22 November 1999, http://news.bbc.co.uk /1/hi/uk_politics/532083.stm
57. 'The Archer Trial: Key Players', BBC News, 19 July 2001, http://news.bbc. co.uk/1/hi/programmes/panorama/ archer/1437286.stm
58. Williams, Rhys, 'Magazine to Name "Gay" Ministers', *Independent*, 15 January 1994, http://www. independent.co.uk/news/uk/ magazine-to-name-gay- ministers-1400026.html
59. Marks, Kathy, 'Bible of Left and Satirical Upstart Are Worlds Apart', *Independent*, 29 January 1993, http:/ /www.independent.co.uk/news/uk/ bible-of-left-and-satirical-upstart-are- worlds-apart-new-statesman-is-80- scallywag-only-a-fledgling-1481386. html
60. Ford, Richard, and Philip Webster, 'Major Asks Magazines for Cash', *The Times*, 6 February 1993
61. Smith, Ramsay, and Gordon Hay, 'What a Major Cook-Up Clare!', *Daily Mirror*, 16 July 1993
62. Panther, Lewis, and Lee Harpin, 'Major Lied to a Judge', *News of the World*, 6 October 2002; Smith and Hay, 'What a Major Cook-Up'
63. Campbell, Alastair, and David Bradshaw, 'The Men Being Sued by

John Major', *Daily Mirror*, 29 January 1993
64. Young, Robin, 'Currie "Insulted" by Link with Evil Film Character', *The Times*, 14 May 1991
65. Garfield, Simon, 'Currie Sues over Negative Image', *Independent*, 25 March 1990
66. Young, 'Currie "Insulted" by Link'
67. Ibid.
68. 'The Secret Diary of Edwina Currie', *Private Eye*, 18 October 2002, http: //www.private-eye.co.uk/sections. php?section_link=columnists&is- sue=1323&article=621
69. 'Currie Affair', *The Times*, 28 September 2002
70. Dougary, Ginny, '"John Was in the Whips' Office, Sometimes Discussing Other People's Affairs, Keeping Very Quiet About His Own": Interview', *The Times*, 28 September 2002
71. 'Major and Currie Had Four-year Affair', BBC News, 28 September 2002, http: //news.bbc.co.uk/1/hi/uk_politics/ 2286008.stm
72. Baldwin, Tom, 'Currie Vents Her Anger at Major's "Shame"', *The Times*, 30 September 2002
73. Dougary,'"John Was in the Whips' Office"'
74. 'Political PR: Conference Eyewitness', *PR Week*, 24 September 2004; Major, John, Speech to 1993 Conservative Party Conference, Blackpool, 8 October 1993, transcript available at Sir John Major website, http://www.johnmajor. co.uk/page1096.html
75. Lawrence, Lucy, 'Major Used Me to Cover Up His Affair', *Sunday Mirror*, 29 September 2002
76. Harding, Luke, David Leigh and David Pallister, *The Liar: The Fall of Jonathan Aitken*, London, Penguin, 1997, pxiv
77. Ibid., p110

78. As detailed at length in ibid.
79. Ibid., p134
80. Ibid., p73
81. Ibid., p78
82. Aitken, Jonathan, *Pride and Perjury: An Autobiography*, London, Continuum, 2003, p220

83. Harding, Leigh and Pallister, p164
84. Ibid., p166
85. Aitken, p221
86. Ibid., p219
87. Ibid., p155
88. Harding, Leigh and Pallister, p139

5. Sins of Spin

1. Heffer, Simon, *Like the Roman: The Life of Enoch Powell*, London, Faber and Faber, 2014, e1270
2. 'Enoch Powell's "Rivers of Blood" Speech', *Telegraph*, 6 November 2007, http://www.telegraph.co.uk/comment /3643823/Enoch-Powells-Rivers-of-Blood-speech.html
3. Heffer, e12812
4. Ibid., e12930
5. '"Rivers of Blood" Speech', *Telegraph*
6. Ibid.
7. Ibid.
8. Heffer, e12829
9. Jones, Rupert, 'My Grandparents, Enoch Powell and the Day They Fell Out over His "Rivers of Blood" Speech', *Guardian*, 22 October 2016
10. Heffer, e12776
11. Ibid., e12424
12. Powell, Enoch, interview, *Frost on Friday*, London Weekend Television (LWT), 3 January 1969
13. 'The Woman Who Never Was', *Document*, BBC Radio 4, 7 March 2007, http://www.bbc.co.uk/programmes/ b007737v
14. Heffer, e12411
15. 'Woman Who Never Was', *Document*
16. Lord Howard of Rising (ed), *Enoch at 100: A Re-evaluation of the Life, Politics and Philosophy of Enoch Powell*, London, Biteback, 2012, e20439

17. 'Twelve Minutes over Tripoli', *Panorama*, BBC 1, 3 April 1987
18. Ibid.
19. 'The President's News Conference', 7 January 1986, transcript available at American Presidency Project, University of California, Santa Barbara, http://www.presidency.ucsb.edu/ws/ ?pid=36812
20. 'Transcript of Address by Reagan on Libya', *New York Times*, 15 April 1986, http://www.nytimes.com/1986/04/15/ world/transcript-of-address-by-reagan-on-libya.html
21. 'Twelve Minutes over Tripoli', *Panorama*
22. Gerstenzang, James, 'The Raid on Libya: 3,200-Mile Mission Showed Long Reach and Precision of US Forces', *Los Angeles Times*, 15 April 1986
23. Malinarich, Nathalie, 'Flashback: The Berlin Disco Bombing', BBC News, 13 November 2001, http://news.bbc.co.uk /1/hi/world/europe/1653848.stm
24. Erlanger, Steven, '4 Guilty in Fatal 1986 Berlin Disco Bombing Linked to Libya', *New York Times*, 14 November 2001, http://www.nytimes.com/2001/11/14/ world/4-guilty-in-fatal-1986-berlin-dis-co-bombing-linked-to-libya.html
25. 'Lockerbie Bomber Freed from Jail', BBC News, 20 August 2009, http:// news.bbc.co.uk/1/hi/scotland/south_ of_scotland/8197370.stm

26. 'Libya to Give Up WMD', BBC News, 20 November 2003, http://news.bbc.co.uk/1/hi/3335965.stm

27. 'Blair Hails Positive Libya Talks', BBC News, 29 May 2007, http://news.bbc.co.uk/1/hi/uk_politics/6699447.stm

28. Quinn, Andrew, 'Clinton Says Gaddafi Must Go', Reuters, 28 February 2011, http://www.reuters.com/article/us-libya-usa-clinton-idUSTRE71Q-1JA20110228

29. 'Libya Unrest: Cameron Warns Gaddafi over Repression', BBC News, 24 February 2011, http://www.bbc.co.uk/news/uk-politics-12564870

30. 'President Obama: Libya Aftermath "Worst Mistake" of Presidency', BBC News, 11 April 2016, http://www.bbc.co.uk/news/world-us-canada-36013703

31. Brown, Gordon, Speech on the Comprehensive Spending Review, House of Commons, 14 July 1998, transcript available at UK Pol Political Speech Archive, http://www.ukpol.co.uk/gordon-brown-1998-speech-on-the-comprehensive-spending-review

32. 'Brown Pumps £21bn into the NHS', BBC News, 15 July 1998, http://news.bbc.co.uk/1/hi/special_report/1998/07/98/spending_review/132436.stm

33. All headlines from 15 July 1998

34. House of Commons Select Committee on Treasury, 'The New Fiscal Framework and the Comprehensive Spending Review: The Comprehensive Spending Review', Treasury – Eighth Report, 27 July 1998, https://www.publications.parliament.uk/pa/cm199798/cmselect/cmtreasy/960/96004.htm

35. House of Commons Select Committee on Treasury, 'Private Finance Initiative: Accounting and Budgetary Incentives', Treasury – Seventeenth Report: Private Finance Initiative, 18 July 2011, https://www.publications.parliament.uk/pa/cm201012/cmselect/cmtreasy/1146/114605.htm

36. 'Full Text: Gordon Brown's Budget Statement', *Guardian*, 17 March 2004, https://www.theguardian.com/money/2004/mar/17/budget.budget20044

37. Chote, Robert, Carl Emmerson and Gemma Tetlow, 'The Fiscal Rules and Policy Framework' in *The IFS Green Budget 2009*, 28 January 2009, Institute of Fiscal Studies, https://www.ifs.org.uk/budgets/gb2009/09chap5.pdf

38. Frith, Maxine, 'Abandoned in Casualty', *Evening Standard*, 21 January 2002, http://www.standard.co.uk/news/abandoned-in-casualty-6311482.html

39. 'The Hospital's Statement', *Evening Standard*, 22 January 2002, http://www.standard.co.uk/news/the-hospitals-statement-6304342.html

40. Hansard, HC (series 6) vol 378, col 882, 23 January 2002, https://www.publications.parliament.uk/pa/cm200102/cmhansrd/vo020123/debtext/20123-02.htm

41. Campbell, Alastair, *The Burden of Power: Countdown to Iraq – The Alastair Campbell Diaries: Volume 4*, London, Arrow, 2013, p147

42. Russell, Ben, 'Care Debate Turns into Row over Race and Spin Dispute', *Independent*, 23 June 2002, http://www.independent.co.uk/life-style/health-and-families/health-news/care-debate-turns-into-row-over-race-and-spin-dispute-5362613.html

43. Ibid.

44. Frith, Maxine, '"My Granny Is Not Racist"', *Evening Standard*, 24 January 2002, http://www.standard.co.uk/news/my-granny-is-not-racist-6300560.html

45. Martin, Nicole, and Sean O'Neill, 'Hospital Sorry for Race Slur on Rose', *Telegraph*, 25 January 2002, http://www.telegraph.co.uk/news/uknews/1382623/Hospital-sorry-for-race-slur-on-Rose.html

46. Craven, Nick, and Michael Seamark, 'My Links with Labour, by Hospital Chief', *Daily Mail*, 25 January 2002

47. Campbell, p147

48. '"Smear" Row Adviser Apologises', BBC News, 7 June 2002, http://news.bbc.co.uk/1/hi/uk_politics/2030685.stm

49. 'Spin Memo Row Duo Quit', BBC News, 15 February 2002, http://news.bbc.co.uk/1/hi/uk_politics/1823120.stm

50. Hines, Nico, 'Alastair Campbell: I Planned My Suicide', *Daily Beast*, 27 March 2014, http://www.thedailybeast.com/articles/2014/03/27/alastair-campbell-i-planned-my-suicide

51. 'Theresa May Speech in Full', Politics.co.uk, 4 October 2011, http://www.politics.co.uk/comment-analysis/2011/10/04/theresa-may-speech-in-full

52. Casciani, Dominic, 'The Case of the Cat Deportation Tale', BBC News, 6 October 2011, http://www.bbc.co.uk/news/uk-politics-15171980

53. Asylum and Immigration Tribunal Appeal IA/14578/2008, 10 December 2008

54. Travis, Alan, 'Catflap: What the Original Ruling Said', *Guardian*, 6 October 2011, https://www.theguardian.com/politics/2011/oct/06/catgate-original-ruling-theresa-may

55. Asylum and Immigration Tribunal Appeal IA/14578/2008, 10 December 2008; Casciani, 'The Case of the Cat Deportation Tale'

56. 'Theresa May Under Fire over Deportation Cat Claim', BBC News, 4 October 2011, http://www.bbc.co.uk/news/uk-politics-15160326

57. Sharman, Jon, 'Brexit: Iain Duncan Smith Makes Series of "Inaccurate" Statements to Attack Supreme Court Ruling', *Independent*, 24 January 2017, http://www.independent.co.uk/news/uk/politics/brexit-ruling-iain-duncan-smith-supreme-court-comments-inaccurate-a7543366.html

58. BBC News, 'Newsnight Reveals Inaccuracies in Iain Duncan Smith's CV', press release, 19 December 2002, http://www.bbc.co.uk/pressoffice/pressreleases/stories/2002/12_december/19/newsnight_ids_cv.shtml

59. 'The Cap Fits for 16,000 Families: Welfare Losers Find Jobs or Cheaper Homes', *The Sun*, 13 April 2013

60. 'Iain Duncan Smith Criticised over Benefit Cap Figures', BBC News, 9 May 2013, http://www.bbc.co.uk/news/uk-politics-22462265

61. Chair of UK Statistics Authority (Andrew Dilnot), letter to Secretary of State for Work and Pensions (Iain Duncan Smith), 9 May 2013, https://www.statisticsauthority.gov.uk/archive/reports---correspondence/correspondence/letter-from-andrew-dilnot-to-rt-hon-iain-duncan-smith-mp-090513.pdf

62. Chair of UK Statistics Authority (Andrew Dilnot), letter to Secretary of State for Work and Pensions (Iain Duncan Smith), 3 May 2013, https://www.statisticsauthority.gov.uk/archive/reports---correspondence/correspondence/work-programme-statistics.pdf

63. Chair of UK Statistics Authority (Sir Michael Scholar), letter to Secretary of State for Work and Pensions (Iain Duncan Smith), 25 January 2012, https://www.statisticsauthority.gov.uk/

wp-content/uploads/2015/12/letter-fromsirmichaelscholartorthoniain duncansmithmp2501201_tcm97-41446. pdf

64. Chair of UK Statistics Authority (Sir Michael Scholar), letter to Patrick Casey, 26 November 2010, https: //www.statisticsauthority.gov.uk/ wp-content/uploads/2015/11/letter-from-sir-michael-scholar-to-patrick-casey-26112010_tcm97-35157.pdf

65. 'Duncan Smith "Clarifies" Commons Slip over Benefit Data', BBC News, 18

November 2010, http://www.bbc.co.uk /news/uk-politics-11792700

66. 'DWP Admits Using "Fake" Claimants in Benefit Sanctions Leaflet', BBC News, 18 August 2015, http://www.bbc.co.uk/ news/uk-politics-33974674

67. Duncan Smith, Iain, interview, *Today*, BBC Radio 4, 15 July 2013; Wintour, Patrick, and Patrick Butler, 'Iain Duncan Smith Defends Use of Statistics over Benefit Cap', *Guardian*, 15 July 2013, https://www.theguardian.com/ politics/2013/jul/15/iain-duncan-smith-statistics-benefits-cap

6. Continental Drift

1. 'A Referendum Stitch-Up: How the EU and British Elites Are Plotting to Fix the Result', leaflet, UKIP and Europe of Freedom and Democracy, 2012, http: //www.ukipmeps.org/uploads/file/ ReferendumStichUp.pdf

2. Cash, Bill, interview, *Paxman in Brussels: Who Really Rules Us?*, BBC 1, 19 May 2016

3. Johnson, Boris, 'Boris Johnson Exclusive: There Is Only One Way to Get the Change We Want: Vote To Leave the EU', *Telegraph*, 16 May 2016, http://www.telegraph.co.uk/opinion /2016/03/16/boris-johnson-exclusive-there-is-only-one-way-to-get-the-change

4. Cabinet Minutes, 2 June 1950, quoted in Christopher Booker and Richard North, *The Great Deception: Can The European Union Survive?*, Continuum, 2005, p66

5. Gaitskell, Hugh, speech, Labour Party Conference, 1961, quoted in Booker and North, p144

6. Booker and North, p145

7. Rey, Jean, speech, Hague Summit, 11 December 1969, available from Archive of European Integration, University of Pittsburgh, http://aei.pitt.edu/1451/1/ hague_1969.pdf

8. Commission on the European Communities, 'Report to the Council and the Commission on the Realisation by Stages of Economic and Monetary Union', document 16.956/II/70-F, 8 October 1970, available from Archive of European Integration, University of Pittsburgh, http://aei.pitt.edu/1002/1/ monetary_werner_final.pdf

9. Bowcott, Owen, 'Treasury Warned Heath that EMU Plan Could Herald European Superstate', *Guardian*, 1 January 2002, https://www. theguardian.com/politics/2002/jan/01 /uk.euro

10. Booker and North, p176

11. Ibid., p179

12. Foreign Office, 'Legal and Constitutional Implications of UK Entry into EEC', briefing paper FCO 30/1048, 1971, available via National Archives,

http://discovery.nationalarchives.gov.
uk/details/r/C11018818

13. HM Government, 'Britain's New Deal
in Europe', leaflet, 1975, reproduced
by Peter Hitchens, 'The 1975
Common Market Referendum
Documents', *Mail on Sunday*,
27 August 2015, http://hitchensblog.
mailonsunday.co.uk/2015/08/
the-1975-common-market-referendum-
campaign-documents.html

14. Waldegrave, William, *A Different
Kind of Weather: A Memoir*, London,
Constable, 2015, p117

15. Commission Implementing Regulation
(EU) No 1333/2011, 'Laying Down
Marketing Standards for Bananas,
Rules on the Verification of
Compliance with those Marketing
Standards and Requirements for
Notifications in the Banana Sector
(Codification)', *Official Journal of the
European Union*, 19 December 2011,
http://eur-lex.europa.eu/legal-content
/EN/TXT/HTML/?uri=CELEX:
32011R1333

16. Lambert, Sarah, 'Putting the Banana
Story Straight', *Independent*, 21
September 1994, http://www.
independent.co.uk/news/putting-the-
banana-story-straight-1450274.html

17. Oliver, Craig, *Unleashing Demons: The
Inside Story of Brexit*, London, Hodder
and Stoughton, 2016, p234

18. Johnson, 'Boris Johnson Exclusive'

19. Purnell, Sonia, *Just Boris: The
Irresistible Rise of a Political Celebrity*,
London, Aurum, 2011, p121

20. *Desert Island Discs*, BBC Radio 4,
4 November 2005, http://www.bbc.
co.uk/programmes/p00935b6

21. Independent Press Standards
Organisation, 'IPSO Resolution
Statement 03284-16: Dyke v Express.
co.uk', 2 August 2016, https://www.

ipso.co.uk/rulings-and-resolution-
statements/ruling/?id=03284-16

22. Chapman, James, 'Eurozone Crisis:
David Cameron Vetoes EU Treaty to
Save Euro', *Daily Mail*, 10 December
2011, http://www.dailymail.co.uk/news
/article-2071952/Eurozone-crisis-Da-
vid-Cameron-vetoes-EU-treaty-save-
euro.html

23. Kirkup, James, 'EU Treaty: Cameron's
Veto Creates New Era for Europe and
Coalition', *Telegraph*, 9 December 2011,
http://www.telegraph.co.uk/news/
politics/david-cameron/8945213/EU-
treaty-David-Camerons-veto-creates-
new-era-for-Europe-and-Coalition.html

24. Wilson, Graeme, and Kevin Schofield,
'Up Eurs', *The Sun*, 10 December 2011,
https://www.thesun.co.uk/archives/
politics/962965/up-eurs

25. Robinson, Nick, 'Britain Uses Its Veto',
BBC News, 9 December 2011, http:
//www.bbc.co.uk/news/uk-politics-
16106307

26. Shipman, Tim, *All Out War: The Full
Story of How Brexit Sank Britain's
Political Class*, London, William Collins,
2016, p8

27. Cameron's statement to the Commons,
quoted at the top of this section,
triggered Miliband's response.
Hansard, HC (series 6) vol 537, col
519, 12 December 2011, https://
www.publications.parliament.uk/pa
/cm201011/cmhansrd/cm111212/
debtext/111212-0001.htm

28. Hansard, HC (series 6) vol 537, col 524,
12 December 2011

29. Miller, Vaughne, 'How Much Legislation
Comes from Europe?', briefing paper
RP10/62, House of Commons, 13
October 2010, http://researchbriefings.
parliament.uk/ResearchBriefing/
Summary/RP10-62; The Bow
Group, 'Who Really Governs Britain',

14 July 2001, https://www.bow
group.org/policy/who-really-
governs-britain; Brown, Martyn, 'Two
Out of Three British Laws Were Made
in Brussels', *Daily Express*, 2 March
2015, http://www.express.co.uk/news
/politics/561286/65-per-cent-British-
laws-made-Brussels-European-Union;
Edmunds, Donna Rachel, '65 Percent
of British Laws Come from Brussels
Says Definitive New Study', Breitbart,
2 March 2015, http://www.breitbart.
com/london/2015/03/02/65-percent-of-
british-laws-come-from-brussels-says-
definitive-new-study

30. Miller, 'How Much Legislation Comes
from Europe?'

31. 'Brexit: UK Sets Out Plan to Replace
All EU Laws', BBC News, 30 March
2017, http://www.bbc.co.uk/news/uk-
politics-39439554

32. May, Theresa, 'Theresa May's Brexit
Speech in Full', *Telegraph*, 17 January
2017, http://www.telegraph.co.uk/
news/2017/01/17/theresa-mays-brexit-
speech-full

33. Cameron, David, speech, Conservative
Party Conference, 1 October 2014,
transcript available at Conservative
Party website, http://press.
conservatives.com/post/98882674910/
david-cameron-speech-to-
conservative-party

34. Pancevski, Bojan, and Tim Shipman,
'Merkel: I Will Block PM on
Immigrants', *Sunday Times*, 26 October
2014, https://www.thetimes.co.uk/
article/merkel-i-will-block-pm-on-im-
migrants-czsj76fzsnd

35. Shipman, p195

36. Ibid., p242

37. Coates, Sam, 'Osborne: Brexit Will Cost
Us £4,300 Per Household', *The Times*,
18 April 2016, https://www.thetimes.

co.uk/article/osborne-brexit-will-cost-
us-4-300-per-household-w8rkrsxff

38. Reuben, Anthony, 'Reality Check:
Would Brexit Cost Your Family £4,300?',
BBC News, 18 April 2016, http://
www.bbc.co.uk/news/uk-politics-eu-
referendum-36073201

39. Ibid.

40. Shipman, p244

41. Oliver, p189

42. 'Osborne Warns of Brexit Budget Cuts',
BBC News, 15 June 2016, http://
www.bbc.co.uk/news/uk-politics-eu-
referendum-36534192

43. Shipman, p252

44. 'Osborne Warns of Brexit Budget Cuts',
BBC News

45. Hansard, HC (series 6), vol 611, col
1752, 15 June 2016, https://hansard.
parliament.uk/Commons/2016-06-15/
debates/517E6CB0-162A-461D-A907-
CD10C3FA7382/Engagements

46. HM Treasury, 'Statement by the
Chancellor Following the EU
Referendum', 27 June 2016, https://
www.gov.uk/government/speeches/
statement-by-the-chancellor-
following-the-eu-referendum

47. Glaze, Ben, 'Jeremy Hunt Dashes Vote
Leave Claims of £350million Brexit
Boost for NHS', *Mirror*, 2 October
2016, http://www.mirror.co.uk/news
/uk-news/jeremy-hunt-dashes-vote-
leave-8964818

48. Office for National Statistics,
'UK Perspectives 2016: The UK
Contribution to the EU Budget', 25
May 2016, http://visual.ons.gov.uk/uk-
perspectives-2016-the-uk-contribution-
to-the-eu-budget

49. Full Fact, 'The UK's EU Membership
Fee', 25 February 2016, https://fullfact.
org/europe/our-eu-membership-fee-
55-million

50. UK Statistics Authority, 'UK Statistics Authority Statement on the Use of Official Statistics on Contributions to the European Union', 27 May 2016, https://www.statisticsauthority.gov.uk/news/uk-statistics-authority-statement-on-the-use-of-official-statistics-on-contributions-to-the-european-union

51. Shipman, p255

52. House of Commons Treasury Committee, 'Oral Evidence: The Economic and Financial Costs and Benefits of UK Membership of the EU', Parliament, 6 April 2016, http://data.parliament.uk/writtenevidence/committeeevidence.svc/evidencedocument/treasury-committee/the-economic-and-financial-costs-and-benefits-of-uks-eu-membership/oral/32135.html

53. Mason, Rowena, 'PM Backs Michael Gove but Suggests Former Aide Was a "Career Psychopath"', Guardian, 18 June 2014, https://www.theguardian.com/politics/2014/jun/18/david-cameron-dominic-cummings-career-psychopath

54. Shipman, p113

55. Ibid., p94

56. Oliver, p130

57. Ibid., p254

58. 'Broken Promises: Who Will Sign the £350m Brexit NHS Cheque', video, Sky News, 15 January 2017, http://news.sky.com/video/broken-promises-who-will-sign-the-163350m-brexit-nhs-cheque-10604870

59. House of Commons Treasury Committee, 'Oral Evidence'

60. Islam, Faisal, 'Post-Brexit Sunderland: "If This Money Doesn't Go to the NHS, I Will Go Mad"', Guardian, 9 August 2016, https://www.theguardian.com/uk-news/2016/aug/09/post-brexit-sunderland-if-this-money-doesnt-go-to-the-nhs-i-will-go-mad

61. Cowburn, Ashley, 'Brexiteers Condemned for Not Backing £350m NHS Amendment to EU Withdrawal Bill', Independent, 8 February 2017, http://www.independent.co.uk/news/uk/politics/brexiteers-condemned-for-not-backing-350m-nhs-amendment-to-eu-withdrawal-bill-a7570336.html

62. Holehouse, Matthew, 'Clegg v Farage: Crunching the Numbers', Telegraph, 27 March 2014, http://www.telegraph.co.uk/news/politics/ukip/10727810/Clegg-v-Farage-Crunching-the-numbers.html

63. Booth, Robert, Alan Travis and Amelia Gentleman, 'Leave Donor Plans New Party to Replace UKIP – Possibly Without Farage in Charge', Guardian, 29 June 2016, https://www.theguardian.com/politics/2016/jun/29/leave-donor-plans-new-party-to-replace-ukip-without-farage

64. Duncan Smith, Iain, interview, The Andrew Marr Show, BBC 1, 26 June 2016

65. Boffey, Daniel, and Toby Helm, 'Vote Leave Embroiled in Race Row over Turkey Security Threat Claims', Guardian, 22 May 2016, https://www.theguardian.com/politics/2016/may/21/vote-leave-prejudice-turkey-eu-security-threat

66. Ibid.

67. European Commission, 'Key Findings of the 2015 Report on Turkey', fact sheet, 10 November 2015, http://europa.eu/rapid/press-release_MEMO-15-6039_en.htm

68. European Commission, 'Six Principles for Further Developing EU–Turkey Cooperation in Tackling the Migration Crisis', press release, 16 March 2016, http://europa.eu/rapid/press-release_

IP-16-830_en.htm; Wright, Ben, 'Reality Check: How Soon Can Turkey Join the EU?', BBC News, 17 March 2016, http://www.bbc.co.uk/news/uk-politics-eu-referendum-35832035

69. Mordaunt, Penny, interview, *The Andrew Marr Show*, BBC 1, 22 May 2016

70. Mason, Rowena, 'Cameron Accuses EU Leave Campaigners of Telling Six Lies', *Guardian*, 7 June 2016, https://www.theguardian.com/politics/2016/jun/07/cameron-accuses-eu-leave-campaigners-six-lies-brexit; *Peston on Sunday*, ITV, 22 May 2016

71. 'Turkey EU Accession Poses Security Risk: Michael Gove', BBC News, 8 June 2016, http://www.bbc.co.uk/news/uk-politics-eu-referendum-36479259

72. Khan, Sadiq, response, *EU Referendum: The Great Debate*, BBC 1, 21 June 2016

73. 'Michael Gove "Shuddered" at UKIP Migrants Poster', BBC News, 19 June 2016, http://www.bbc.co.uk/news/uk-politics-eu-referendum-36570759

74. Farage, Nigel, interview, *Peston on Sunday*, ITV, 19 June 2017

75. Shipman, p297

76. Travis, Alan, 'Lasting Rise in Hate Crime After EU Referendum, Figures Show', *Guardian*, 7 September 2016, https://www.theguardian.com/society/2016/sep/07/hate-surged-after-eu-referendum-police-figures-show

7. Where Power Lies

1. Moore, Charles, *Margaret Thatcher: The Authorized Biography, Volume 1: Not For Turning*, London, Allen Lane, 2013, p667

2. Ibid., p711

3. Ibid.

4. Ibid., p712

5. Ibid., p713

6. Rossiter, Mike, *Sink the Belgrano*, London, Corgi, 2008, p333

7. Chippindale, Peter, and Chris Horrie, *Stick It Up Your Punter! The Uncut Story of the Sun Newspaper*, London, Pocket Books, 1999, p140

8. Hansard, HL (series 5) vol 429, col 1074, 4 May 1982, http://hansard.millbanksystems.com/lords/1982/may/04/the-falkland-islands

9. Hansard, HC (series 6) vol 33, col 103W, 29 December 1982, http://hansard.millbanksystems.com/written_answers/1982/nov/29/general-belgrano

10. Hansard, HC (series 6) vol 34, col 895, 21 December 1982, http://hansard.millbanksystems.com/commons/1982/dec/21/falklands-campaign

11. Dalyell, Tam, *Misrule: How Mrs Thatcher Has Misled Parliament*, London, Hamish Hamilton, 1987, p37

12. Hansard, HC (series 6) vol 23, col 19, 4 May 1982, http://hansard.millbanksystems.com/volumes/6C/23

13. Moore, p714

14. Dalyell, p53

15. Hansard, HC (series 6) vol 34, col 59W, 14 December 1982, http://hansard.millbanksystems.com/written_answers/1982/dec/14/general-belgrano

16. Hansard, HC (series 6) vol 34, col 199W, 16 December 1982, http://hansard.millbanksystems.com/written_answers/1982/dec/16/general-belgrano

17. Andrews, Nigel, 'Margaret Thatcher Rejoices – and Splits the Country in Two', *Financial Times*, 8 December 2007, https://www.ft.com/content/72b2bfea-a13d-11dc-9f34-0000779fd2ac

18. 'History of the BBC: The Falklands Conflict 1982', BBC, n.d. (accessed 5 May 2017), http://www.bbc.co.uk /historyofthebbc/research/culture/ bbc-and-gov/falklands

19. *Nationwide* (On the Spot), BBC 1, 24 May 1983, transcript available at Margaret Thatcher Foundation, http:// www.margaretthatcher.org/document /105147

20. Ibid.

21. Ibid.

22. *BSE Inquiry Report, Volume 1: Findings and Conclusions*, London, Her Majesty's Stationery Office, 2000, pxx, available at National Archives, http:// webarchive.nationalarchives.gov.uk/ 20060715141954/http://bseinquiry.gov. uk/report/contents.htm

23. Hansard, HC (series 6) vol 274, col 375, 20 March 1996, http://hansard. millbanksystems.com/commons/1996/ mar/20/bse-health

24. *BSE Inquiry Report, Volume 1*, pxvii

25. 'Madness: Special Report – The BSE Crisis', *Observer*, 29 October 2000, https://www.theguardian.com/uk/2000 /oct/29/bse.focus1

26. *BSE Inquiry Report, Volume 1*, pxix

27. Assinder, Nick, 'Phillips Report Packs a Punch', BBC News, 26 October 2000, http://news.bbc.co.uk/1/hi/uk_politics /992883.stm

28. *BSE Inquiry Report, Volume 3: The Early Years, 1986–88*, London, Her Majesty's Stationery Office, 2000, section 2.53, available at National Archives, http://webarchive.nationalar- chives.gov.uk/20060715141954/http: //bseinquiry.gov.uk/report/volume3/ toc.htm

29. Ibid., section 5.21

30. Ibid., section 5.69

31. Ibid., section 5.101

32. Ibid., section 5.30

33. Ibid., sections 5.62, 5.67

34. *BSE Inquiry Report, Volume 4: The Southwood Working Party, 1988–89*, London, Her Majesty's Stationery Office, 2000, section 2.4, available at National Archives, http:// webarchive.nationalarchives.gov.uk/ 20060715141954/http://bseinquiry.gov. uk/report/volume4/chapter2.htm

35. Ibid., section 10.42

36. *BSE Inquiry Report, Volume 1*, pxxiii

37. Ibid., pxxvi

38. Ibid., pxxvii

39. Ibid.

40. Ibid., pxxiii

41. 'On This Day: 16 May 1990 – Gummer Enlists Daughter in BSE Fight', BBC News, http://news.bbc.co.uk/ onthisday/hi/dates/stories/may/16/ newsid_2913000/2913807.stm

42. Ibid.

43. *BSE Inquiry Report, Volume 1*, pxviii

44. Ibid., pxxvii

45. Ibid., pxviii

46. Godlee, Fiona, Jane Smith and Harvey Marcovitch, 'Wakefield's Article Linking MMR Vaccine and Autism Was Fraudulent', *BMJ* 342, 6 January 2011, http://www.bmj.com/content/342/bmj. c7452

47. Moriarty, Richard, Lauren Veevers and Tom Newton Dunn, 'Hillsborough: The Real Truth', *The Sun*, 12 September 2012, https://www.thesun.co.uk /archives/news/915727/hillsbor- ough-the-real-truth

48. *The Report of the Hillsborough Independent Panel*, London, Her Majesty's Stationery Office, September 2012, p25, http://hillsborough. independent.gov.uk/report/ main-section/part-2/chapter-12/ page10a

49. Ibid., p349, http://hillsborough. independent.gov.uk/report/

main-section/part-2/chapter-12/page-4
/index.html

50. Ibid., p16, http://hillsborough.
independent.gov.uk/report/Section-1/
summary/page-8/index.html

51. Ingham, Sir Bernard, letter to Graham
Skinner, 30 December 1996, quoted
in David Bartlett, 'Sir Bernard Ingham
1996 Letter: Liverpool Should "Shut Up"
About Hillsborough', *Echo*, 16 January
2013, http://www.liverpoolecho.co.uk/
news/liverpool-news/sir-bernard-
ingham-1996-letter-3324915

52. Ingham, Sir Bernard, letter to
Hillsborough campaigners, 8 July
1996, quoted in David McCarthy,
'Police and FA Guilty of Hillsborough
Hooliganism, Not Fans', *Daily Record*,
27 April 2016, http://www.dailyrecord.
co.uk/sport/football/football-news/
david-mccarthy-police-fa-guilty-
7839720

53. 'Summary of Chapter 11: Review and
Alteration of Statements', *Report of The
Hillsborough Independent Panel*, http:
//hillsborough.independent.gov.uk/
report/Section-1/summary/page-13

54. *Interim Report of the Taylor Inquiry
into the Hillsborough Stadium Disaster*,
London, Home Office, August 1989,
p96, http://hillsborough.independent.
gov.uk/repository/HOM000028040001.
html

55. Ibid., p104

56. Ibid., pp105–6

57. Slocock, Caroline (Private Secretary, 10
Downing Street), letter to Peter Storr,
Home Office, 3 August 1989, evidence
to Hillsborough Independent Panel,
http://hillsborough.independent.gov.uk
/repository/HOM000013060001.html

58. Straw, Jack, interview, *Today*, BBC
Radio 4, 13 September 2012, http:
//news.bbc.co.uk/today/hi/today/
newsid_9751000/9751006.stm

59. *Report of the Hillsborough Independent
Panel*, p365, http://hillsborough.
independent.gov.uk/repository/
SYP000046060001.html

60. Ibid., p361, http://hillsborough.
independent.gov.uk/report/
main-section/part-2/chapter-12/page-8
/index.html

61. 'Hillsborough Inquests: The Questions
the Jury Had to Consider', BBC News,
26 April 2016, http://www.bbc.co.uk/
news/uk-england-merseyside-
35401436

62. Quoted in Steven Swinford,
'Hillsborough: MP Finally
Apologises After 23 Years',
Telegraph, 13 September 2012, http://
www.telegraph.co.uk/sport/football/
news/9542091/Hillsborough-MP-
finally-
apologises-after-23-years.html

63. Robertson, Geoffrey, *The Justice Game*,
London, Vintage, 2011, p314

64. Trewin, Ion, *Alan Clark: The
Biography*, London, Weidenfeld and
Nicolson, 2009, p350; Neil, Andrew,
Full Disclosure, London, Pan, 1996,
p404

65. Quoted in Robertson, *Justice Game*,
pp338–9

66. Ibid., p335

67. Ibid., p332

68. Quoted in ibid., p326

69. Ibid.

70. Quoted in ibid., p318

71. Lewis, James, 'Interview With UK
Secretary Of State For Justice Ken
Clarke – Transcript', website of
International Bar Association, 8
September 2016 (interview conducted
in November 2011), www.ibanet.org/
Article/NewDetail.aspx?ArticleUid=-
F4A4D433-36F9-4D3B-A3CA-ED94A30E-
F09A

72. Robertson, *Justice Game*, p320

73. Oborne, Peter, *The Rise of Political Lying*, New York, Free Press, 2005, p19
74. Trewin, p360
75. Ibid., p350
76. Robertson, p337
77. Quoted in ibid., p338
78. Norton-Taylor, Richard, *Truth is a Difficult Concept: Inside the Scott Inquiry*, London, Fourth Estate, 1995, p33
79. Ibid., p32
80. Waldegrave, William, *A Different Kind of Weather: A Memoir*, London, Constable, 2015, p249
81. Robertson, p331
82. Oborne, p268
83. Norton-Taylor, p65
84. Ibid., p67
85. Ibid., p68
86. Ibid., p264
87. Ibid., p89
88. Ibid., p25
89. Ibid., p223
90. Scott, Sir Richard, *Report of the Inquiry into the Export of Defence Equipment and Dual-Use Goods to Iraq and Related Prosecutions*, London, Her Majesty's Stationery Office, 1996, p1799
91. Rawnsley, Andrew, *The End of the Party: The Rise and Fall of New Labour*, London, Penguin, 2010, p36
92. Blair, Tony, *A Journey: My Political Life*, London, Hutchinson, 2010, p386
93. Blair, Tony, speech, Labour Party Conference, Brighton, 28 September 2004, transcript available at BBC News, http://news.bbc.co.uk/1/hi/uk_politics/3697434.stm
94. Blair, Tony, Prime Minister's Press Conference, Sedgefield, 3 September 2012, transcript available at National Archives, http://webarchive.national archives.gov.uk/20060802134639/http:/ /number10.gov.uk/page3001
95. Campbell, Alastair, *The Burden of Power: Countdown to Iraq – The Alastair Campbell Diaries* vol. 4, London, Hutchinson, 2012, pp291, 293
96. Powell, Sandra (on behalf of Alastair Campbell), email to Jonathan Powell, 5 September 2002, evidence to Hutton inquiry, http://webarchive.national archives.gov.uk/20051219094446/http:/ /the-hutton-inquiry.org.uk/content/cab /cab_11_0017.pdf
97. Smith, Godric, email to Daniel Pruce and Alastair Campbell, 11 September 2002, evidence to Hutton inquiry, http: //webarchive.nationalarchives.gov.uk/ 20051219094446/http://the-hutton-inquiry.org.uk/content/cab/cab_ 11_0023to0024.pdf
98. Kelly, Tom, email to Alastair Campbell, 18 September 2002, evidence to Hutton inquiry, http://webarchive.national archives.gov.uk/20051219094446/http:/ /the-hutton-inquiry.org.uk/content/cab /cab_11_0091to0092.pdf
99. Prince, Rosa, 'Civil Servants Had Serious Concerns over Iraq "Dodgy Dossier"', *Telegraph*, 13 March 2009, http://www.telegraph.co.uk/news/ politics/labour/4980103/Civil-servants-had-serious-concerns-over-Iraq-dodgy-dossier.html
100. 'Q&A: The Weapons Evidence', BBC News, 20 July 2004, http://news.bbc. co.uk/1/hi/uk_politics/3895967.stm
101. 'Inquiry Calls over Iraq Dossier', BBC News, 12 March 2009, http://news.bbc. co.uk/1/hi/uk_politics/7939726.stm; Rawnsley, p114
102. Rawnsley, p114
103. Powell, Jonathan, email to Alastair Campbell, 19 September 2002, evidence to Hutton inquiry, http:// webarchive.nationalarchives.gov.uk/ 20051219094446/http://the-hutton-

inquiry.org.uk/content/cab/
cab_11_0103.pdf

104. Hansard, HC (series 6) vol 417, col
822, 4 February 2004, http://hansard.
millbanksystems.com/commons/2004/
feb/04/lord-huttons-report

105. Chilcot, Sir John, *The Report of the
Iraq Inquiry*, Section 4.2: Iraq WMD
Assessments, July to September 2002,
p116, http://www.iraqinquiry.org.uk/
media/248177/the-report-of-the-iraq-
inquiry_section-42.pdf

106. 'Timeline: The 45-Minute Claim', BBC
News, 13 October 2004, http://news.
bbc.co.uk/1/hi/uk_politics/3466005.
stm

107. Ibid.

108. Ibid.

109. Ibid.

110. Lord Hutton, *Report of the Inquiry into
the Circumstances Surrounding the
Death of Dr David Kelly*, p131, http:/
/webarchive.nationalarchives.gov.uk/
20051219094446/http://the-hutton-
inquiry.org.uk/content/report/index.
htm

111. Ibid., p124

112. Chilcot, p231

113. Hutton, p131

114. Hansard, HC (series 6) vol 390, col
3, 24 September 2002, https://www.
publications.parliament.uk/pa/
cm200102/cmhansrd/vo020924/debtext
/20924-01.htm

115. Powell, email to Campbell, 19
September 2002

116. Blair, p453

117. Lord Butler, *Review of Intelligence on
Weapons of Mass Destruction*, London,
Her Majesty's Stationery Office, 2004,
p126, http://webarchive.national
archives.gov.uk/20090120202433/
http:/archive.cabinetoffice.gov.uk/
butlerreview/report/report.pdf

118. Ibid.

119. Ibid., p127

120. Chilcot, p6

121. Rawnsley, p100

122. Hansard, HC (series 6), vol 399, col
25, 3 February 2003, https://www.
publications.parliament.uk/pa/
cm200203/cmhansrd/vo030203/debtext
/30203-06.htm

123. 'Downing Street Dossier Plagiarised',
Channel 4 News, 6 February 2003, http:
//www.channel4.com/news/articles/
politics/domestic_politics/downing
%2bst%2bdossier%2bplagiarised
%2b%2b%2b/253293.html

8. Breaking Their Word

1. 'Commander in Chief Lands on USS
Lincoln', CNN, 2 May 2003, http://
edition.cnn.com/2003/ALLPOLITICS/05
/01/bush.carrier.landing

2. Murphy, Jarrett, 'Text of Bush Speech',
CBS/Associated Press, 1 May 2003,
http://www.cbsnews.com/news/text-
of-bush-speech-01-05-2003

3. 'Bush Lands Aboard USS Abraham
Lincoln', Fox News, 2 May 2003, http:/
/www.foxnews.com/story/2003/05/02/

bush-lands-aboard-uss-abraham-
lincoln.html

4. Lyke, M. L., 'Commander in Chief's
Visit Sets Aircraft Carrier's Crew Abuzz',
Seattle Post-Intelligencer, 1 May 2003,
http://www.seattlepi.com/news/article/
Commander-in-chief-s-visit-sets-
aircraft-1113821.php

5. Quoted in Kate Phillips, 'Bush: "I Was
Unprepared for War"', *New York Times*,
1 December 2008, https://thecaucus.

blogs.nytimes.com/2008/12/01/
bush-i-was-unprepared-for-war

6. 'Barack Obama: All US Troops to Leave Iraq in 2011', BBC News, 21 October 2011, http://www.bbc.co.uk/news/world-us-canada-15410154

7. Murphy, 'Text of Bush Speech'

8. Murphy, Jarrett, '"Mission Accomplished" Whodunit', CBS/Associated Press, 29 October 2003, http://www.cbsnews.com/news/mission-accomplished-whodunit

9. Conason, Joe, 'Joe Conason's Journal: Bush's "Top Gun" Get-Up', *Salon*, 2 May 2003, http://www.salon.com/2003/05/02/topgun

10. 'Bush Lands Aboard USS Abraham Lincoln', Fox News

11. 'Gordon Brown Steps In to Secure HBOS Rescue', *The Times*, 17 September 2008, https://www.thetimes.co.uk/article/gordon-brown-steps-in-to-secure-hbos-rescue-f66m33jbbdm

12. 'UK Banks Receive £37bn Bail-Out', BBC News, 13 October 2008, http://news.bbc.co.uk/1/hi/business/7666570.stm

13. Titcomb, James, 'The Government Has Made Back Half of the £20.5bn It Paid to Bail Out Lloyds', *Telegraph*, 12 May 2015, http://www.telegraph.co.uk/finance/newsbysector/epic/lloy/11598849/Government-cuts-Lloyds-stake-below-20pc.html

14. Treanor, Jill, 'UK Government Starts Royal Bank of Scotland Sell-Off', *Guardian*, 3 August 2015, https://www.theguardian.com/business/2015/aug/03/uk-government-starts-royal-bank-of-scotland-sell-off-rbs

15. Treanor, Jill, 'RBS Reports £7bn Loss and Says It Will Not Make Profit Until 2018', *Guardian*, 24 February 2017, https://www.theguardian.com/business/2017/feb/24/rbs-loss-profit-bank

16. Rawnsley, Andrew, 'The Weekend Gordon Brown Saved the Banks from the Abyss', *Guardian*, 21 February 2010, https://www.theguardian.com/politics/2010/feb/21/gordon-brown-saved-banks

17. Stratton, Allegra, Toby Helm and Rajeev Syal, 'RBS Bankers May Still Receive Bonuses Despite Treasury Probe into Pay', *Guardian*, 8 February 2009, https://www.theguardian.com/uk/2009/feb/08/rbs-bankers-could-receive-bonuses

18. Treanor, Jill, '"Fred Goodwin's Folly" Given New Use by RBS Chief Executive', *Guardian*, 4 March 2015, https://www.theguardian.com/business/2015/mar/04/fred-goodwin-folly-edinburgh-rbs-rbs-mcewan

19. 'Former RBS CEO Goodwin Paid £1.3 Million for 2008', Reuters, 8 March 2009, http://uk.reuters.com/article/uk-rbs-pay-idUKTRE52854520090309

20. 'Supplementary Memorandum from UK Financial Investments: Annex', House of Commons Treasury Committee, https://www.publications.parliament.uk/pa/cm200809/cmselect/cmtreasy/144/144iii04.htm

21. Pierce, Andrew, 'Sir Fred Goodwin Agrees to Pension Cut', *Telegraph*, 19 June 2009, http://www.telegraph.co.uk/finance/newsbysector/banksandfinance/5570311/Sir-Fred-Goodwin-agrees-to-pension-cut.html

22. House of Commons Treasury Committee, *Banking Crisis: Reforming Corporate Governance and Pay in the City*, London, Her Majesty's Stationery Office, 12 May 2009, https://www.publications.parliament.uk/pa/cm200809/cmselect/cmtreasy/519/51906.htm

23. House Treasury Committee, *Banking Crisis*

24. Ibid.

25. 'Brown Vows to Claw Pension Back', BBC News, 27 February 2009, http://news.bbc.co.uk/1/hi/uk_politics/7914993.stm

26. Hencke, David, 'Harriet Harman Increases Pressure over Sir Fred Goodwin's Pension', *Guardian*, 1 March 2009, https://www.theguardian.com/politics/2009/mar/01/harriet-harman-sir-fred-goodwin

27. 'Sir Fred Goodwin's Letter to Lord Myners Regarding His Pension', *Telegraph*, 26 February 2009, http://www.telegraph.co.uk/finance/newsbysector/banksandfinance/4840511/Sir-Fred-Goodwins-letter-to-Lord-Myners-regarding-his-pension.html

28. Ibid.

29. Treanor, Jill, 'Fred Goodwin Pension Row: 90% of RBS Shareholders Vote Against Pay Report', *Guardian*, 3 April 2009, https://www.theguardian.com/business/2009/apr/03/fred-goodwin-pension-rbs-agm

30. 'After Sir Fred, RBS Slashes Pensions of Ordinary Staff', *Scotsman*, 25 August 2009, http://www.scotsman.com/news/after-sir-fred-rbs-slashes-pensions-of-ordinary-staff-1-766885

31. Johnston, Philip, 'A Giant Bonus for Foes of Capitalism', *Telegraph*, 26 February 2009, http://www.telegraph.co.uk/comment/columnists/philipjohnston/4841142/A-giant-bonus-for-foes-of-capitalism.html

32. Peston, Robert, 'Reducing Sir Fred Goodwin's Pension', BBC News, 18 June 2009, http://www.bbc.co.uk/blogs/thereporters/robertpeston/2009/06/reducing_sir_fred_goodwins_pen.html

33. Fraser, Douglas, 'Fred Goodwin: A Very British Humiliation', BBC News, 31 January 2012, http://www.bbc.co.uk/news/uk-scotland-scotland-business-16823381.

34. Dunkley, Emma, 'Goodwin Not to Face Scottish Prosecution over RBS', *Financial Times*, 12 May 2016, https://www.ft.com/content/e71ccfd4-1848-11e6-bb7d-ee563a5a1cc1

35. Yeomans, Jon, 'Sir Philip Green Puts £363m into Pension Fund of Collapsed Retailer After Threats to Strip His Knighthood', *Telegraph*, 28 February 2017, http://www.telegraph.co.uk/business/2017/02/28/sir-philip-green-puts-363m-bhs-pension-fund

36. Brook, Stephen, 'Mulcaire "Dealt with News Int Staff Other than Goodman", Judge Said', *Guardian*, 21 July 2009, https://www.theguardian.com/media/2009/jul/21/news-world-phone-hacking

37. Weaver, Matthew, 'Cameron Ignored High-Level Warnings About Andy Coulson, Ashcroft Claims', *Guardian*, 5 October 2015, https://www.theguardian.com/politics/2015/oct/05/cameron-ignored-high-level-warnings-about-andy-coulson-ashcroft-claims

38. 'Rebekah Brooks and Andy Coulson Had Affair, Phone-Hacking Trial Hears', BBC News, 31 October 2013, http://www.bbc.co.uk/news/uk-24762474

39. 'Rebekah Brooks Reveals "LOL" Texts from Cameron', BBC News, 11 May 2012, http://www.bbc.co.uk/news/uk-politics-18032027

40. 'Leveson: "We're Definitely in This Together", Brooks Told PM', BBC News, 14 June 2012, http://www.bbc.co.uk/news/uk-18437287

41. Seal, Mark, 'Seduced and Abandoned', *Vanity Fair*, 19 February 2014, http://www.vanityfair.com/style/2014/03/wendi-deng-note-tony-blair

42. 'Trial And Error', *Private Eye*, 11 July 2014

43. Davies, Nick, 'Murdoch Papers Paid £1m to Gag Phone-Hacking Victims', *Guardian*, 9 July 2009, https://www.theguardian.com/media/2009/jul/08/murdoch-papers-phone-hacking

44. Coulson, Andy, testimony, 21 July 2009, quoted in House of Commons Culture, Media and Sport Committee, *Press Standards, Privacy and Libel: Second Report of Session 2009–10*, Volume II, London, Her Majesty's Stationery Office, 2010, p322, https://www.publications.parliament.uk/pa/cm200910/cmselect/cmcumeds/362/362ii.pdf

45. Doward, Jamie, and Toby Helm, 'David Blunkett in Secret NI Payout over Phone-Hacking Claims', *Observer*, 10 December 2011, https://www.theguardian.com/media/2011/dec/10/david-blunkett-ni-phone-hacking-claims

46. Neate, Rupert, 'David Blunkett Renews £49,500 Contract as News International Adviser', *Guardian*, 1 February 2012, https://www.theguardian.com/media/2012/feb/01/david-blunkett-news-international-adviser

47. Brooks, Rebekah, memorandum to the House of Commons Culture, Media and Sport Committee, 4 January 2010, https://www.publications.parliament.uk/pa/cm200910/cmselect/cmcumeds/362/362we37.htm

48. Wells, Matt, 'Sun Editor Admits Paying Police Officers for Stories', *Guardian*, 12 March 2003, https://www.theguardian.com/media/2003/mar/12/sun.pressandpublishing

49. Murdoch, Rupert, testimony, Leveson inquiry, 25 April 2012, http://webarchive.nationalarchives.gov.uk/20140122145147/http://www.levesoninquiry.org.uk/wp-content/uploads/2012/04/Transcript-of-Afternoon-Hearing-25-April-2012.txt

50. 'Special Report: Phone-Hacking Scandal: Trial and Error', *Private Eye*, 11 July 2014, p21

51. 'Andy Coulson Quits Downing Street Communications Role', BBC News, 21 January 2011, http://www.bbc.co.uk/news/uk-politics-12251456

52. 'Andy Coulson Jailed for 18 Months over Phone Hacking', BBC News, 4 July 2014, http://www.bbc.co.uk/news/uk-28160626

53. 'Cameron Apologises over Andy Coulson Appointment', BBC News, 24 June 2014, http://www.bbc.co.uk/news/uk-politics-27998411

54. Croft, Jane, Kiran Stacey, Jim Pickard and John Aglionby, 'Judge Hits at David Cameron over Coulson Comments', *Financial Times*, 25 June 2014, https://www.ft.com/content/7abc08ba-fc65-11e3-86dc-00144feab7de

55. Oliver, Jonathan, and David Smith, 'Nick Clegg Is Nearly as Popular as Winston Churchill', *Sunday Times*, 18 April 2010, https://www.thetimes.co.uk/article/nick-clegg-is-nearly-as-popular-as-winston-churchill-t9gn20hnmbm

56. Burkeman, Oliver, 'Nick Clegg – the British Obama?', *Guardian*, 19 April 2010, https://www.theguardian.com/politics/2010/apr/19/nick-clegg-obama

57. 'General Election 2010: Lib Dems Take Lead in New Poll', *Telegraph*, 18 April 2010, http://www.telegraph.co.uk/news/election-2010/7605260/General-Election-2010-Lib-Dems-take-lead-in-new-poll.html

58. Merrick, Jane, and Brian Brady, 'Cleggmania Spreads Across Britain', *Independent*, 17 April 2010, http://www.independent.co.uk/news/uk/politics/cleggmania-spreads-across-britain-1947687.html

59. Ibid.

60. National Union of Students, '1000 Candidates Sign Vote for Students Pledge to Oppose Tuition Fees Hike', press release, 26 April 2010, https://www.nus.org.uk/en/news/lib-dem-and-labour-mps-would-vote-together-to-oppose-tuition-fee-rise

61. Watt, Nicholas, 'Secret Documents Show Liberal Democrats Drew Up Plans to Drop Flagship Student Pledge Before Election', *Guardian*, 12 November 2010, https://www.theguardian.com/politics/wintour-and-watt/2010/nov/12/nickclegg-danny-alexander

62. Blair, Tony, *A Journey: My Political Life*, London, Hutchinson, 2010, p480

63. Ibid., p483

64. Rawnsley, p748

65. Watt, 'Secret Documents'

66. Cameron, David, 'Our Health Priorities', speech, Royal College of Pathologists, London, 2 November 2009, transcription available at http://conservative-speeches.sayit.mysociety.org/speech/601253

67. The King's Fund, Projects: 'Health and Social Care Act', 10 February 2015, https://www.kingsfund.org.uk/projects/health-and-social-care-act

68. Ibid.

69. Hansard, HC (series 6) vol 512, col 166–7, 22 June 2010, https://www.publications.parliament.uk/pa/cm201011/cmhansrd/cm100622/debtext/100622-0004.htm

70. Office for National Statistics, 'Government Deficit and Debt', statistical bulletin, 20 October 2016, https://www.ons.gov.uk/economy/governmentpublicsectorand taxes/publicspending/bulletins/ukgovernmentdebtanddeficit foreurostatmaast/aprtojune 2016

71. Hansard, HC (series 6) vol 502, col 359, 9 December 2009, https://www.publications.parliament.uk/pa/cm200910/cmhansrd/cm091209/debtext/91209-0004.htm

72. Hansard, HC vol 512, col 166–7, 22 June 2010

73. Summers, Deborah, 'David Cameron Warns of "New Age of Austerity"', *Guardian*, 26 April 2009, https://www.theguardian.com/politics/2009/apr/26/david-cameron-conservative-econom-ic-policy1

74. Hansard, HC vol 512, col 166–7, 22 June 2010

75. Office for National Statistics, 'Government Deficit and Debt'

76. 'George Osborne: Deficit Cut Is Taking Longer than Planned', BBC News, 2 December 2012, http://www.bbc.co.uk/news/uk-politics-20571621

77. Full Fact, 'Did George Osborne Promise to Eliminate the Deficit by This Year?', 26 November 2015, https://fullfact.org/economy/did-george-osborne-promise-eliminate-deficit-year

78. 'A Dangerous Gamble: George Osborne's Fiscal Charter Makes Little Economic Sense', *The Economist*, 17 October 2015, http://www.economist.com/news/britain/21674777-george-osbornes-fiscal-charter-makes-little-economic-sense-dangerous-gamble

79. Quoted in Stewart, Heather, and Larry Elliott, 'Budget 2016: Osborne "Has Only 50–50 Chance" of Hitting Surplus Target' ", *Guardian*, 17 March 2016, https://www.theguardian.com/uk-news/2016/mar/17/budget-2016-osborne-chances-of-delivering-surplus-50-50-ifs.

80. Office of Budget Responsibility, 'A Brief Guide to the Public Finances', briefing, 8 March 2017, http://budgetresponsibility.org.uk/forecasts-in-depth/brief-guides-and-explainers/public-finances

81. House of Commons, 'Register of Members' Financial Interests: As at 2 May 2017: Osborne, Mr George (Tatton)', https://www.publications.parliament.uk/pa/cm/cmregmem/170502/osborne_george.htm

82. 'Cameron Defends Change over Election Vote Rules', BBC News, 14 May 2010, http://news.bbc.co.uk/1/hi/uk_politics/8681624.stm

83. Travis, Alan, 'Fixed Five-Year Parliamentary Term Will Tie Both Leaders' Hands', *Guardian*, 13 May 2010, https://www.theguardian.com/politics/2010/may/12/fixed-five-year-parliamentary-term

84. May, Theresa, interview, *Andrew Marr Show*, BBC 1, 4 September 2016, http://www.bbc.co.uk/programmes/p046sm5x

85. Hughes, Laura, 'No 10 Rejects Calls for Theresa May to Hold an Early General Election', *Telegraph*, 7 March 2017, http://www.telegraph.co.uk/news/2017/03/07/no-10-inists-theresa-may-not-planning-early-general-election

86. Parker, George, and Jim Pickard, 'Downing Street Denies Theresa May Will Call Snap General Election', *Financial Times*, 20 March 2017, https://www.ft.com/content/af09826a-0d64-11e7-b030-768954394623

87. Rayner, Gordon, Christopher Hope and Kate McCann, 'Theresa May Denies Breaking Election Tax Promise over National Insurance as 100 Tory MPs Prepare to Join Budget Rebellion', *Telegraph*, 9 March 2017, http://www.telegraph.co.uk/news/2017/03/09/theresa-may-insists-national-insurance-rise-budget-honours-manifesto

88. 'Full May Announcement on Snap Election', BBC News, 18 April 2017, http://www.bbc.co.uk/news/av/uk-politics-39627177/theresa-mays-full-announcement-on-calling-snap-election

89. Ibid.

90. 'Election: Theresa May Urges Voters to "Strengthen My Hand"', BBC News, 25 April 2017, http://www.bbc.co.uk/news/uk-wales-politics-39698499

91. Prime Minister's Office, 'The Government's Negotiating Objectives for Exiting the EU: PM's Speech', news release, 17 January 2017, https://www.gov.uk/government/speeches/the-governments-negotiating-objectives-for-exiting-the-eu-pm-speech

9. Whose Truth Is It Anyway?

1. Mance, Henry, 'Britain Has Had Enough of Experts, Says Gove', *Financial Times*, 3 June 2016, https://www.ft.com/content/3be49734-29cb-11e6-83e4-abc22d5d108c

2. @ShaunMcCluskey (Shaun McCluskey), Tweet, 26 August 2014, 6:03 p.m., and others; graphic reproduced in Waterson, Jim, 'These Scottish Nationalists Think There's a Conspiracy to Hide a Secret Oilfield', BuzzFeed, 2 September 2014, https://www.buzzfeed.com/jimwaterson/secret-oilfields-of-scotland

3. @David_Cameron (David Cameron), Tweet, 23 July 2014, 1:45 a.m.; photograph reproduced in Waterson, 'These Scottish Nationalists Think There's a Conspiracy'

4. 'Downing Street Silent on Cameron's Secret Shetland Visit', Newsnet.scot, 7 August 2014, http://newsnet.scot/

archive/downing-street-silent-on-camerons-secret-shetland-visit

5. McAlpine, Joan, 'It's Time to Take a Close Look at Some of London's Lies over Scots Oil Wealth', *Daily Record*, 25 August 2014, http://www.dailyrecord.co.uk/news/politics/joan-mcalpine-its-time-take-4103855

6. Waterson, 'These Scottish Nationalists Think There's a Conspiracy'

7. Ibid.

8. Gosden, Emily, 'BP Oil Spill in North Sea Forces Shutdown of Clair Platform', *Telegraph*, 3 October 2016, http://www.telegraph.co.uk/business/2016/10/03/bp-shuts-north-sea-platform-after-oil-leak

9. Laville, Sandra, '1,400 Investigated in Child Abuse Inquiry, Including Politicians', *Guardian*, 20 May 2015, https://www.theguardian.com/uk-news/2015/may/20/1400-suspects-operation-hydrant-politician-and-celebrity-child-sex-abuse-inquiry

10. 'The Paedophile MP – How Cyril Smith Got Away with It', *Dispatches*, Channel 4, 12 September 2013

11. Gray, David, and Peter Watt, *Giving Victims a Voice: A Join Report into Sexual Allegations Made Against Jimmy Savile*, Metropolitan Police Service and the National Society for the Prevention of Cruelty to Children, January 2013, https://www.nspcc.org.uk/globalassets/documents/research-reports/yewtree-report-giving-victims-voice-jimmy-savile.pdf

12. Symonds, Tom, 'Historical Abuse Inquiry: Police Examine "Possible Homicide"', BBC News, 14 November 2014, http://www.bbc.co.uk/news/uk-30052726

13. Bracchi, Paul, and Stephen Wright, 'Nick: Victim or Fantasist?', *Daily Mail*, 18 September 2015, http://www.dailymail.co.uk/news/article-3240661/Nick-Victim-fantasist-Rape-Torture-Murders-extraordinary-claims-one-man-against-leading-Establishment-figures-Police-called-story-credible-true-s-not-shred-evidence-allegations.html

14. Ibid.

15. 'The VIP Paedophile Ring: What's the Truth?', *Panorama*, BBC 1, 6 October 2015

16. Syal, Rajeev, 'Westminster Paedophile Claims: Harvey Proctor Accuses Police of Witch-Hunt', *Guardian*, 25 August 2015, https://www.theguardian.com/uk-news/2015/aug/25/westminster-paedophile-claims-harvey-proctor-accuses-police-of-witch-hunt

17. De Simone, Daniel, 'Operation Midland Cost £2.5m, Says Met Police', BBC News, 9 August 2015, http://www.bbc.co.uk/news/uk-37027144

18. Evans, Martin, '"I Witnessed Tory MP Strangle Child", Claims Abuse Victim', *Telegraph*, 18 December 2014, http://www.telegraph.co.uk/news/uknews/crime/11301666/I-witnessed-Tory-MP-strangle-child-claims-abuse-victim.html

19. Henriques, Sir Richard, 'An Independent Review of the Metropolitan Police Service's Handling of Non-Recent Sexual Offence Investigations Alleged Against Persons of Public Prominence', 31 October 2016, p67, http://news.met.police.uk/documents/report-independent-review-of-metropolitan-police-services-handling-of-non-recent-sexual-offence-investigations-61510

20. Ibid., p66

21. Ibid., p26

22. 'Exaro: The Ultimate Wind-Up', *Private Eye*, 10 February 2017

23. Ford, Richard, 'Brittan Defends Role over Lost "Westminster Paedophile

File'", *The Times*, 3 July 2014, https://www.thetimes.co.uk/article/brittan-defends-role-over-lost-westminster-paedophile-file-q7kwskhdrcj

24. *Private Eye*, 29 June 1984

25. Slack, James, 'Revenge! Drugs, Debauchery and the Book That Lays Dave Bare', *Daily Mail*, 21 September 2015, http://www.dailymail.co.uk/news/article-3242494/Revenge-PM-s-snub-billionaire-funded-Tories-years-sparked-explosive-political-book-decade.html

26. Ashcroft, Michael, and Isabel Oakeshott, 'British Prime Minister and an Obscene Act with a Dead Pig's Head', *Daily Mail*, 25 September 2015, http://www.dailymail.co.uk/news/article-3242550/Cameron-pig-bemused-look-face-future-PM-took-outrageous-initiation-ceremony-joining-Oxford-dining-society.html

27. Ibid.

28. Marsden, Sam, 'Read in full: the emails that reveal Vicky Pryce's plot to 'nail' cheating Chris Huhne', *Telegraph*, 7 March 2013, http://www.telegraph.co.uk/news/politics/liberaldemocrats/9874347/Read-in-full-the-emails-that-reveal-Vicky-Pryces-plot-to-nail-cheating-Chris-Huhne.html

29. Oakeshott, Isabel, interview, *Channel 4 News*, 21 September 2015, https://www.youtube.com/watch?v=rm_Bli5h0Ns

30. Malvern, Jack, 'Cameron's Pig Head Incident May Be a Porkie, Says Author', *The Times*, 9 October 2015, https://www.thetimes.co.uk/article/camerons-pig-head-incident-may-be-a-porkie-says-author-s9xq28dwr9w

31. 'Cameron: "People Will See Straight Through Ashcroft's Book"', *ITV News*, 28 September 2015, http://www.itv.com/news/2015-09-28/cameron-people-will-see-straight-through-ashcrofts-book/

32. Kerr, Jacob, 'Donald Trump Exaggerates Crowd Size at Phoenix Rally', *Huffington Post*, 15 July 2015, http://www.huffingtonpost.com/entry/donald-trump-crowd-size_us_55a56d2de4b04740a3de3d26

33. Lizza, Ryan, 'John McCain Has a Few Things to Say About Donald Trump', *New Yorker*, 16 July 2015, http://www.newyorker.com/news/news-desk/john-mccain-has-a-few-things-to-say-about-donald-trump

34. Reilly, Katie, 'Here Are All the Times Donald Trump Insulted Mexico', *Time*, 31 August 2016, http://time.com/4473972/donald-trump-mexico-meeting-insult

35. Johnson, Jenna, and Mary Jordan, 'Trump on Rally Protester: "Maybe He Should Have Been Roughed Up"', *Washington Post*, 22 November 2015, https://www.washingtonpost.com/news/post-politics/wp/2015/11/22/black-activist-punched-at-donald-trump-rally-in-birmingham

36. Ibid.

37. Mekelburg, Madlin, and John Reynolds, 'The Brief: Nov. 16, 2015', *Texas Tribune*, 16 November 2015, https://www.texastribune.org/2015/11/16/brief-nov-16-2015

38. Kessler, Glenn, 'Trump's Outrageous Claim That "Thousands" of New Jersey Muslims Celebrated the 9/11 Attacks', *Washington Post*, 22 November 2015, https://www.washingtonpost.com/news/fact-checker/wp/2015/11/22/donald-trumps-outrageous-claim-that-thousands-of-new-jersey-muslims-celebrated-the-911-attacks

39. Trump, Donald, interview, *This Week*, ABC News, 22 November 2015, transcript available at http:/

/abcnews.go.com/Politics/week-transcript-donald-trump-ben-carson/story?id=35336008

40. Campbell, Carol Ann, 'Jersey City Muslims Confront Wide Suspicion', *Star-Ledger*, 18 September 2001, http://www.nj.com/news/index.ssf/2015/11/from_the_archives_jersey_city_muslims_confront_wid.html

41. Kessler, 'Trump's Outrageous Claim'

42. Farmer, John Jr, 'I Was in Charge in N. J. on 9/11 and Trump's Claims Never Happened', *Star-Ledger*, 24 November 2015, http://www.nj.com/opinion/index.ssf/2015/11/nj_attorney_general_on_911_says_trumps_jersey_city.html

43. Ibid.

44. Turkel, Dan, 'Video Appears to Show Donald Trump Mocking a Reporter's Physical Condition During a Speech', *Business Insider*, 26 November 2015, https://www.businessinsider.com.au/trump-appears-to-be-mocking-the-physical-condition-of-a-reporter-during-a-south-carolina-rally-2015-11

45. Kessler, 'Trump's Outrageous Claim'

46. Ibid.

47. Nolte, John, 'Trump 100% Vindicated: CBS Reports "Swarm" on Rooftops Celebrating 9/11', Breitbart, 2 December 2015, http://www.breitbart.com/big-journalism/2015/12/02/trump-100-vindicated-cbs-reports-swarms-on-roofs-celebrating-911

48. Kessler, 'Trump's Outrageous Claim'

49. Santucci, John, and Alana Abramson, 'Trump Says He Heard from "Hundreds" Who Saw 9/11 Celebrations in US', ABC News, 23 November 2015, http://abcnews.go.com/Politics/trump-heard-hundreds-911-celebrations-us/story?id=35380110

50. Nashrulla, Tasneem, 'Three Lies About Birtherism to Look Out for in Donald Trump's Speech', BuzzFeed, 16 September 2016, https://www.buzzfeed.com/tasneemnashrulla/three-lies-about-birtherism-to-look-out-for-in-donald-trumps

51. DelReal, Jose A., 'Trump Draws Scornful Rebuke for Mocking Reporter with Disability', *Washington Post*, 26 November 2015, https://www.washingtonpost.com/news/post-politics/wp/2015/11/25/trump-blasted-by-new-york-times-after-mocking-reporter-with-disability

52. Ibid.

53. Haberman, Maggie, 'Donald Trump Says His Mocking of *New York Times* Reporter Was Misread', *New York Times*, 26 November 2015, https://www.nytimes.com/2015/11/27/us/politics/donald-trump-says-his-mocking-of-new-york-times-reporter-was-misread.html

54. DelReal, 'Trump Draws Scornful Rebuke'

55. Gillman, Ollie, and Ashley Collman, 'Trump Denies Ever Having Met the Disabled Reporter He Is Accused of Cruelly Mimicking and Says the "Poor Guy" Should Stop Using His Disability to "Grandstand"', *Daily Mail*, 26 November 2016, http://www.dailymail.co.uk/news/article-3334489/Donald-Trump-slammed-outrageous-impression-disabled-New-York-Times-reporter.html

56. Haberman, 'Donald Trump Says His Mocking… Was Misread'

57. Savransky, Rebecca, 'Trump Falsely Claims He Got Biggest Electoral College Win Since Reagan', *The Hill*, 16 February 2017, http://thehill.com/business-a-lobbying/donald-trump-falsely-claims-biggest-electoral-win-since-reagan

58. 'President Trump's Interview with Time on Truth and Falsehoods', *Time*, 23 March 2017, http://time.com/4710456/

donald-trump-time-interview-truth-falsehood

59. @JeremyCorbyn4PM, Tweet, 7 May 2016, time unknown [subsequently deleted]; screengrabbed in Belam, Martin, 'Why that Chart Demonstrating Jeremy Corbyn's Election Success Is Misleading', *Guardian*, 9 May 2016, https://www.theguardian.com/politics/2016/may/09/why-that-chart-demonstrating-jeremy-corbyns-election-success-is-misleading

60. See, for example, Melvin, Melanie Kathleen, Facebook post, 28 November 2015, https://www.facebook.com/photo.php?fbid=10153812759904885&set=a.10153693650834885.1073741830.754579884&type=3&theater

61. 'Suspected Paedophile Ring Exposed', DC PizzaGate Blog, 7 November 2016 (updated 20 April 2017), https://dcpizzagate.wordpress.com

62. Ibid.

63. Various internet postings gathered at 'Chuck E. Sleaze', Snopes, 21 November 2016, http://www.snopes.com/pizzagate-conspiracy

64. Editorial Board, '"Pizzagate" Shows How Fake News Hurts Real People', *Washington Post*, 25 November 2016, https://www.washingtonpost.com/opinions/pizzagate-shows-how-fake-news-hurts-real-people/2016/11/25/d9ee0590-b0f9-11e6-840f-e3ebab6bcdd3_story.html

65. Freeman, Hadley, 'Sandy Hook Father Leonard Pozner on Death Threats: "I Never Imagined I'd Have To Fight For My Child's Legacy"', *Guardian*, 2 May 2017, https://www.theguardian.com/us-news/2017/may/02/sandy-hook-school-hoax-massacre-conspiracists-victim-father

66. Infowars.com Audience Insights and Demographic Analytics, https://www.quantcast.com/infowars.com; Medick, Veit, 'Meet Donald Trump's Propagandist', *Spiegel*, 28 February 2017, http://www.spiegel.de/international/world/a-visit-to-the-infowars-studios-of-alex-jones-a-1136654.html

67. Bradner, Eric, 'Trump Praises 9/11 Truther's "Amazing" Reputation', CNN, 2 December 2015, http://edition.cnn.com/2015/12/02/politics/donald-trump-praises-9-11-truther-alex-jones

68. 'Bombshell: Hillary Clinton's Satanic Network Exposed', Infowars, 4 November 2016, https://www.infowars.com/bombshell-hillary-clintons-satanic-network-exposed

69. Transcript available at 'Infowars Denies It Promoted "Pizzagate" Conspiracy Theory After Deleting Content from Its Website', Media Matters, 24 February 2017, https://www.mediamatters.org/blog/2017/02/24/infowars-denies-it-promoted-pizzagate-conspiracy-theory-after-deleting-pizza-gate-content-its-website/215465

70. Goldman, Adam, 'The Comet Ping Pong Gunman Answers Our Reporter's Questions', *New York Times*, 7 December 2016, https://www.nytimes.com/2016/12/07/us/edgar-welch-comet-pizza-fake-news.html

71. Yuhas, Alan, '"Pizzagate" Gunman Pleads Guilty as Conspiracy Theorist Apologizes over Case', *Guardian*, 25 March 2017, https://www.theguardian.com/us-news/2017/mar/25/comet-ping-pong-alex-jones

72. Kang, Cecilia, and Adam Goldman, 'In Washington Pizzeria Attack, Fake News Brought Real Guns', *New York Times*, 5 December 2016, https://www.nytimes.com/2016/12/05/business/media/com-

et-ping-pong-pizza-shooting-fake-news-consequences.html

73. Jones, Alex, 'A Note to Our Listening, Viewing and Reading Audiences Regarding Pizzagate Coverage', Infowars, 24 March 2017, https://www.infowars.com/a-note-to-our-listening-viewing-and-reading-audiences-concerning-pizzagate-coverage

74. Warzel, Charlie, 'Alex Jones Suffers Defeat in Custody Hearing', BuzzFeed, 28 April 2017, https://www.buzzfeed.com/charliewarzel/jones-trial-verdict; Tilove, Jonathan, 'In Travis County Custody Case, Jury Will Search for Real Alex Jones', *Austin American-Statesman*, 16 April 2017, http://www.mystatesman.com/news/state--regional-govt--politics/travis-county-custody-case-jury-will-search-for-real-alex-jones/rnbWzMHnFCd-5SOPgP3A34J

75. Kang, Cecilia, 'Fake News Onslaught Targets Pizzeria as Nest of Child-Trafficking', *New York Times*, 21 November 2016, https://www.nytimes.com/2016/11/21/technology/fact-check-this-pizzeria-is-not-a-child-trafficking-site.html

76. Twitter search by author, 17 May 2017, 11:36 a.m.

Conclusion

1. 'Register of Members' Financial Interests As at 8 June 2015': Boris Johnson, https://www.publications.parliament.uk/pa/cm/cmregmem/150608/johnson_boris.htm; Register of Lords' Interests, http://www.parliament.uk/mps-lords-and-offices/standards-and-interests/register-of-lords-interests/?letter=P

2. Blair, Tony, *A Journey: My Political Life*, London, Penguin, 2011, p516

3. Kertscher, Tom, 'Is Donald Trump the Only Major-Party Nominee in 40 Years Not to Release His Tax Returns?', Politifact, 28 September 2016, http://www.politifact.com/wisconsin/statements/2016/sep/28/tammy-baldwin/donald-trump-only-major-party-nominee-40-years-not

4. O'Sullivan, Jack, 'The Politics of the BBC (Ben Bradshaw, Candidate)', *Independent*, 3 March 1997, http://www.independent.co.uk/news/media/the-politics-of-the-bbc-ben-bradshaw-candidate-1270807.html

5. Cadwallader, Carole, 'The Great British Brexit Robbery: How Our Democracy Was Hijacked', *Observer*, 7 May 2017, https://www.theguardian.com/technology/2017/may/07/the-great-british-brexit-robbery-hijacked-democracy

INDEX

ABOUT
THE AUTHOR

Adam Macqueen has been reporting for *Private Eye* since the early days of Tony Blair's government. He covered the epic phone-hacking trial of Rebekah Brooks and Andy Coulson for the magazine, and writes the regular 'Number Crunching' and 'Focus on Fact' features.

His books include *The Prime Minister's Ironing Board and Other State Secrets* (2013) and the *Sunday Times* top ten bestseller *Private Eye: The First 50 Years, an A–Z* (2011).

He lives in Hastings with his husband, the painter Michael Tierney.